The Philosophy of Advaita

Sage Vidyāraṇya in Processsion
(From a painting in the Hampī ruins)
Courtesy: The Department of Archaeology, Government of India and Dr V. Raghavan

The Philosophy of Advaita

With Special Reference to Bhāratītīrtha-Vidyāraṇya

T.M.P. Mahadevan

With a Foreword by

S. Radhakrishnan

DK®
PRINTWORLD
Publishers of Indian Traditions

Cataloging in Publication Data — DK
[Courtesy: D.K. Agencies (P) Ltd. <docinfo@dkagencies.com>]

Mahadevan, T.M.P. (Telliyavaram Mahadevan Ponnambalam), 1911-1983, **author.**
The philosophy of Advaita: with special reference to Bhāratītīrtha-Vidyāraṇya / T.M.P. Mahadevan ; with a foreword by S. Radhakrishnan.
pages cm
Reprint of revised edition: 1957.
Revision of the author's thesis (doctoral).
ISBN: 9788124611548

1. Advaita. 2.Philosophy, Indic. 3. Bhāratītīrtha. 4. Mādhava, -1386. l. Title.

LCC B 132.A3M34 2025 | DDC 181.482 23

ISBN: 978-81-246-1154-8

First published by Ganesh & Co. (Madras) in 1938
Revised edition published in 1957
Retypesetted edition published in 2025

Printed and published by:
D.K. Printworld (P) Ltd.
Regd. Office : "Vedaśrī", F-395, Sudarshan Park
ESI Hospital Metro Station, New Delhi - 110015
Phones : (011) 4172 2626, 98713 94815
e-mail : indology@dkprintworld.com
Web : www.dkprintworld.com

To
Svami Rajesvaranandaji
With Love, Veneration and Gratitude

Books by T.M.P. Mahadevan

- *The Philosophy of Advaita*
- *The Upaniṣads (An Anthology)*
- *The Fundamentals of Logic*
- *Whither Civilization and Other Broadcast Talks*
- *Gauḍapāda: A Study in Early Advaita*
- *Time and the Timeless*
- *The Idea of God in Śaiva-Siddhānta*
- *Outlines of Hinduism*
- *A Morning Prayer and Hymn to Dakṣiṇāmūrti*
- *Īśāvāsya Upaniṣad*

Foreword

I HAD an opportunity of reading Dr Mahadevan's book, a few months ago, and thought it was a masterly survey of the Advaita doctrine, as set forth in the writings of Vidyāraṇya. While Śaṅkara's system is fairly well known to English readers, later developments of the Advaita philosophy are not so well known. If we look at the growth of Indian religious and philosophical systems, we find that utmost liberty of thought compatible with the maintenance of the fundamental presuppositions is permitted and Vidyāraṇya develops the Advaita position in a striking way. It is not my purpose here to traverse the ground covered so well by the writer. I should like to say that Dr Mahadevan expounds Vidyāraṇya's views with great clarity and penetration; his book fills a distinct need and will be a worthy addition to the literature in English on the subject.

1 June 1938 **S. Radhakrishnan**
Oxford

Publisher's Note

This volume, *The Philosophy of Advaita*, is a re-typeset and re-laid out version of the revised edition of 1957. We have attempted to value-add to this much-in-demand work in a few ways.

1. We have incorporated the up-to-date diacritics for all Indology terms and Sanskrit words.
2. For spelling, we have gone by *New Oxford Spelling Dictionary*, 2014 edition.
3. As far as acronyms and abbreviations are concerned, we have followed *New Oxford Dictionary for Writers and Editors*, 2014 revised edition.
4. Bibliography is updated in best possible manner. Many incomplete citations in footnotes have been completed and listed in the Bibliography.
5. **Index has been prepared afresh making it more exhaustive**.

We firmly believe that these value additions should help our readers in understanding, absorbing and analysing the contents effortlessly. Happy Reading!

Preface to the Revised Edition

THIS is a revised edition of my doctoral thesis first published in 1938. The thesis was written during the years 1933-35 under the guidance of the late Professor S.S. Suryanarayana Sastri. After the publication of this work which represents an important phase of the post-Śaṅkara dialectics, I have had occasion to bring out a study of the philosophy of the great pre-Śaṅkara Advaitin, Ācārya Gauḍapāda. This work entitled *Gauḍapāda: A Study in Early Advaita* was published by the University of Madras in 1952 (second edition, 1954). Just at present a translation of Sureśvara's *Sambandha-Vārttika*, with introduction, notes and extracts from three unpublished commentaries, is in the press, and will be released shortly by the University. Thus my studies in Advaita which started in 1933 have been a source of solace to me; and it is my conviction that they will continue to inspire me.

The scope of the present work is indicated in the Preface to the first edition. While revising this work I have made no substantial change. The first edition was sponsored by Messrs Luzac & Company, London. The present one is published by Messrs Ganesh & Company, Madras, who are well known for their books on Indian philosophy and religion.

Dr V.A. Devasenapathi and Shri P.K. Sundaram, my colleagues in the Department of Philosophy, University of Madras, have helped me in preparing the revised edition for the press and by reading the proofs. Mr James Hoyt Knapp Norton, a young American scholar who has come to my Department to study Indian philosophy, has been responsible for revising the Index. To these friends I am grateful. To the Department of Archaeology, Government of India, and to Dr V. Raghavan, Professor of Sanskrit, University of Madras, I am indebted for supplying a photograph of Vidyāraṇya which appears as frontispiece to this edition. I am thankful to Messrs Ganesh & Company for sponsoring this publication, and to the Vasanta Press, Adyar, for printing this book expeditiously and well.

University of Madras **Mahadevan**
12 November 1957

Preface to the First Editon

In the present work an attempt has been made to present the philosophy of Advaita with special reference to Bhāratītīrtha-Vidyāraṇya. Bhāratītīrtha is a great name in the history of Advaita after Śaṅkara. One of the most favoured books which has found a permanent place in a study of the Advaita system is the *Pañcadaśī*. But the work which is more important for Advaita dialectics is the *Vivaraṇa-Prameya-Saṁgraha* which is a summary of the topics dealt with in the *Vivaraṇa* of Prakāśātman, which is a gloss on Padmapāda's *Pañcapādikā,* which in its turn is a commentary on the *Śāṅkara-Bhāṣya* on the first four aphorisms of the *Vedāntasūtra.* Another work of Bhāratītīrtha from which I have drawn material is the *Dṛg-Dṛśya-Viveka.* But since a systematic treatment of the Advaita philosophy was not possible from a knowledge of these treatises alone, I had also to draw largely from the works of other preceptors like Dharmarāja, Vimuktātman, Citsukha and Appayya Dīkṣita.

The mass of Advaita literature has grown enormously in the post-Śaṅkara period, necessitated by charges and countercharges. The believer in a faith does not need much argumentation. He learns from his teacher the principal tenets of the system he comes to believe in; and because the method of exposition is direct, appealing more to the heart than to the head, there is not much room for disputation. But the *darśana*s (lit. points of view or visions) are not mere faiths demanding simple belief; they are philosophical systems as well. And so, the exponent of each metaphysical tradition has to maintain his position as against those of his opponents through dialectics.

Much of this wordy warfare may appear to be quibble to those who are sceptical about philosophical pursuits. But, nevertheless, it shows the intellectual virility and argumentative skill of the philosophers of India. The present thesis purports to be a modest study of Advaita dialectics with particular reference to the works of Bhāratītīrtha.

In the first two chapters the epistemological position of Advaita is considered. Though the Advaitin admits six *pramāṇa*s (means of valid knowledge), the final court of appeal is Scripture. The knowledge of *Brahman* that results therefrom is unsublatable and ultimate. Truth, according to the Advaitin, is that knowledge which is never contradicted; and error is born of *avidyā* which it is not possible to determine either as real or as unreal. In the three chapters that follow, the definition of *Brahman* as existence–intelligence–bliss is examined. In the sixth chapter the *sākṣī* (witness) is defined as the real self of the *jīva*, and it is shown to be non-different from *Brahman*. In chapter seven there is a discussion about *Īśvara* and the *jīva* and their mutual relation. The difference between Pratibimbavāda and Avaccheda-vāda is pointed out, and incidentally there is brought out the divergence of views as between the Bhāmatī and the Vivaraṇa schools. In the next chapter the doctrine of *māyā* is treated from three different levels, and it is discussed how and why it appears to be a riddle to the inquiring mind. The last two chapters are concerned with the way and the goal. All Advaitins maintain that the principal means to release is *jñāna;* but some of them tend to give a place, though a secondary one, to contemplation and devotion. *Mokṣa* in the system of Advaita, as in the other schools of Vedānta, means not only cessation of sorrow but also attainment of positive bliss, though attainment here is figurative, as *Brahman* is eternally attained and ever realized.

To my knowledge this is the first attempt that has been made to present systematically the philosophy of Advaita as expounded by Bhāratītīrtha-Vidyāraṇya and to assess the contribution of that great scholar-saint to the Vivaraṇa school in particular and to Advaita metaphysics in general. It is hoped that the present treatise will help students of Indian philosophy in getting to know the main concepts of Advaita doctrine in relation to other systems of Indian thought and thereby make for extending, in however small a measure, the frontiers of knowledge.

The accomplishment of this work would have been well nigh impossible but for the help of my revered brother Svami Rajesvaranandaji at every stage of its production and publication. My first duty is to record my deep indebtedness to him. Especially in a task of this kind the value of the guidance of one who leads the life of an Advaitin cannot be adequately expressed. The seeds of Advaita sown by the Svami early in my life have grown under his constant care. Conscious as I am of my ignorance of the many intricacies of Advaita, if I have succeeded, though in a poor measure, to present the philosophical system in an intelligible way, it is not a little due to the impressions that were formed even before I had crossed the early teens of my life.

I am deeply indebted to Mr S.S. Suryanarayana Sastri, Head of the Department of Philosophy in the University of Madras, who guided my work throughout. An adept in metaphysical ways of thinking Mr Sastri has led me by the hand, steadied my faltering steps and shown me the direction whence to expect gleams of truth. Not only did he lend me his translations of such classic treatises on Advaita like the *Vivaraṇa, Vivaraṇa-Prameya-Saṁgraha, Iṣṭasiddhi* and *Siddhāntaleśa*; he trained me also to hunt in the treasure-house of knowledge. I express my sincere gratitude to Mr P.N. Srinivasachariar, my professor at college, who gave me the knowledge which has served as the foundation of my efforts. His advice has always been valuable and his example an inspiration.

To Sir S. Radhakrishnan I acknowledge my indebtedness for the very kind interest he has taken in my work and for the

Foreword he has written. And to the University of Madras I owe my obligations for affording me all facilities for preparing the thesis. My thanks are also due to Vidyāratnākara Kodavasal Narasimhachariar and Vedānta-śiromaṇi K.R. Lakshmana Sastri with whom I read some of the Sanskrit texts, and to all those who have contributed, in one way or other, to the success of this undertaking.

Madras **Mahadevan**
1 August 1938

Abbreviations

AitUp	*Aitareya Upaniṣad*
BhG	*Bhagavadgītā*
BrahmaUp	*Brahmabindu Upaniṣad*
BṛUp	*Bṛhadāraṇyaka Upaniṣad*
BṛVārt	*Bṛhadāraṇyaka-Upaniṣad-Bhāṣya-Vārtika*
ChāUp	*Chāndogya Upaniṣad*
ĪśaUp	*Īśa Upaniṣad*
JābālaUp	*Jābāladarśana Upaniṣad*
KaivalyaUp	*Kaivalya Upaniṣad*
KaṭhaUp	*Kaṭha Upaniṣad*
KauṣīUp	*Kauṣītaki Upaniṣad*
KenaUp	*Kena Upaniṣad*
MahānārUp	*Mahānārāyaṇa Upaniṣad*
MaitrīUp	*Maitrī Upaniṣad*
MāUp	*Māṇḍūkya Upaniṣad*
MemEdn	*Memorial Edition of Śaṅkara's Works,* Vāṇı Vilās Press
MuṇḍUp	*Muṇḍaka Upaniṣad*
MśV	*Mīmāṁsā-Śloka-Vārttika*
PD	*Pañcadaśī*
PraśnaUp	*Praśna Upaniṣad*

śl	*śloka*
SLS	*Siddhāntaleśasaṁgraha*
ŚvetUp	*Śvetāśvatara Upaniṣad*
TaitUp	*Taittirīya Upaniṣad*
TC	*Tattvacintāmaṇi*
TPH	Theosophical Publishing House
TS	*Tarkasaṁgraha*
VedSū	*Vedāntasūtras*
VP	*Vedānta-Paribhāṣā*
VPS	*Vivaraṇa-Prameya-Saṁgraha*

Contents

Introduction

IN these pages an attempt is made to present the philosophy of Advaita from a study of the *Vivaraṇa-Prameya-Saṁgraha, Pañcadaśī* and *Dṛg-Dṛśya-Viveka*. Tradition ascribes the authorship of the *Vivaraṇa-Prameya-Saṁgraha* to Vidyāraṇya whom it identifies with Mādhava, the son of Māyaṇa and the brother of Sāyaṇa and Bhoganātha.[1] The *Pañcadaśī* is thought to be the work of Vidyāraṇya and Bhāratītīrtha. With regard to the authorship of the *Dṛg-Dṛśya-Viveka*, opinion is divided. Brahmānanda Bhāratī, one of the commentators on the work, regards Bhāratītīrtha as its author. In some manuscripts bearing the commentary of Ānandajñāna it is found that Śrī Śaṅkarācārya is saluted as its author. Niścaladāsa, in his *Vṛtti-Prabhākara*, ascribes the book to Vidyāraṇya.

Vidyāraṇya seems to have lived in the fourteenth century CE as the family *guru* of Harihara I and Bukka, the founders of the Vijayanagara kingdom, and appears to have occupied the *gaddī* of the Śṛṅgerī Maṭha from *c.*1377 to 1386 CE. Tradition attaches great importance to Vidyāraṇya. He is regarded as having been the friend, philosopher and guide of the early rulers of Vijayanagara, and in the field of religion and philosophy he is classed with the greatest of the post-Śaṅkara Advaitins.

---

1 See *Parāśara-Mādhavīya:*
śrīmatī jananī yasya sukīrtir māyaṇaḥ pitā
sāyaṇo bhogānathaś ca mano-buddhī sahodarau ।
baudhāyanam yasya sūtram śākhā yasya ca yājuṣī
bhāradvājam yasya gotram sarvajñaḥ sa hi mādhavaḥ ॥

The tendency of late has been to discard the traditional identity between Vidyāraṇya and Mādhava. Mādhava, the reputed author of such works as the *Parāśarasmṛti-Vyākhyā, Vyavahāra-Mādhava, Kāla-Mādhavīya, Jīvanmukti-Viveka* and *Jaiminīya-Nyāyamālā-Vistāra,* was the brother of Sāyaṇa, the author of the *Veda-Bhāṣya.* Both of them were politicians connected with the founding and development of the Vijayanagara Empire. But Vidyāraṇya, it is said, was only "an insignificant ascetic who presided over the Śṛṅgerī Maṭha from *c.*1377 to 1386 CE".[2] The works that are definitely attributed to Vidyāraṇya are only the *Pañcadaśī* and the *Vivaraṇa-Prameya-Saṁgraha.*[3]

The major portion of the contention of those who are against identifying Vidyāraṇya with Mādhava is based on the argument from silence. It is said that the several inscriptions which refer to Vidyāraṇya and his several predecessors and successors in the Śṛṅgerī Maṭha do not identify him with Mādhava, that the few inscriptions that refer to Mādhavācārya and his brother Sāyaṇa never indicate any connection between him and Vidyāraṇya, that the works of Mādhava and those of Vidyāraṇya do not bear testimony to the identity-theory and that no work can be cited either of contemporary authors or even of writers who flourished one or two centuries later which might clearly prove the identity. The other main argument advanced against the identity-theory is that it is extremely belated.

It is admitted that Bhāratītīrtha and Vidyātīrtha were the preceptors of Mādhava, for Mādhava himself tells us that he was favoured by them. While Vidyāraṇya in his works praises Śaṅkarānanda and Vidyātīrtha, it is said, nowhere he refers to Bhāratītīrtha. Mādhava acknowledges Bhāratītīrtha as his preceptor, but Vidyāraṇya in the *Vivaraṇa-Prameya-Saṁgraha*

---

[2] See the article in the *Indian Historical Quarterly,* XII(2): 241-50, "The Mādhava-Vidyāraṇya Theory" by M.A. Doraiswamy Iyengar, 1933.

[3] See the article "Vidyāraṇya and Mādhavācārya" by Rama Rao in the *Indian Historical Quarterly,* vol. VI, p. 701.

and the *Pañcadaśī* does not mention the name of Bhāratītīrtha at all. Hence, it is asked how both Mādhava and Vidyāraṇya can be identical.

Further, it is observed, throughout the works of Mādhava, King Bukka I is referred to as the patron, while the inscriptions of Vidyāraṇya are all of the reign of Harihara II (1377–1404). It is also contended that none of the inscriptions relating to Vidyāraṇya shows any connection between him and the building of the capital city of the Vijayanagara Empire, and that in those inscriptions the capital is called Vijayanagara and not Vidyānagara.[4] Even supposing that Vidyānagara was another name of the same city, it is said, the ascetic connected with the name and foundation of the empire, if any, should have been Vidyātīrtha, the preceptor of Mādhava and not Vidyāraṇya. Since Mādhava as well as his father were family ministers and teachers of the dynasty of Saṅgama and since Mādhava's teacher was Vidyātīrtha, the Pontiff of the Kāñcī Kāmakoṭi Maṭha, it is likely that, when Saṅgama's son founded a new empire with Mādhava as the chief minister, the latter sent for his teacher from which time Vidyātīrtha must have taken his seat at Śṛṅgerī. From these and other considerations it is sought to be proved that the identity-theory is an invention of later admirers of Vidyāraṇya, who were anxious to make him the author of as many works as possible.

From the evidence we have on hand it cannot be conclusively proved that Mādhava and Vidyāraṇya were identical. But the identity-theory seems to be more probable than the opposite theory.[5] From two copper-plate grants both dated 1336 CE we gather that Harihara I went out hunting in the forest on the southern bank of the Tuṅgabhadrā, where he saw a hound and

---

4 R. Rama Rao's article on "The Origin of Mādhava-Vidyāraṇya Theory" in the *Indian Historical Quarterly*, vol. VII, pp. 78-92.

5 See N. Venkata Ramanayya, 1933, *Vijayanagara: Origin of the City and the Empire*, chap. II, pp. 48f.

a hare together in spite of their natural enmity, that he narrated this incident to Vidyāraṇya who was practising asceticism in the temple of Virūpākṣa and who advised Harihara to found a city on the spot called Vidyānagara, and that Harihara accordingly built the city from which he began to rule his kingdom. To question the authenticity of these grants on the grounds that the formation of the letters is modern and that the incident which they record, viz. a hound and a hare being on good terms, is legendary, is not sound.

> It is not impossible that Harihara I should have built a capital for himself on the advice of Vidyāraṇya; nor is it unlikely that the city of Vidyānagara or Vijayanagara should have been built about 1336.[6]

The evidence of the copper-plate grants is corroborated by a few inscriptions of the Tuḷuva period which declare that the city of Vidyānagara was built by King Harihara I and named Vidyānagara in the name of Vidyāraṇya Śrīpāda. Two inscriptions dated respectively 1538 and 1559 CE state that Harihara Rāya built Vidyānagara in the name of Vidyāraṇya.

These evidences go to prove that Vidyāraṇya was connected with the founding of the Vijayanagara Empire, that Vijayanagara had another name Vidyānagara almost from the very beginning, that the assertion that the inscriptions referring to Vidyāraṇya are all of the reign of Harihara II is groundless, and that it is needless to connect the name Vidyanāgara with Vidyātīrtha.

> If the name Vidyānagara was really derived from Vidyāraṇya as the Tuḷuva inscriptions would have us believe, it cannot be denied that he had some share direct or indirect in building the city.[7]

---

6 See N. Venkata Ramanayya, 1933, op. cit., pp. 48f.

7 See *Descriptive Catalogue*, vol. XII, no. 7067.

It is evident from the inscriptions that Vidyāraṇya's counsel was sought by all the early kings of the Vijayanagara Empire. Of Harihara II it is said, "By the grace of Vidyāraṇya-muni, he acquired the empire of knowledge unattainable by other kings." We learn that when Vidyāraṇya paid a visit to Varanasi where he stayed for some time (about 1356 CE), Bukka I desired that Vidyāraṇya should return to Vijayanagara. He was not sure that his request would be complied with. So he secured a *śrīmukha* from the senior Śrīpāda of Śṛṅgerī commanding Vidyāraṇya to return to Vijayanagara and despatched it to Vidyāraṇya together with his own request. It is said that Vidyāraṇya came back "as he had great respect for his *guru*". That Vidyāraṇya was famous during the time of the early kings of Vijayanagara for his wisdom and piety and that it is possible that the kings did seek his advice are evident from an inscription of Harihara II in which we find the following passage:

> May the wonderful glances of Vidyāraṇya which resemble showers of camphor dust, garlands of *kalhāra* flower, rays of the moon, sandal paste and waves of milk ocean, and which shower the nectar of compassion, bring you happiness. Can he be Brahmā? We do not see four faces. Can he be Viṣṇu? He has not got four arms. Can he be Śiva? No oddness of the eye is observed. Having thus argued for a long time, the learned have come to the conclusion that Vidyāraṇya is the supreme light incarnate.

The considerations we have set forth above point to the greater probability of the identity-theory being true. Though the contention that Vidyāraṇya was not Mādhavācārya and that he had nothing to do with the Vijayanagara empire is unconvincing, the distinction which the opponents of the identity-theory make between the author of such works as the *Parāśara-Mādhavīya*, etc. and the author of the *Pañcadaśī* and the *Vivaraṇa-Prameya-Saṁgraha*, etc. seems to be true. There appears to be a confusion between Vidyāraṇya and Bhāratītīrtha. It is possible for the reason we shall give below that both Mādhava and Bhāratītīrtha had the surname Vidyāraṇya. It was said by the opponents of the identity-theory that works of Mādhava, while referring to Bhāratītīrtha, do not make mention of Vidyāraṇya. That may be because, while Bhāratītīrtha was the preceptor of Mādhava, the word Vidyāraṇya was the surname of the author. It was shown that the *Pañcadaśī* and the *Vivaraṇa-Prameya-Saṁgraha* do not mention the name of Bhāratītīrtha and that therefore these are the works of Vidyāraṇya and not of Mādhava. While it may be conceded that they are not the works of Mādhava, it is probable that the name of Bhāratītīrtha is not mentioned in them by the author, not because Bhāratītīrtha was not the preceptor of the author of these works, but because Bhāratītīrtha himself was their author. The colophon to one of the manuscripts[8] available in the Tanjore Palace Library makes use of the name Bhāratītīrtha-Vidyāraṇya. This shows the possibility that Bhāratītīrtha also might have had the surname Vidyāraṇya.

Appayya Dīkṣita in his *Siddhāntaleśa* attributes the *Vivaraṇa-Prameya-Saṁgraha* to Bhāratītīrtha. He calls the work *Vivaraṇopanyāsa*. That the *Vivaraṇa-Prameya-Saṁgraha* had also the other name *Vivaraṇopanyāsa* is borne out by the fact that the colophon at the end of the first *varṇaka* names the work as *Vivaraṇopanyāsa*.[9] Appayya Dīkṣita attributes several chapters of the *Pañcadaśī* to Bhāratītīrtha while he makes no mention of Vidyāraṇya (i.e. Mādhava). That Rāmakṛṣṇa Paṇḍita at the beginning of his commentary on the *Tṛptidīpa*[10] mentions Bhāratītīrtha as the author is no ground for stating that the earlier chapters are the work of Mādhava-Vidyāraṇya. The mention of Bhāratītīrtha in the *Tṛptidīpa* may indicate

[8] *vivaraṇopanyāse bhāratītīrtha-vacanam* । – *SLS*, vol. II, p. 93

[9] *iti śrī vivaraṇopanyāse prathama-varṇakam samāptam* । – *VPS*, p. 108

[10] *tṛptidīpākhyam prakaraṇaṁ ārabhamāṇaḥ śrī bhāratītīrthagurus tasya śruti-vyākhyāna-rūpatvāt tadvyākhyām śrutim ādau paṭhati* ।
– *PD*, p. 209

his authorship not of that chapter alone nor of that and the succeeding chapters alone but of the whole book. Rāmakṛṣṇa Paṇḍita no doubt pays obeisance to both Vidyāraṇya and Bhāratītīrtha. But this would at best prove that Rāmakṛṣṇa was probably the disciple of both and not that the Pañcadaśī was the work of both. Niścaladāsa's evidence, according to which the first ten chapters are the work of Mādhava-Vidyāraṇya and the other five that of Bhāratītīrtha, cannot be relied upon; for Appayya who lived very much earlier than Niścaladāsa must have known better about the authorship of the *Pañcadaśī* than the latter. The *Dṛg-Dṛśya-Viveka* is also attributed by Appayya to Bhāratītīrtha-Vidyāraṇya.[11] Since Brahmānanda Bhāratī, one of the commentators, also acknowledges Bhāratītīrtha as the author of the *Dṛg-Dṛśya-Viveka*, we are led to think that the evidence of Appayya is correct. One other work which is ascribed to Bhāratītīrtha is the *Vaiyāsikanyāya-mālā* which serves as a good guide to the study of Śaṅkara's *Sūtrabhāṣya.*

From the evidence afforded by the *Siddhāntaleśa* of Appayya Dīkṣita which is supported by other evidences we have set forth above, we are led to the conclusion that Bhāratītīrtha was the author of the three works and that the name Vidyāraṇya was an appellation which was common to both Mādhava and Bhāratītīrtha. It is possible that either was referred to sometimes by one name and sometimes by the other and that therefrom resulted the confusion.

Bhāratītīrtha-Vidyāraṇya was the senior contemporary of Mādhava-Vidyāraṇya. One of the inscriptions dated 1386 CE records thus:

> The swan Bukka sports happily near the lotus Bhāratītīrtha which, having sprung from Vidyātīrtha possesses the fragrance of joy from a knowledge of non-dualism and expands by the rays of the sun of Vidyāraṇya.

---

[11] See *SLS*, vol. II, p. 22.

From this passage we understand that Vidyātīrtha was Bhāratītīrtha's preceptor and that Bhāratītīrtha was Mādhava-Vidyāraṇya's preceptor. Both Bhāratītīrtha and Mādhava seem to have been eminent Advaitins; and both of them were connected with the early kings of Vijayanagara. In a copy of a copper plate inscription found in a *kaḍita* in the Śṛṅgerī Maṭha dated 1380 Vidyāraṇya's (Mādhava's) feats are stated to be more wonderful than those of Brahmā, seeing that he can make the eloquent dumb and the dumb the most eloquent, and Bhāratītīrtha is described as the refuter of the doctrines of Bhaṭṭa (Kumārila), Buddha, Jina, Guru (Prabhākara), the Logicians and the Cārvākas, and the establisher of the Advaita doctrine. Another inscription dated 1386 states:

> The impressive and dignified discourses delivered by Bhāratītīrtha when expounding various works treating of obscure subjects resemble the uninterrupted flow of the Ganges from the slopes of the Himālayas.

Beyond the facts we have given above nothing is known about the details of Bhāratītīrtha's life. He lived in the fourteenth century CE; he was the predecessor of Mādhava-Vidyāraṇya in occupying the pontifical seat of the Śṛṅgerī Maṭha. He was famous for his exposition of Advaita and was revered by the early kings of Vijayanagara. While the passages from the inscriptions which we have quoted refer to the prowess and occult powers of Mādhava-Vidyāraṇya, they speak of Bhāratītīrtha as a great scholar and exponent of Advaita.

1

The Ways of Knowing

VEDĀNTA is the Science of Reality which it defines as the one Being without a second. It aims at the knowledge of that by knowing which everything else becomes known. *Brahman* is all-that-which-is, and after knowing that, there remains nothing else to be known. Self-knowledge (*ātma-vidyā*) is the end of knowledge (*vedānta*). *Ātmānam viddhi* "sums up the law and the prophets".[1] The principal means to self-knowledge is the study of scripture to which reflection and meditation are auxiliaries, and calmness, restraint, etc. serve as the modus operandi (*VPS*, p. 2). When the purport of the major texts of the Vedānta is cognized, there arises a certain psychosis of the internal organ whose sphere is *Brahman*. This is what is called *Brahman*-intuition which removes all misery and brings in its train unexcellable bliss (*VPS*, p. 2).

The Mechanism of Knowledge

Before entering into the details of the central doctrine of Advaita, viz. the non-difference of the *jīva* from *Brahman*, it is necessary to examine the mechanism of knowledge. Before trying to understand how *Brahman* is known, it is useful to inquire into the nature of the empirical usage in respect of cognitions. Epistemology is the portal to philosophy. "Almost the first

[1] S. Radhakrishnan, 1923, *Indian Philosophy*, vol. I, p. 28, London: George Allen & Unwin.

question which everyone of the Hindu systems of philosophy tries to settle is, How do we know? In thus giving the Noetics the first place,"says Max Müller, "the thinkers of the East seem to me again superior to most of the philosophers of the West." [2]

The process of knowing implies the subject who knows and the object that is known. An act of cognition involves the triple forms (*tripuṭī*), the cognizer, the object cognized and the means of cognition. The justification of the empirical usage of the cognizer, means of cognition, etc. is impossible, says the Advaitin, in the non-Advaitic systems like those of the Sāṁkhyas and the Naiyāyikas (*VPS*, pp. 70-72).[3] Egoity (*ahaṁkāra*) which is inert, according to the Sāṁkhyas, cannot be the cognizer. Nor can cognizership belong to the self. The self is intelligent, but non-active; and cognizership, which consists in being transformed in the form of the act called *pramāṇa*, cannot be an attribute of the self. Though these objections may be urged against the Advaitin, he effectively refutes them, as we shall see later and explains how the empirical usage is intelligible. The Sāṁkhya may argue that even without cognizership, the self, which is self-luminous intelligence, may manifest objects. But if that were so, then, even because of the omnipresence of the self, there is the contingence of the simultaneous manifestation of everything.

Unlike the Sāṁkhyas and the Advaitins who hold that cognition is not originated, the Naiyāyikas maintain that it is originated in the omnipresent self. Even thus, if cognition be inherent in the entire self, it is not possible to account for the restriction of cognition to particular objects. If cognition be pervasive of the entire self, since there is nothing which controls it, there is the contingence of the simultaneous manifestation of all objects. Nor may it be said that merit (*dharma*) and

---

2 Max Müller, 1899, *Six Systems of Indian Philosophy*, p. xii, London: Longmans, Green & Co.

3 In all polemical discussions the final position (*siddhānta*) is established by a refutation of the rival (*pūravapakṣa*) views.

demerit (*adharma*) are the controllers. Merit may bring about the cognition of those objects which generate happiness; and demerit may serve as the controller in respect of the cognition of those objects which produce misery. But in respect of things which are to be treated with indifference, merit and demerit are not the controllers. Nor is there a rule that cognition manifests its own generator. The sense of sight, for example, which generates cognition is not manifested by it. Whether cognition be regarded as a quality or an act, it cannot be generalized that it apprehends the object which generates it. To avoid the defects in the view that cognition is inherent in the entire self, it may be stated that it is inherent only in that part of the self which is defined by the body. Even thus, if the part which is defined by the body be natural to the self, there is the contingence of the self having parts. If that part be due to adjuncts, and if cognition apprehend only those objects which are conjoined thereto, then there would be no cognition of external things which are not conjoined to the body. If cognition apprehend what is conjoined to the part of the self which is outside the body, then, nothing could prevent the simultaneous manifestation of all external things. Those views which attempt to escape from these difficulties by regarding the self as atomic in size or of the size of the body fare no better in explaining the empirical usage of cognizer, means of cognition, etc.

The Advaitin states the possibility of the empirical usage thus: Nescience which is of the nature of an existent is the cause of all empirical distinctions. It obscures the omnipresent, intelligent self, and transforms itself in the form of the world of diverse kinds.

> Of these, that transformation of nescience which resides in the body and is called the internal organ, being prompted by merit and demerit, goes out through the channel of the eyes, etc. pervades suitable objects like the pot, and becomes of their respective forms. – *VPS*, p. 71

This is compared to the water flowing from the tank to the fields through channels and assuming the forms of the respective fields. Just as the molten metal which is poured into a crucible puts on the shape of the latter, the mind which pervades an object assumes the form of that object (*PD* IV.28). Or, even as the light of the sun takes on the shape of the object which it illumines, the intellect which enlightens everything, assumes the form of the object which it reveals (*PD* IV.29). As the *vārtikakāra* (Sureśvara) observes, from the cognizer, i.e. the reflection of intelligence (*cidābhāsa*) which resides in the intellect, there arises *pramāṇa* which is of the nature of a psychosis of the internal organ (*antaḥkaraṇa-vṛtti*). The *pramāṇa,* on reaching the object of cognition, e.g. a pot, assumes the form of that object (*PD* IV.30). A psychosis is a transformation of the internal organ. And transformation of the internal organ is intelligible, since the internal organ, like milk, etc. has parts. The psychosis connects the cognizer and the object cognized. The same internal organ resides in the body, goes out through the channels of the senses, pervades the object and manifests it. That part of the internal organ which is defined by the body is called egoity; that part which connects egoity with the object is termed cognitive psychosis; and that part, which pervades the object, assumes the form of the object and invests it with the character of objectness, is known as fitness for manifestation (*abhivyakti-yogyatā*). Because the internal organ with its three parts is a product of the *sattva*-constituent of nescience, it mirrors intelligence; and although intelligence is impartite, it appears as if split up into three forms on account of the difference in the parts of the internal organ which manifests it. The aspect of intelligence which is defined by egoity is the cognizer (*pramātā*); the aspect of intelligence which is defined by the cognitive psychosis is the means of cognition (*pramāṇa*); the aspect of intelligence defined by the element of fitness for manifestation present in the object is the cognition (*pramiti*). Thus, the Advaitin attributes the empirical usage in respect of cognition to the work of nescience which presents the impartite intelligence as if it was split up into parts. The distinctions of cognizer, means of cognition, etc. are the creation of *avidyā*.[4] It is thus that the Advaitin accounts for the empirical usage of distinctions involved in acts of cognition.

The Function of Psychosis

The function of psychosis is to manifest objects. The intelligence which is defined by pot, cloth, etc. is called the object-defined intelligence. That which manifests it is a transformation either of the internal organ or of nescience. Such a transformation either of the internal organ or of nescience is what is known as a psychosis (*vṛtti*).[5] Since the *jīva* or the cognizer is of the nature of intelligence, it may be doubted, why it should not manifest objects without the help of psychoses. The reply to this objection as given by the Vivaraṇa view which is summarized in the *Vivaraṇa-Premeya-Saṁgraha* is as follows (*SLS*, vol. II, pp. 33f.): *Brahman*-intelligence, because it is the material cause of all things, manifests them. But the *jīva*-intelligence, which has nescience for its adjunct, is not the material cause of all things. Just as for the generality, cowness, which is omnipresent, there is conjunction only with cows and not with horses, etc. so also for the omnipresent *jīva*-intelligence, there is natural conjunction with the internal organ and not with objects. Since there is no conjunction of the *jīva* with objects, there is need for psychoses to bring about that conjunction. The psychosis which is a transformation of the internal organ goes out through the

---

4 It must, however, be said, in fairness to the Sāṁkhya, that such an explanation is handy even to him.

5 See *Tattvānusandhāna*, p. 111:
viṣaya-caitanyā-'bhivyañjako-'ntaḥkaraṇā-'jñānayoḥ pariṇāma viśeṣaḥ vṛttiḥ ।
The term *psychosis* is used by modern psychologists to indicate an abnormal state of mind. But here it is employed to mean a transformation either of the mind or of its cause, nescience.

senses to the object and pervades it. Thence arises the cognition of the object. Just as the bare fire, which is incapable of burning even a blade of grass, burns when it is associated with a ball of iron, even so the *jīva*-intelligence, though unable to manifest objects, does so when it is associated with the psychoses of the internal organ. This mode of explaining the need for psychoses is on the assumption that the *jīva* is omnipresent and that its adjunct is nescience. When, however, the *jīva* is regarded as finite because of its adjunct, the internal organ, it is easy to establish that since there is no relation between the *jīva* and the object, a psychosis is needed to manifest the non-difference of the *jīva* from the object-defined-intelligence. Or else, though the *jīva* be regarded as omnipresent, since it is veiled by nescience, it does not by itself manifest objects. The function of the psychosis is to destroy the ignorance veiling the *jīva*. Being manifested in this manner by the psychosis, the *jīva* illumines that object which is pervaded by the psychosis. Thus, the dependence of the *jīva* on the psychoses is either for bringing about the association of the object with intelligence, or for manifesting the non-difference of the *jīva* from the object, or for lifting the veil of ignorance that obscures the *jīva*-intelligence. There is not the destruction of obscuration (*āvaraṇa*) by the psychoses, in which case there is the contingence of release even by the pot-cognition. What is called the manifestation of intelligence by the internal organ is the overpowering (*abhibhava*), not the destruction (*vināśa*), of obscuration (*VPS*, p. 72).

If intelligence be omnipresent, it may be asked how there is restriction of cognition of particular objects (*prati-karma-vyavasthā*). It was argued above that in the view of the Sāṁkhyas, who hold the self-intelligence to be omnipresent, there is the contingence of the simultaneous manifestation of all things. It is possible to urge the same objection against the Advaitin who regards intelligence as omnipresent. But this contention will not bear reasoning. What is meant by saying that in the view of the Advaitin there is not the restriction of cognition to particular objects? Is it inferred that the happiness, misery, etc. experienced by one person should be experienced by all, because of the oneness of intelligence of all persons? Or, is it urged that when a particular person experiences a certain object, say, a pot, the whole world should be experienced by him, because of the omnipresence of his intelligence? The first inference is not valid. The Advaitin does not say that bare intelligence is the cause of the experience of objects. Intelligence is obscured by nescience; and hence it is incapable of manifesting objects. It is only that intelligence which is manifested by the internal organ that is the cause of the experience of objects.[6] Since for each person, the internal organ is different, the non-experience by a particular person of the happiness, misery, etc. experienced by another is intelligible. The second contention that, when a person experiences a pot, he should experience the whole world, is also unsound. The internal organ of each person is finite and particular; and it does not relate simultaneously to the entire world. Nor may it be said that even for the finite, as for the rays of the sun, there may be the capacity to manifest all objects together; for in the case of the transformation of the internal organ, the causal aggregate consisting in merit, demerit, the sense of sight, etc. is restricted. When the causal aggregate is not restricted, there is, no doubt, the simultaneous manifestation of all things, as in the case of the *yogin* who obtains occult powers.

The assumption of the internal organ is, it was said, for the sake of associating the self with objects. Without association with objects, no cognition of them is possible. The self, which

6 Such an answer is available even for the Sāṁkhya. In truth, the solutions for the present problem given by the Sāṁkhya and the Advaitin are more or less the same. The self, though intelligent, is non-active and the intellect which is a product of matter is inert. But since the intellect is constituted of the *sattva*-element (intelligence-stuff) and is translucent, it reflects the intelligence-self and brings about the experience of objects.

is non-attached intelligence, is not associated with the objects. A psychosis which is a transformation of the internal organ is needed in order that the association of the self with the object may be effected. It was also observed that there is a natural association between the self and the internal organ which is itself a product of nescience. Now, it may be asked how there is association of the non-attached intelligence with the internal organ. If the self be associated with the internal organ, it ceases to be non-attached; and if there be attachment for the self, there may as well be direct association for it with objects of sense. Nor may it be said that, even though there is association of the self with objects, the internal organ is required in order to manifest objects; for, when there is established the manifestation of objects even from the association with intelligence, it is futile to assume an internal organ over and above intelligence. When it is proved that the assumption of the internal organ as the adjunct of the self is unwarranted, it is easily established that in the case of the omnipresent self there cannot intelligibly be restriction of cognition to particular objects.

The Advaitin seeks to answer this contention by cross-examining his opponent. He begins by stating that in the case of *Brahman* the simultaneous manifestation of all objects is a contingence of the acceptable. The *jīva*-intelligence, however, though omnipresent, is not capable of manifesting the entire world. Since it is obscured by nescience, it does not by itself illumine objects. It is only through association with the internal organ that the self apprehends objects. Nor may it be said that association with the internal organ is unintelligible in the case of the self which is unattached; for, as was remarked above, just as the generality, cowness, though omnipresent, associates with the individual that has a dewlap, etc. not with any other individual, even so the omnipresent self associates with the internal organ, not with anything else. If this example be unacceptable, let there be the illustration of the radiance of the lamp, which though pervasive of colour, taste, odour, etc. manifests colour alone to the exclusion of the rest. Thus, there is the requirement of the internal organ for the sake of bringing about the association of intelligence with objects.

If the internal organ be instrumental to the apprehension of what is associated therewith, it may be contended that there is the contingence of the constant cognition of *Brahman*, for *Brahman*, being the material cause of all, is associated with all things including the internal organ. But the Advaitin replies that the mere existence of the internal organ is not enough to manifest objects. In order that there may be the cognition of an object, the psychosis of the internal organ must take on the form of the object. And since there is no psychosis of the internal organ which has assumed the form of *Brahman*, there is not the contingence of the *jīva*'s constant apprehension of *Brahman*. If the mere association of the internal organ with an object be the cause of the manifestation of that object, there is the contingence of the cognition of mind, etc. which are present in the internal organ itself.

Thus, it is the assumption by the psychosis of the internal organ, of the form of the object which it pervades, that restricts the *jīva*'s cognition of things.

Psychoses, we have said, may be transformations either of nescience or of the internal organ. Where there is not present the activity of the internal organ and yet there is cognition, there, the cognition is due to the psychoses of nescience, e.g. the perception of happiness, etc.

Psychoses may lead either to valid (*pramā*) or false (*apramā*) knowledge. *Pramā* (valid knowledge) is defined as that knowledge which is unsublated and unestablished by any other means.[7] The knowledge of something which is not contradicted and which is novel is *pramā*. Unsublatability and novelty are marks of valid knowledge. That which is the distinctive cause

7 *VP*, p. 15: *anadhigatā-'bādhitā-'rtha-viṣayaka-jñānatvam pramātvam* ।

of arriving at valid knowledge is *pramāṇa*. *Pramāṇa* is the instrument (*karaṇa*) of valid knowledge. Following the way of Bhāṭṭas in empirical matters,[8] the Advaitin admits of six *pramāṇas* (ways of knowing) – perception (*pratyakṣa*), inference (*anumāna*), analogy (*upamāna*), verbal testimony (*āgama*), presumption (*arthāpatti*) and non-cognition (*anupalabdhi*).

PERCEPTION (PRATYAKṢA)

The theory of perception is the basis on which the superstructure of a *Weltanschauung* is built. No generalization about the nature of the world can afford to neglect enquiring into the nature of the perceptual process. In the discussion on the function of psychoses we have already pointed out how the cognition of an object takes place. What distinguishes *pratyakṣa* is its directness or immediacy. Valid knowledge from *pratyakṣa* is defined as the *pramāṇa*-intelligence which is non-different from the object-defined-intelligence. When the psychosis of the internal organ goes out through the channel of the senses, pervades the object and puts on the form of the object, there is brought about the non-difference of the intelligence which is inherent in the means of valid knowledge from the object-defined-intelligence.[9] This is *pratyakṣa*. Perception is possible only of things which are present and are capable of being perceived. The events of yesterday are not objects of perception, because they are not facts of the present time. Mind, though present, cannot be perceived, because it is not capable of being an object of perception. Knowledge derived from perception can be valid only when it is not sublated by any other evidence. Judged by this test only the knowledge of *Brahman* can be *pramā*; and the Vedānta which leads to that knowledge can alone be the *pramāṇa*. But still, since empirical knowledge remains unsublated up to the cognition of *Brahman*,

---

8 *vyavahāre bhaṭṭa-nayaḥ* ।

9 *abādhita-vartamāna-yogya-viṣaya-caitanyā-'bhinna-pramāṇa-caitanyam pratyakṣa-pramā* ।

it is also regarded as valid. Empirical validity belongs to the knowledge of the world; *Brahman*-knowledge is absolutely valid.

According to the Ābhāsavāda (theory of reflection) expounded in the *Pañcadaśī*, there are four factors in an act of perception:

1. the intelligence which has the internal organ as its attribute together with the reflection of intelligence is the perceiving agent;
2. the intelligence qualified by the psychosis together with the reflection of intelligence is the means of valid knowledge;
3. the intelligence defined by pot, etc. is the object-intelligence; and
4. the reflection of intelligence which is generated by the relation of the psychosis with pot, etc. is the fruit-intelligence (*phala-cetanā*).

If a pot is to be known, there must result in it the reflection of intelligence brought about by the contact of the psychosis with the pot (*PD* VIII.4-17). The intelligence which is in the intellect and which has assumed the form of the pot makes known the pot. The known-ness of the pot, however, is caused by *Brahman*-intelligence.

If the known-ness of the pot be due to *Brahman*-intelligence, it may be asked, what purpose is served by the presence of the intellect? The author of the *Pañcadaśī* replies that the intellect or the internal organ is the instrument for making the pot known. Prior to the intellectual cognition of the pot, the pot is made manifest by *Brahman*-intelligence, not as known, but as a thing unknown; and after the mental psychosis has come into contact with the pot, the same intelligence manifests the pot as known. Both the statements, "I know the pot" and "I do not know the pot", have Brāhmaṇas their basis.

It may be urged that, while it is intelligible that *Brahman* should illumine the unknown-ness of an object, because of the absence of an apparatus of perception, it does not stand to reason that *Brahman*-intelligence is required for manifesting the known-ness of the object also, for in the latter case there is the activity of the internal organ through the channel of the senses, which alone is the cause of perception. The answer which the Advaitin gives to this contention is that both the known-ness and unknown-ness of an object are attributes manifested by *Brahman*.

Just as *Brahman*-intelligence is required for the sake of manifesting the known-ness and the unknown-ness of an object, the *ābhāsa* (reflection of intelligence) is needed in order to enable the psychosis of the intellect to illumine the object. The intellect, which is inert, non-intelligent, like pot, etc. is powerless to manifest any object. Let us imagine a wall studded with pieces of mirror. When the rays of the sun are reflected in the mirrors, we may well say that the wall is illumined both by the reflected rays and the direct rays of the sun. But when there is neither the sun nor the reflection of its rays, the wall is not illumined. Minds are, like mirrors, ineffectual in themselves to reveal objects. Reflection is necessary, if the mirrors are to illumine the wall, and the sun too is needed, if there is to be reflection at all. It is only that intellect which is endowed with the reflection of intelligence that is capable of accomplishing the perception of an object. The known-ness of a pot means the generation of the fruit, viz. the *cidābhāsa* (reflection of intelligence) in that pot. When a psychosis comes into contact with the pot there is generated in the pot a reflection of intelligence; and it is this reflection that reveals the pot and is called the fruit (*phala*).

What is called the fruit in the perceptual process is not *Brahman*-intelligence, for even prior to the perception of an object it existed and will continue to exist when the perceptual process has come to an end. The fruit that is generated in the external objects of perception is not intelligence per se; it is only the reflection of intelligence (*cidābhāsa*). The words of Sureśvara are sometimes quoted as evidence for the statement that *Brahman* itself is the fruit (see *PD* VIII.11, 13). But the real intention of that great preceptor is to declare merely that the fruit, viz. the reflection of intelligence, is similar to *Brahman*. What is generated in the object of perception is a reflection of *Brahman*-intelligence which in turn illumines the objects. The *ābhāsa* (reflection) is an appearance of which *Brahman* is the reality.

Brahman-intelligence illumines the psychosis, the *ābhāsa* and the object of perception, whereas the *ābhāsa* reveals the object alone. Thus, the object is illumined by two intelligences, the real intelligence that is *Brahman* and the reflection that is the *ābhāsa*. First, the object is known and then, there is the knowledge that the object is known. The latter kind of knowledge is called by the Logicians reflective cognition (*anuvyavasāya-jñāna*). This is identified in the Vedānta with *Brahman*-intelligence, since the admission of a reflective psychosis leads to infinite regress. The perceptual process discloses two distinct stages. The first is the perception of the object and the second is the cognition that the object is perceived. "This is a pot", we observe, and later on add, "I know this pot". The first of these statements indicates the activity of the *ābhāsa* and the second points to the fact that *Brahman* is the basic intelligence which accounts for the known-ness of the object. Without the *ābhāsa* there cannot be the perception of the object and without *Brahman*-intelligence there cannot be the generation of the *ābhāsa* which stands to *Brahman* as a reflection to its image.

The channels which carry the psychoses of the internal organ to the objects wherein the reflection of intelligence is generated, are the cognitive senses (*jñānendriya*s). The psychoses of the internal organ go out to the objects through the pathways of the senses and generate in them reflections of intelligence; thence the objects are revealed.

The followers of the various schools of thought have different views about *indriya*s (senses) (*VPS*, p. 185). The Saugatas (Buddhists) maintain that the senses are but the orbs. But the Saugata view does not stand to reason. Snakes, etc. though devoid of orbs like the ear-cavity, cognize sound. And in the case of trees, which have no orb whatever, there is the cognition of objects.[10] We learn that the trees perceive, since there is the sacred teaching "Therefore, the trees see". That the trees are not inert things but intelligent beings is evident from the prohibition of injury to them. Thus, the Saugata view that the senses are the orbs is defective.

According to the Mīmāṁsakas, the senses are the capacities of the orbs. They think that, instead of assuming another substance possessed of capacity, it is more in keeping with parsimony to assume capacity alone in the things already cognized. But as against this view, the Advaitin maintains that there is the greatest parsimony in postulating a capacity for the self, which consists in generating cognitions in sequence. Surely, to assume one substance with capacity is more parsimonious than to assume many capacities in the various sensory orbs. The Mīmāṁsaka may turn round and say that the transformation of the omnipresent self as cognition in the region of the orbs is unintelligible. But this objection cannot properly be raised by him; for he too admits that in the region of the body the self is transformed as cognition. Thus, without the assumption of capacities in the orbs, the co-presence and co-absence of the orbs and cognitions may be explained on the postulation that the self transforms itself as cognitions in those regions of the body which are called the sensory orbs. Hence the view of the Mīmāṁsaka that the capacities of the orbs are the senses is not sound.

Others hold that the senses are substances other than the orbs and that they are denoted by the words *cakṣus* (eye), etc.

---

[10] That plants and even metals are sentient is borne out by the researches of Sir J.C. Bose.

because of their connection with the particular orbs. Even this view is defective, since there is no evidence for stating that the senses are substances other than the orbs and their capacities. It cannot be inferred that cognitions of colour, etc. are caused by instruments on the ground that they are activities of an agent like the activity of cutting a piece of wood. It is not conclusively proved that activities of agents are caused by instruments. In that activity of the agent, for example, which consists in directing the instrument, there is not the requirement of another instrument. Otherwise, there would be infinite regress. Nor may it be said that the senses are known from the scriptural text, "From this the vital air is generated, mind and all the senses" (*MuṇḍUp* II.i.3); for even those who have no knowledge of the sacred lore are cognizant of the existence of the senses. It cannot be maintained that like the mind, the senses are also cognized by the witness, for they are not made known by the witness alone independent of the *probans* like the cognition of colour, etc. Hence, even the third view of the senses is faulty.

On the ground that the three views mentioned above are defective, it cannot be concluded that there are no senses at all. What the vulgar regard as the senses are the orbs and not the senses proper. The senses which are other than the orbs are known from revelation alone. They cannot be perceived; they can only be inferred. The *indriya* is the instrument (*karaṇa*) of perception.

What is the cause of *indriyas* (*VPS*, p. 186)? The Sāṁkhyas declare the senses to be the products of individuation (*ahaṁkāra*). Whether the individuation be understood to be something personal or to be the primal nature, there is no evidence whatever for the assertion that individuation is the parent of the senses. The Purāṇas cannot be quoted as supporting the view that primal nature, which is the *prius* of creation and is called individuation, is the cause of the senses; for there is conflict with scripture which declares:

> Mind, dear one, is the product of food (earth), the vital air is the product of water, speech is the product of fire.
>
> – *ChāUp* VI.v.4

From this text we learn that the senses are the products of the elements. Hence, the passages of the Purāṇas must be understood as stating that the senses are dependent on individuation, not its products.

The Logicians (Tārkikas) base their conclusions that the senses are elemental on abstract reasoning. But that too is unsound, for they can cite no evidence in their favour. They cannot argue that the senses are elemental, because they have parts and that they have parts, because of their medium size; for the *probans* are not established (*hetv-asiddhi*), since there is no sublation even if the senses be atomic in size. It may be said that, if the senses be atomic in size, there is the contingence of the presentation of the object too being atomic. But this contention cannot validly be lodged by the Logicians according to whom the mind, which is atomic, cognizes substances like the self. The reasoning which establishes the elemental nature of the senses may be stated thus: of the five, colour, sound, odour, taste and touch, the sense of sight manifests colour alone. In order that the sense of sight may manifest colour, it must have as its material cause that substance which has colour as its quality. *Tejas* (fire) is that which has colour as its distinctive quality. Hence the sense of sight is a modification of the element, fire. In this way it can be reasoned out that the other senses are also elemental. But this mode of reasoning has a flaw; and there is inconclusiveness (*anaikāntikatva*) in the case of the sense of hearing, which though manifesting sound alone is not the product of ether which has sound as its quality. According to the Logician, the sense of hearing is ether defined by the cavity of the ear. Admitting that in respect of the sense of hearing the above reasoning does not help to determine its elemental nature, it may be said that the syllogistic reasoning, which establishes the sense of sight, etc. to be products of elements, is perfectly valid. But even here undue extension (*atiprasaṅga*) cannot be prevented. If it be said that, because the sense of sight manifests colour, it must be the product of that substance which has colour as its quality, then it must be maintained that mind is a product of the four elements, since it manifests colour, odour, taste and touch. Nor may it be said that since mind apprehends even what is not an element, e.g. the self, it is not a product of elements; for, in that case, it is easy to state that the sense of sight, etc. are not products of elements, since they cognize number, size, etc. If it be said that, on the principle that a thing is produced by its distinctive content, there is established the elemental character of the senses, then let the mind be generated by its distinctive content, the self. Thus, reasoning cannot establish the elemental nature of the senses. It is only from revelation that we come to know that the senses are elemental.

The senses of hearing, touch, sight, taste and smell are products respectively of ether, air, fire, water and earth, and they are located respectively in the ear-cavities, skin, orbs of the eyes, tongue and nose. Since they are subtle, they are inferred from their effects and known from revelation. For the most part they go out and grasp external objects. But sometimes they turn inward and apprehend objects that are within the body. For instance, when the ear-cavities are shut, the inner sound is heard (*PD* II.6-8).

The Yogas (i.e. followers of the Yoga system) consider the senses to be omnipresent (*VPS*, p. 187). But their view is without evidence. On the analogy of the omnipresent ether, they say that the self, the senses and the mind are omnipresent, since their activity is seen everywhere. This inference is not valid. It is in no way established that their activity covers the entire world. Nor may it be said that because they are active wherever there is body, they are omnipresent; for, since body is not omnipresent, the activity of the senses, etc. which pervade the body cannot be omnipresent. Then it may be thought that, just as ether is omnipresent because of the conditioning of its motion by pot, etc. the senses are omnipresent, since their movement is conditioned by the body. But this too does not stand to reason. If the conditioning of the movement of an object by something else be determinative of its omnipresence, then the parts of the body may well be omnipresent, since their movement is conditioned by the vital air. Further, if the senses were omnipresent, there would be the simultaneous cognition of all things. Therefore, the senses are not omnipresent.

How do the senses manifest objects (*VPS*, p. 187)? The Saugatas hold that they reveal objects even without reaching to them. Here, they must be asked whether the senses of sight and hearing alone are effective without reaching to the object, or whether the rest of the senses also are so effective. The rest of the senses do not manifest objects without reaching to them. Otherwise, there is the contingence of the cognition of the touch and odour of a thing which is distant. Even in the case of the senses of hearing and sight, it is not possible to demonstrate that they are effective without reaching to the object. Since these two are external senses like the sense of smell, they are effective only by reaching to the object. Nor may it be said that, if the sense of sight be effective only by reaching to the object, there would be no instantaneous cognition of the distant luminaries like the pole-star; for quick travel of the sense of sight, which is of the nature of light, to great distances is intelligible. As for what the Logicians say that reaching, in the case of sound, consists in the inherence in the sense of hearing, that is unsound. If that were so, the cognition would be of the form, "The sound is here in the sense of hearing". But what we actually experience is the apprehension of the sound *there*. Hence, it must be assumed in conformity with experience that the sense of hearing goes out to the object and apprehends sound. Thus, it is settled that the senses are elemental, finite and effective by reaching to the object.

It has been said that mind flows through the channels of the senses and apprehends objects. One section of the Lokāyatas (materialists) thinks that mind is the self (*VPS*, p. 188). The Logicians regard mind as eternal, partless and atomic in size. But eternality cannot be attributed to the mind, because it is finite like pot. It is not possible to argue that, because mind is a partless substance, it is eternal; for the partlessness of mind is not established. Mind is with parts, because it is an instrument, like the sense of sight, etc. Further, scripture declares that mind is made of food (earth); and what is made of food cannot be a partless substance. It may be asked how, if the mind be with parts, there is no obstruction for it by corporeal objects. The Advaitin answers that the non-obstruction is intelligible even because there is no going away of the mind from the body so long as there is life. There exists at the time of death non-obstruction even for the sense of sight, etc. which are admitted to be with parts. Hence, mind is not partless. It is not also atomic in size, for it is with parts and it has conjunction (*saṁyoga*) and disjunction (*vibhāga*). If mind be omnipresent, there is the contingence of the simultaneous cognition of every thing, because of its conjunction with all the senses. But there is no such defect if the mind be considered to be of medium size. That the mind of an elephant assumes the size of an ant when it takes birth as an ant is intelligible through a decrease in the parts of the mind.

According to the Śākyas (Bauddhas), in a series of cognitions, the immediately antecedent cognition is the instrument of the subsequent cognition, and it is itself called *manas* (mind) (*VPS*, p. 188). This view is not valid. The generation of the subsequent cognition by the prior cognition does not take place without dependence on a rule of pervasion. This is so because the cognition of the *probans* generates the cognition of the *probandum* only in dependence on the pervasion. The Śākya cannot maintain that in the case of verbal knowledge, there is the generation of the cognition of sense by the cognition of the word without dependence on pervasion; for in his view, verbal knowledge is included in inference; and if it be a mode of inferential knowledge, then the pervasion is certainly required for the knowledge of the sense to arise. Leaving the view that the immediately antecedent cognition generates the subsequent one, it may be stated that it confers on the latter its form. But since form and that which has form are non-different, and since form which is the nature of a thing is not dependent on any other, what the Śākya now maintains is also faulty. Hence, it must be admitted that *manas* is some other thing which has parts.

Whether *manas* is an *indriya* or not is a disputed question. Vācaspati Miśra regards *manas* as a sense organ. From the statement made by Śaṅkara in his commentary on the *Vedāntasūtra* that, while scripture (*śruti*) holds mind to be not an *indriya,* the traditional code (*smṛti*) characterizes it as an *indriya,* Vācaspati concludes that Śaṅkara's view favours the doctrine of the traditional code. In internal perception there is not the activity of the external senses; there is only the function of the mind. Perception is brought about through the channel of the sense; and since in internal perception there is not the activity of the external senses, mind itself should be regarded as a sense organ. If mind be not characterized as an *indriya,* we must either say that cognition of happiness, etc. is not a case of perception or that *indriya* is not the instrument (*karaṇa*) of perception.

According to the *Vivaraṇa* view, *manas* is not an *indriya.* Admitting that the cognition of happiness, etc. is an internal perception, the *vivaraṇakāra* does not agree to the statement that all cases of perception are to be caused by the activity of the senses. As for what we have said above that the senses are instruments of perception, that refers only to the cases of external perception. Mind is an auxiliary to *pramāṇa.* It is the locus, not the instrument, of valid knowledge.[11] Since happiness, etc. are made known by the witness-intelligence, there is no need

[11] *Bheda-dhikkāra or A Critique of Difference,* p. 3.

for any other *karaṇa.* The experience, "I perceive this with the mind", is not an evidence for stating that mind is an instrument of perception. Mind, which is the material cause of cognition, is also the efficient cause of the superimposition of cognition, etc. on the self. Thus, the experience, "I perceive this with the mind", is intelligible even without assuming the mind to be an instrument of valid knowledge. That the mind is the material cause of cognition is established by the scriptural text, "Desire, resolve, etc. ... are the mind alone" (*BṛUp* III.28). Further, such usage as, "Our minds know this", makes known the mind to be the cognizer and not the instrument of cognition. Scripture expressly declares that *manas* is not a sense organ in the text, "Greater than the senses are the objects; greater than the objects is the mind" (*KaṭhaUp* III.10).

As for what was said that, if mind be not an *indriya,* internal perception cannot be called perception, that is unsound. To define perception as knowledge generated by sense-contact with the object[12] is not correct. What is characteristic of perception is immediacy (*aparokṣatva*), not sense-contact;[13] and that immediacy is achieved when there is the non-difference of the *pramāṇa* intelligence with the object-defined intelligence. Hence, the cognition of happiness, etc. though there be no sense-contact, is perceptual, because it is immediate.

In the *Pañcadaśī,* Bhāratītīrtha does not strictly adhere to all the doctrines of the *Vivaraṇa* view which he so ably expounds in his *Vivaraṇa-Prameya-Saṁgraha.* As we shall have occasion

---

12 *indriyā-'rtha-sannikarṣa-janyaṁ-jñānaṁ pratyakṣam, TS,* p. 29.

13 The Neo-Naiyāyikas, however, point out the defect in the older definition. Gaṅgeśa defines perception as direct or immediate knowledge and Bhāsarvajña defines it as the means to clear and direct experience. *samyag-aparokṣā-'nubhava-sādhanaṁ-pratyakṣam, Nyāyasāra,* p. 7.
According to Prabhākara, perception is direct apprehension, *sākṣāt pratītiḥ.*

to point out later on, he tries to make compromises with the *Bhāmatī* view and present an eclectic conception of Advaita. In the *Pañcadaśī*, he characterizes *manas* as the internal *indriya*.[14] In passing, it may be mentioned that the recognition of *manas* as an *indriya* accounts for giving mental concentration (*dhyāna*) a place, though a secondary one, in the mode of realizing *Brahman* and regarding it as a means to *Brahman*-knowledge.

The function of mind is to go out to the object through the senses and manifest it. This, it is able to do because of its capacity to reflect intelligence. Since mind is considered in Indian thought to be a product of primal nature (*prakṛti*) and therefore material, the "going out" of the mental psychosis is not metaphorical, but actual. In Western philosophy, mind is very often confused with spirit and hence it is contrasted with matter. The mind–body problem appears to be insoluble for modern psychology because of the antithesis that is drawn between body and mind. Materialistic metaphysics and behaviouristic psychology agree with the Vedānta insofar as they regard mind as a product of matter; but they go against the spirit of the Vedānta when they do not accept a self as the basis of both mind and body. Without the self which is of the nature of intelligence no cognition is possible. Mind which is inert, a product of food, is ineffectual of itself to illumine objects.

The Vedānta view, that mind goes out to the object in order to grasp it, explains the perceptual process better than the impressionistic view of the West.[15] Mind is not a mere *tabula rasa*, a recorder of impressions received from without. It is not at all passive in perception. Modern psychologists are beginning to

---

14 *PD* II.12. See Rāmakṛṣṇa Paṇḍita's commentary: *tasya antarindriyatvam sanimittakam āha*, p. 42.

15 See Jadunath Sinha, 1934, *Indian Psychology: Perception*, p. 137: "And it is much easier to conceive the *out-going* of the mind intelligized by the conscious self to the object than the *in-coming* of the unconscious object to the mind."

stress the importance of the activity of the mind in perceiving objects. They have relinquished the common-sense point of view according to which perception is a simple act, a passive state, a kind of receptivity. Perception is "a mixed state, a cerebro-sensory phenomenon produced by an action on the senses and a reaction of the brain".[16] It is "the process by which the mind completes, with the accompaniment of images, an impression of the senses".[17]

> The perception of an external object is determined by apperception as well as by sensation. ... Every perception is a synthesis, or combination, of the part constituted by apperception and the part contributed by sensation.[18]

> The general law of perception is this: that whilst part of what we perceive comes through our senses from the object before us, another part (and it may be the larger part) always comes out of our own mind.[19]

The stimuli are said to issue forth from the object, strike the sense organs and stimulate the nerves which carry them to the cerebral centre where they are interpreted as sensations. Modern psychology recognizes only the interpretative activity of mind. According to the Vedānta, mind participates even in the collection of the raw material of perception. It cooperates with the senses, flows through the channels made by them, pervades the object and manifests it. The Vedānta view will not appear to be fantastic when we bear in mind the failure of the Western theories to explain how the various stimuli received from an external object give us a knowledge of the object *as a whole.*

---

16 E.S., Robinson and F.R. Robinson, 1923, "Alfred Binet on Perception", p. 239.

17 Ibid., p. 241.

18 Robinson, E.S. and F.R. Robinson, 1923, "Lightner Witmer on Perception", p. 243.

19 William James, 1892, *Psychology: A Briefer Course*, chap. XX, p. 329.

The mind is conceived by the Vedāntin to be active in perceiving an object and not a passive recorder of impressions. In indeterminate perception, however, the Vedāntin seems to acknowledge that the activity of the mind consists in nothing more than running into and filling a mould which is not fundamentally different from passive functioning. But in determinate perception, acquired perception and recognition, there is not only a presentative process but also a representative process which involves the active imagination of the mind. In determinate perception, the mind, by its analytico-synthetic function of dissociation and association, breaks up the "manifold of intuitions", renders it definite and determinate and refers it to the empirical unity of apperception. In the visual perception of fragrant sandal which is a case of acquired perception there is a representative element involved. To explain this kind of perception the Naiyāyika assumes a super-normal sense-contact called *jñāna-lakṣaṇa-sannikarṣa* (contact through the cognition of an object revived in memory). The Vedāntin, finding no use for such an assumption, regards the acquired perception as a mixed mode of consciousness, a psychic compound of a presentative element and a representative element. Recognition is a case of perception involving not only peripheral stimulation but also the revival of residual impressions. All these cases of perception reveal that the mind is extremely active in the process of knowing.[20]

The Naiyāyikas and the followers of Vācaspati Miśra consider *manas* to be the instrument (*karaṇa*) of internal perception. But, according to the *Vivaraṇa* view, happiness, misery, etc. which are objects of internal perception are manifested by the pure witness-intelligence (*kevala-sākṣī-bhāṣya*). In the perception of an external object, there has to be brought about the non-difference of the subject-intelligence which is within and the object-

[20] See Jadunath Sinha, 1934, *Indian Psychology: Perception*, chaps V & VI.

defined-intelligence which is without; hence the psychosis of the internal organ has to go out to the object through the channel of the sense. But in the case of internal perception, where the psychosis and the object are not different, there is not needed either the going out of the psychosis or any extraneous sense organ. Just as the fire which pervades a ball of iron illumines the ball without depending on any extraneous light, the reflection of intelligence pervading the psychoses reveals them (*PD* VIII.19). Since the subject-intelligence and the object-intelligence, i.e. the psychosis-defined-intelligence, are within, their non-difference is achieved even without the external activity of *manas*. When the witness-intelligence is sufficient to illumine the objects of internal perception, it is prolix to assume the *manas* to be a sense organ.

INFERENCE (ANUMĀNA)[21]

What is distinctive of the perceptual knowledge of objects both external and internal is its immediacy. Unlike perception, inference (*anumāna*) yields mediate knowledge. Even *śabda*, *upamāna* and *arthāpatti* give us only mediate knowledge. But the knowledge which results from inference is caused by the cognition of *probans* (*liṅga* or *hetu*). The cognition that there must be fire on the hill which has smoke is the classic example of inferential knowledge. What is of utmost importance in inferential knowledge is *vyāpti-jñāna* (knowledge of the pervasion). *Vyāpti* is the concomitance of the *probans* and the *probandum*. When we know through previous observation that wherever there is smoke there is fire, and when we now behold smoke issuing forth from yonder hill, we at once infer that there must be fire on the hill. The cognition that there is fire on the hill is based on the knowledge that wherever there is smoke there

21 Although Bhāratītīrtha does not discuss all the *pramāṇa*s in the three works we are examining, a short account of the six means of knowledge is given in this chapter so that the other doctrines of the Advaita as expounded by him may become intelligible.

is fire. The latter kind of knowledge is what is known as *vyāpti-jñāna*. *Vyāpti* (pervasion) is the coexistence of the *probandum* with the *probans*, in all the loci wherein the *probans* may be found.[22] That which pervades is the *probandum* and is called the *vyāpaka* (pervader); and that which is pervaded is the *vyāpya*. Fire is the pervader and smoke, is the pervaded. Wherever there is smoke, there is fire; but it does not follow from this that wherever there is fire there must be smoke. Since in the case of fire and smoke, the *vyāpaka* and the *vyāpya* are not coextensive, the pervasion that obtains between fire and smoke is called *viṣama-vyāpti* (unequal pervasion). But where the *vyāpaka* and the *vyāpya* are coextensive, there the positions of the *probandum* and the *probans* may validly be interchanged. The inference of smoke from fire fed by wet fuel is as valid as the deduction of fire fed by wet fuel from smoke. As between the two terms, "fire fed by wet fuel" and "smoke" there is *sama-vyāpti* (equipollence).

The instrument which generates inferential knowledge is *vyāpti-jñāna*. The residual impression of the pervasion (*vyāpti-saṁskāra*) and the perception of the *probans* (*liṅga-darśana*) are the causes of inference (*VPS*, p. 36). The pervasion of one thing by another is understood when they are observed to be co-present without any inconstancy.[23] There must be an essential connection between the two phenomena which are said to be in the relation of the pervader and the pervaded. That alone is the criterion of a valid knowledge of *vyāpti*. The observation of the *vyāpti* only once is enough, and *bhūyo-darśana* (repeated observation) is not needed, if that relation is known to be vital. Any number of observations of crows being black cannot serve to establish a relation of *vyāpti* between crow-ness and black-ness, for the two are not essentially related; and there can conceivably be crows which are white. While the Naiyāyikas regard co-absence (*vyatireka*) also as that which intimates *vyāpti*, the Advaitins

---

22 *VP*, p. 151: *vyāptiśca aśeṣasādhanāśrita-sādhya-sāmānādhikaraṇya-rūpā* ।

23 *VP*, p. 152: *sā ca vyabhicārādarśane sati sahacāra-darśanena gṛhyate* ।

maintain that the observation of co-absence is not necessary. When two phenomena are observed to be co-present without any exception whatever, a relation of *vyāpti* can be said to exist between them. This is why the Advaitins (most of them) accept only one type of inference, viz. the *anvayī*, rejecting the Naiyāyika classification of inference into *kevalānvayī*, *kevala-vyatirekī* and *anvaya-vyatirekī*.

The Logicians make a distinction between *svārthānumāna* and *parārthānumāna*, the inference which is intended for the satisfaction of one's own reasoning and the inference which is given out for convincing others. The former consists of three propositions, while the latter contains five. The premising of what is to be proved is called *pratijñā*, e.g. the hill is with fire. *Hetu* is the statement of the reason, e.g. because it has smoke. Next, the *vyāpti* is stated and illustrated, e.g. wherever there is smoke there is fire, as in the hearth. This is known as *udāharaṇa*. Then, the presence of the *probans* in the subject is indicated, e.g. there is fire-pervaded smoke on the hill. This is *upanaya*. The first premise is then repeated as the conclusion (*nigamana*), e.g. therefore, this hill has fire. This is the full-fledged five-membered syllogism of the Logician. The Advaitin holds that even for convincing others three propositions would be sufficient.[24] Either the first two or the last two propositions can be omitted. Whether the first three or the last three members are taken, the *udāharaṇa*, which contains the statement of the invariable, universal relation, is preserved. The five-membered syllogism of the Naiyāyika is mechanical and cumbersome. The *pratijñā* and the *nigamana* are verbatim the same.[25] The *hetu* and the

24 Cf. *Tattva-Pradīpikā*, p. 247, Citsukha's criticism of the five-membered syllogism. He seems to think that only two members, viz. *vyāpti* and *pakṣa-dharmatā*, are essential and they are indicated by the *udāharaṇa* and *upanaya*.

25 The Logician, however, defends his position by asserting that the *nigamana* is the statement of a proved certain conclusion, while the *pratijñā* only premises it as provable.

upanaya state the same fact.[26] Hence, it is superfluous to have five propositions even in order to demonstrate the validity of an inference to others.

The Logicians of the West make a distinction between formal and material logic, deduction and induction. Bacon, Mill and others revolted against the logic of their predecessors because they found it to be purely formal and mechanical. The Indian syllogism, however, is free from the defects of formalism. It is both formal and material, deductive and inductive. The *udāharaṇa* (illustration) is essential for establishing the validity of an argument. It was because the early Logicians did not lay stress on pure forms that an elaborate system of figures and moods was not laid out.

We have observed that the objects of inference are mediate. But according to the Advaita all things are superimposed on the self and it is the self that is the source of illumination. If the objects of inference as well as those of perception are superimpositions on the self, why should the former be mediate and the latter immediate? (*VPS*, pp. 82-83). There is no use of evading this question by stating that intelligence is not the generator of immediate cognition; for what else can regulate immediacy? The sense organ cannot be the regulator; for in the cognition of happiness, etc. though there be no sense organ, they are perceived as immediate. If the internal organ be the regulator, then as there is the function of the internal organ even in the inferential cognition of objects, the immediacy of those objects is difficult to avoid.

To this, the Advaitin replies that, whereas in the case of perception the objects serve as the causal correlates and manifestors of intelligence, the objects of inference do not possess the twofold attribute which is the regulator of immediacy. In an

[26] The Logician states the difference between the two thus: the *hetu* states the cognition of the *probans;* the *upanaya* states the cognition of *probans* as pervaded by the *probandum.*

act of perception the pot, etc. which are objects, are the causal correlates, and they function as manifestors because they are the originators of psychoses of the internal organ. Such an activity of the objects is not invariably observed in the case of inference. Inference may be based even on objects which do not belong to the present. As for the usage in respect of the object of inference, in the form, "He knows the rain", that is figurative. There is not any positive attribute called content-ness pertaining to the object of inference. Thus, the difference is intelligible as between the objects of perception and those of inference.

ANALOGY (UPAMĀNA)

Upamāna is admitted by the Mīmāṁsakas and the Advaitins to be an independent means of valid knowledge. It is what may be called analogical reasoning or comparison. The knowledge that is gained through this *pramāṇa* is the knowledge of similarity.[27] *Upamāna* (comparison) is neither *anumāna* nor perception.

A townsman is told that the *gavaya*, which is an inhabitant of the forest, bears a resemblance to the cow. He goes to the forest, finds the *gavaya* and notices its similarity to the cow. And then he compares the cow with the *gavaya* and knows that the cow resembles the *gavaya*. This cognition of his is the result of *upamāna*. The judgement, "The cow is like the *gavaya*", is not born of perception, because the cow about which the judgement is made is not an object presented to sense. Nor is *upamāna* partly perception and partly memory; for what we have therein is a unitary act of knowledge, a single pulsation of intelligence.

The Naiyāyika account of *upamāna* differs from that of the Advaitin. A person who has not seen the *gavaya* is informed that the wild animal resembles a cow. He casually comes across a *gavaya*, and remembers what he has heard from his friend about the resemblance of the *gavaya* to the cow. And he comes to know that what the word *gavaya* denotes is the class of objects which

---

27 *VP*, p. 176: *sādṛśya-pramākaraṇam upamānam* ।

resembles the cow. Thus, according to the Naiyāyika, *upamiti* (knowledge resulting from *upamāna*) consists in the knowledge of the relation between a name and the object denoted by it. Knowledge of similarity is the instrument of such cognition.

The Advaitin's objection to this account of the Logician is that it does not make out a case for regarding *upamāna* as a separate *pramāṇa*. That the word *gavaya* denotes the class of objects similar to the cow can be known either through verbal testimony or through inference. Hence, it is only the knowledge of the similarity to the *gavaya* that is present in the cow through the instrumentality of the knowledge of the similarity to the cow which is present in the *gavaya* that constitutes *upamiti-pramā*.[28]

PRESUMPTION (ARTHĀPATTI)

Presumption (*arthāpatti*) is the postulation of what explains through the knowledge of what is to be explained.[29] When a certain fact is to be explained, we assume something which accounts for it. *Arthāpatti* is that process of knowledge which makes something intelligible by assuming something else. When it is known that a particular person is alive and when he is not to be found in his house, we assume, in order to reconcile the two facts of his living and of his absence from home, that he must be somewhere outside his house. The knowledge of what is to be explained, viz. the absence from home of the person who is alive, is instrumental to the knowledge of what explains, viz. that the person exists somewhere outside his house.[30]

Arthāpatti is of two kinds, presumption from what is seen (*dṛṣṭārthāpatti*) and presumption from what is heard (*śrutārthāpatti*). Scripture declares, "The knower of self crosses sorrow" (*ChāUp* VIII.i.3). The host of bondage which is indicated

---

[28] *VP*, p. 177: *gavaya-niṣṭha-gosādṛśya-jñānaṁ karaṇam goniṣṭha-gavaya-sādṛśya-jñānaṁ phalam* ।

[29] *VP*, p. 236: *upapādya-jñānena upapādaka-kalpanaṁ arthāpattiḥ* ।

[30] *VP*, p. 237: *upapādya-jñānaṁ, karaṇaṁ, upapādaka-jñānam phalam* ।

by the word "sorrow" is determined to be illusory, since nothing which is real is removable by knowledge. This is an instance of *śrutārthāpatti*. When there is the sublation of the cognition of silver in nacre by the cognition of nacre, the illusoriness of silver is assumed so that the reality of nacre that is perceived may become intelligible. This is presumption from what is seen (*dṛṣṭārthāpatti*).

The suggestion that *arthāpatti* may be included in inference is turned down by pointing out that if an instance of *arthāpatti* be reduced to the syllogistic form, the major premise will not indicate any positive pervasion (*anvaya-vyāpti*). It will take the form of *vyatireka-vyāpti* which is, for the Advaitin, not a valid inference.

NON-COGNITION (ANUPALABDHI)

The Bhāṭṭas and the Advaitins who follow them in matters empirical, hold that non-existence (*abhāva*) is known through non-cognition (*anupalabdhi*). The non-existence of knowledge in general, says the Advaitin, is known by the witness. But the non-existence of a particular cognition is known by non-cognition.[31] The valid knowledge of non-existence is that which is gained through non-cognition of the capable.[32] If in a particular locus, say, the ground, there be the non-existence of something, say, the pot, then, that non-existence is known by non-cognition. The locus of non-cognition is called the correlate (*anuyogī*) and that of which there is the non-existence in the locus is known as the counter-correlate (*pratiyogī*). Non-cognition can yield knowledge of the non-existence only of those objects which are capable of being cognized were they present in the respective loci along with the other causes of cognition. Otherwise, the non-existence of pot in a place which is enshrouded in darkness and of merit

31 *VPS*, p. 16: *sākṣi-vedyo jñānamātrā-'bhāvaḥ jñāna-viśeṣā-'bhāvas tu vyavahāre bhaṭṭa-naya ity abhyupagamena ṣaṣtha-māna-gamyaḥ* ।

32 *Tattvānusandhāna*, p. 207: *yogyā-'nupalabdhi-karaṇikā pramā abhāva-pramā* ।

and demerit in the self would be cognized through *anupalabdhi.* But since the presence of pot in a dark place is not perceptible, its non-existence cannot be the object of non-cognition. Similarly, since merit and demerit are super-sensuous, their non-existence cannot be known by *anupalabdhi.* Hence, in order that the non-existence of a particular object may be known by non-cognition, it is essential that the existence of that object must be capable (*yogya*) of being cognized.

The Prābhākaras do not accept non-cognition as the *pramāṇa* which makes known non-existence. They hold that non-existence has no reality apart from the existence of a thing. An object is known to be existent with reference to itself and non-existent with reference to other objects. The non-existence of a thing is the existence of another. The Sāṁkhyas also regard the non-existence of pot on the ground as but the existence of the bare ground. Both these schools maintain that non-existent is *perceived.* The perception of the bare locus, say, the ground, makes known the non-existence of the counter-correlate, say, the pot.

The Advaitin criticizes this view of the Prābhākaras and the Sāṁkhyas. If the perception of the bare locus, e.g. the ground, yield the cognition of non-existence, then, even when there is the existence of pot on the ground, there must be the cognition of its non-existence, since there is present the perception of the locus. It may be said that because there is an existent, viz. pot on the ground, there is not the cognition of non-existence. Then, there is this contingence that when a cloth is perceived to be on the ground, there would not be the cognition of the non-existence of pot. Further, if the perception of the bare locus be instrumental to the cognition of non-existence, then as there is the non-existence of innumerable things on the perceived locus, the ground, there must be the cognition of the non-existence not only of pot but of all those things. But that is not testified to by our experience. Hence the theory that non-existence is known by perception is extremely defective.

The Naiyāyikas advocate what may be called the adjectival theory of non-existence. They do not, like the Prābhākaras and the Sāṁkhyas, identify non-existence with the bare existence of the locus. They regard non-existence as an attribute of the locus. The ground is *qualified* by the non-existence of pot. Since the qualities of an object are given in the perception of that object, the quality called non-existence is also made known by the perception of the locus of non-existence. For every act of perception there is needed some mode of contact (*sannikarṣa*); and that kind of contact which leads to the perception of non-existence is technically called *viśeṣaṇatā.*

The Advaitin rejects this view, because it is defective. *Viśeṣaṇatā* cannot be a mode of sense-contact.[33] If mere *viśeṣaṇatā* were the contact, there should be the cognition of the non-existence of pot even in a place which is hidden by a wall, since that place is *qualified* by the non-existence of pot. The Logician cannot with justification say that the contact of the locus and the sense organ is also the cause of the cognition of non-existence; for according to him, in the cognition of the non-existence of sound there is no sense-contact with the locus which is itself the sense of hearing, viz. the ear-defined ether. If sense-contact with the locus were also the cause of the cognition of non-existence, there is the contingence of the non-perception of the non-existence of sound. Nor may it be said that there is sense-contact with the non-existence which is the qualification of that locus where, if the counter-correlate existed, it would be perceived; for what is meant by the words "cognition of the counter-correlate in the locus of its existence"? Will there be sense-contact with the non-existence which is the qualification of a locus where the existence of the counter-correlate is occasionally cognized? If sense-contact be admitted in such a case, then, since there is occasional cognition of pot, etc. even in a place that is now hidden, there is the contingence of the perception of the non-existence. To remedy

[33] *Bheda-dhikkāra* (or A Critique of Difference), p. 6.

this defect, it may be stated that there must be constant cognition of the counter-correlate if it existed in the locus, and then alone the non-existence of that counter-correlate can be perceived. But constant cognition is impossible even in the case of sound which is constantly present in the sense of hearing. Sound is heard only when there is the presence of the necessary auxiliaries.

Since cognition of non-existence is intelligible even by non-cognition, it is futile to assume *viśeṣaṇatā* as a mode of sense-contact which makes known non-existence. Non-cognition is not perceptual in character. As for the activity of the sense organ in non-cognition that is exhausted even with the cognition of the locus. The locus is perceived, not non-existence. Hence, non-cognition must be recognized as the *pramāṇa* which makes known non-existence.

Four varieties of non-existence are recognized by the Nyāya. The non-existence of an object before it comes into being is *prāg-abhāva.* Pot is non-existent prior to its production. Antecedent non-existence is the basis on which judgements about future phenomena are made. This kind of non-existence is beginningless, but it comes to an end when the object in question is brought into being. *Pradhvaṁsā-bhāva* is annihilative non-existence. It is a phenomenon which happens to an object when that object is destroyed. When a pot is broken, the pot ceases to exist. The annihilative non-existence of the pot has a beginning, but no end. The same pot which is destroyed can never come into existence again. The third variety is *atyantā-bhāva* (absolute non-existence). If in a locus a thing is never present, then it is said that there is in that locus the absolute non-existence of that thing, e.g. in ether there is the absolute non-existence of taste, odour, etc. This kind of non-existence is held to be eternal by the Logicians. The last mode of *abhāva* is reciprocal non-existence (*anyonyā-bhāva*). It makes known *bheda* (difference) of one object from another. As between pot and cloth there is reciprocal non-existence.

The author of the *Vedānta-Paribhāṣā* accepts the Naiyāyika classification of non-existence (*VP*, p. 259). But he does not subscribe to the statements that annihilative non-existence is without an end and that absolute non-existence is eternal. The annihilative non-existence of pot is destroyed when there is the destruction of the potsherds. Nor may it be said that when the annihilative non-existence is destroyed, there must be the existence of pot again; for, since the destruction of the potsherds implies the destruction of the pot as well, there is not the contingence of the re-emergence of the pot. Otherwise, even when the pot, which is of the nature of the destruction of its *prāg-abhāva*, is destroyed, there is the contingence of the re-emergence of the *prāg-abhāva*. It may be said that where the locus of destruction is eternal, there, the destruction is also eternal. But if such a locus be other than intelligence, then that locus cannot be eternal. If the locus of destruction be intelligence, then, what is called the destruction of what is superimposed is nothing but the bare substrate, viz. *Brahman*-intelligence. The Naiyāyika view that *atyantābhāva* is eternal does not fit in with the scheme of Advaita wherein nothing other than the Absolute is eternal.

Nṛsiṁhāśramin in the *Bheda Dhikkāra* records that it is unnecessary to admit of varieties in non-existence. All cases of non-existence can be reduced to the form of absolute non-existence. For instance, in the cognitions "the ground is not pot" and "there is no pot on the ground", there is no difference whatever in the sense of the negation. Potness is the determinant of counter-correlated-ness in both cases; and in both the instances there is admitted the cognition of the ground not having pot-ness. Thus, it is needless to make distinctions in non-existence.[34]

Whether modes of non-existence be recognized or not, the Advaitins agree with the Bhāṭṭas in admitting the *pramāṇa* of non-cognition as making known the non-existence of particular objects. The non-existence of knowledge in general, however,

34 *Bheda-dhikkāra* (or A Critique of Difference), p. 34.

as the *Vivaraṇa-Prameya-Saṁgraha* puts it, is revealed by the witness.

VERBAL TESTIMONY (ŚABDA OR ĀGAMA)

Words are the vehicles of thought. *Śabda* means "sound" and "word". *Śabda-pramā* is knowledge derived from the authority of words. Verbal testimony is a valid means of knowledge. To the Mīmāṁsakas and the Advaitins who regard Truth as revealed by scripture, *śabda-pramāṇa* is vitally important. Just as in empirical usage, the testimony of a trustworthy person makes known truth, in the sphere of the supersensuous, scripture is of use as the revelation of what is true.

The Buddhists do not accept scripture as authoritative (*VPS*, p. 31). Words, they say, are not recallers of tilings and *vākya* (sentence) is not a means of valid knowledge. Words cannot recall associated things, because as between words and things the modes of relation, like conjunction, etc. are not possible. Nor can the word *sambandha* (relation) mean the capacity to generate knowledge; for whether the capacity to generate knowledge be interpreted as the capacity to generate experience or as the capacity to generate memory, that is not present in words. Words, when they are in the form of a sentence, generate the experience of the sentence-sense; but they by themselves cannot generate experience in respect of their own senses. Even at the time of learning the meaning of words, the words do not by themselves convey their senses. The senses of words are known by other means. Hence, words cannot generate the experience of their senses. Nor have words the capacity to generate memory. The alleged capacity in words cannot generate memory, as uncognized, for the instrument of memory is what is itself cognized. Nor is it possible to say that the capacity, which is known to exist in words, generates memory; for capacity cannot be known prior to the production of its effect. Were it to generate memory only after it is known, there is reciprocal dependence (*parasparāśraya*) as between the origination of memory and cognition of capacity. The defect of reciprocal dependence may be sought to be overcome by examining how the senses of words are first learnt. On hearing the words "bring the cow", a person brings the cow, and when ordered to "take the cow", he leads the cow away. Through the activity of the intermediate elder (*madhyama-vṛddha*), a child learns the meanings of the words "cow", "bring", "take", etc. This, the child is able to do through insertion and elimination of words. It infers that the cognition of the sense of particular words is the cause of a certain kind of activity, since the latter follows on the former. In this manner, since at the time of learning, the capacity of words to generate their senses is known, later on when those words are uttered, the memory of their senses is generated. Hence, it may be thought that there is not the said reciprocal dependence. Even thus, is the determination of capacity at the time of learning in respect of words alone, or is it in respect of those related to particular things? Not the first, since there is the contingence of the non-establishment of restriction in applying a particular word to a particular thing. The second alternative leads to infinite regress (*anavasthā*) in that in order to determine the capacity of a word to be related to a particular object another relation is needed and for that another and so on. If it be said that capacity establishes both itself and the other, even then, at the time of memory, the thing cannot be remembered from the cognition of the mere word, since there is the contingence of non-restriction. Nor can the memory be caused by the perception of the word possessing a capacity whose sphere is the thing; for, since the thing is seen at the same time when there is the perception of the word, the memory generated by the word is futile. Nor is it valid to hold that the memory is from the perception of the word and the residual impression generated by the cognition of capacity; for that much is not enough to produce memory. To say that a particular thing is the recaller and another the recalled, there must be between them some other relation such as similarity, opposition, causality, etc. But no such relation is observed to obtain as between a word and thing. Hence, the Buddhists conclude that words are not recallers of things and that the sentence is not a means of valid knowledge.

As against the Buddhist view, the Advaitin maintains that there is no defect whatever in the memory of a thing being caused by the perception of the word and the residual impression of capacity. It does not stand to reason to say that, because as between a word and thing there is no relation like that of similarity, etc.; a word, though it has capacity, does not recall a thing, for it is a contradiction to hold that there is capacity without the generation of the effect. What has capacity must generate the effect. Hence, words which have capacity produce the recollection of the things which they signify. Since words are capable of connoting their senses, they are valid as means of knowledge.

What does a word primarily recall or indicate, a particular (*vyakti*) or a class (*jāti*)? The Sāṁkhyas hold that a word signifies a particular or individual. In our experience we meet with particulars alone, not with generalities. When we mention the word "cow", we mean by that word a particular cow. The Jainas or the Ārhatas maintain that the word denotes *ākṛti* (configuration) of the parts. The word "cow" denotes the generic form of cows. The reference to individuals is only indirect. The Mīmāṁsakas, the Vedāntins and those of their way of thinking regard words as primarily signifying generalities (*jāti*). The word "cow" stands for the essential nature of cow, viz. cowness. It is not the generic form (*ākṛti*) but the essential attribute that is signified by the word. The Naiyāyikas argue that a word means all the three – *vyakti* (individual), *jāti* (generality) and *ākṛti* (configuration). Some of the later Naiyāyikas are of the opinion that a word signifies neither a pure particular nor a bare generality. What it denotes is an individual qualified by a class (*jātiviśiṣṭa-vyakti*).[35] The Advaitins criticize this view on the ground that the generality which is connoted by the word "cow" is the basis for applying that word to an individual cow. What they mean by generality or class is the essential nature of the individuals that constitute a class.

Besides the primary sense (*mukhyārtha* or *śakyārtha*), a word has also an implied or secondary sense (*lakṣyārtha*). When the primary meaning of a word does not fit in with the context in which it appears, the secondary sense of the word is to be accepted. The secondary implication of a word is that which is related to what is primarily indicated by that word.[36] There are three kinds of secondary implication. *Jahallakṣanā* (exclusive implication) is the implication of some sense which is other than the sense primarily indicated by the word but which is related to the latter while the primary sense is completely given up.[37] In the phrase "the village on the Ganges", the primary sense of the word "Ganges", viz. the river, is relinquished and the bank which is related to the river is implied. *Ajahallakṣaṇā* (non-exclusive implication) is the implication of a sense, which being other than the primary sense of the word, is yet related to it, this primary sense not being given up.[38] The word "school" in the sentence "the school works today" indicates the inmates of the school, but still the primary sense of the word is not rejected. When part of the primary sense of a word is discarded and part of it accepted, there is for that word exclusive–non-exclusive implication (*jahadajahallakṣaṇā*).[39] This type of implication is also called *bhāga-tyāga-lakṣaṇā*. In the judgement of identity, "This

35 D.M. Datta, 1932, *Six Ways of Knowing*, pp. 259f.

36 *śakya-saṁbandhaḥ lakṣaṇā.*

Vākyavṛtti 47, *Mem. Ed.*, vol. 15: *mānāntara-virodhe tu mukhyārthasyā-'parigrahe* । *mukhyārthenā- 'vinābhūte pratītir lakṣaṇocyate* ॥

37 *śakyārtha-parityāgena tat-saṁbandhy arthāntare vṛttiḥ jahallakśanā* ।

38 *śakyārthā- 'parityāgena tat-saṁbandhy arthāntare vṛttiḥ ajahallakṣaṇā* ।

39 *śakyaikadeśa-parityāgenaikadeśe vṛttiḥ jahad-ajahallakṣanā* ।

is that Devadatta", the exclusive–non-exclusive implication is understood. The meaning of the word "this" is Devadatta qualified by present time, etc. and the sense of the word "that" is the same Devadatta qualified by past time, etc. In this judgement part of the meaning of the words "this" and "that", viz. Devadatta, is taken and the other part of their meanings, viz. "qualified by present time" and "qualified by past time", is rejected. In construing the sense of the major texts like, "That thou art" and "I am *Brahman*", exclusive–non-exclusive implication is employed.

Words that have a syntactical unity constitute a sentence (*VPS*, pp. 257-58). How is the meaning of a sentence known? Do the words that form a sentence indicate the construed meaning, besides their own senses? Or do they present their individual meanings alone? The Prābhākaras hold that the words convey their own senses as well as the construed meaning of the sentence. Their theory is termed Anvitābhidhānavāda. The Bhāṭṭas maintain that the words signify their own senses alone. The sentence-sense is later on cognized by the construction of the meanings of words. This view is known as Abhihitānvayavāda (*Mānameyodaya*, pp. 94-98). Words connote their own senses. The word "cow" is used in such contexts as "Bring the cow", "Bind the cow", etc. While the word "cow" is present in both these sentences, the words "bring" and "bind" are inconstant. Hence, the word "cow" is not invariably related to any other sense than its own. Every word at first signifies its own meaning. Then the meanings of all the words in a sentence are put together and the sense of the sentence is construed. First, the senses of words arise from words; and then from the senses of words the sentence-sense is construed.[40]

The Prābhakāras object to the Abhihitānvayavāda of the Bhāṭṭas. The words of a sentence, even at the very first, cause the cognition of their relation in the sentence. Further, it is prolix to

---

40 *padebhyaḥ padārthāḥ padārthebhyaḥ saṁsarga ity abhihitānvayaḥ* ।

interpose, between the sentence and the cognition of its sense, the meanings of the words and their capacities. The view of the Bhāṭṭas disregards these two facts, and hence it is defective. What is central in a sentence is the verb which is declarative of what is to be accomplished (*kārya*).[41] All other words in the sentence have syntactical connection with the *kārya*. Nothing has meaning if it be not related to what is to be accomplished (*kārya*). From the sentence, "Bring the cow, with the stick", there is cognized the syntactical connection of the "cow" and "stick" with the act of bringing. The act of bringing is, no doubt, not known from the sentence, "Bind the cow"; but still, even there, the cow is cognized only as related to an act, e.g. binding. Instead of stating that words originate a knowledge of their senses and later from their senses the sentence-sense is construed, it is in keeping with parsimony to say that words themselves make known their relation. And an examination of how the meanings of words are learnt shows that all words are related to what is to be accomplished.

Though in empirical matters, the Advaitins pursue the path of the Bhāṭṭas, they are divided among themselves on the present question. Eminent preceptors of Advaita like Vācaspati and Citsukha advocate the view of the Bhāṭṭas. But the author of the *Vivaraṇa* and Bhāratītīrtha in the *Vivaraṇa-Prameya-Saṁgraha* hold that both the views are equally valid for the purpose of Advaita. The *Vivaraṇa* view, which is explained by Bhāratītīrtha, gives a different account of the Anvitābhidhānavāda from that of the Prābhākara. It is not necessary, says the *vivaraṇakāra* (author of *Vivaraṇa*), for every word in a sentence to be related to the verb alone. Relation may be to an attribute, substance, act, causal-correlate, etc. In the sentence "Bring the white

41 A distinction is made between the *kārya* and the *kriyā*. The reaching of a place is the *kārya* or what is to be accomplished. The act of walking is the *kriyā*. *Kārya*, in Prābhākara terminology, is equivalent to *apūrva*.

cow", the attribute "white" is related to the substance which is associated with the generality, viz. cow, the substance is related to the causal-correlate, the sense of the case-ending and again the substance as qualified by the sense of the case-ending is related to the act, and the act is related to the *niyoga kārya* (what is to be accomplished by the injunction). Thus, the relation of the attribute, etc. with what is to be accomplished (*kārya*) is not direct. Hence, because of parsimony, it must be admitted that the word has capacity in respect of its sense as associated with the sense of some other word, not necessarily with the sense of the verb. If this be not accepted, there is the contingence of the sentence being merely a restatement; for, the capacity of words is discerned in those senses which are associated with what is to be accomplished and which are known by other *pramāṇas*, and then the same is cognized by the *vākya-pramāṇa*. Hence the sentence must surely be a re-statement of what is already known by other *pramāṇas*. Nor may it be said that the meanings of all words are directly related to what is to be accomplished and that while the former are subsidiaries (*śeṣa*), the latter is the principal (*śeṣī*); for as between the word-senses and the *kārya* the relation of subsidiaries and the principal cannot be established. How is the *kārya* the principal? It is not the master (*svāmin*), because it is inert. It is not the whole (*avayavī*), because the other word-senses are not its parts or members. It is not what is to be achieved (*sādhya*), for everywhere it is action (*kriyā*) that is achieved by the causal-correlates. It is not what is ultimately to be achieved, since the fruit, heaven, etc. is alone what is to be thus achieved. Hence, words must be regarded as making known their senses as in association with the senses of other words, be they verbs or otherwise. If there be capacity only for those words which are associated with the *kārya*, then, what about the word *kārya* which has no other *kārya* to be related to? It cannot be said that there is the other *kārya* which is of the nature of the stem-sense; for there is not, at first, for the stem-sense, the nature of what is to be accomplished. It is fallacious to say that all words have capacity only in respect of what is to be accomplished. There is knowledge of sense even from such statements like "Devadatta went out after taking his meal", which do not indicate anything that is to be accomplished. There is no rule that meanings of words are to be learnt only by observing the intermediate elder carrying out some commands. Even from the teachings of the *Nighaṇṭu* and Grammar, learning is possible. Hence, without depending on what is to be accomplished, words intimate their senses as associated with the senses of other words (*anyānvita-svārtha*). It may be objected that in the view of *anvitā-bhidhāna* since the word "cow" will be associated with such words as "bring", "bind", etc. and the word "bring" will be associated with words like "cow", "horse", etc. the sense of the sentence, "Bring the cow", will not be definite and distinct. This objection will appear pointless, when we take into account the context in which the words appear. In the sentence "Bring the cow", the word "cow" is not related to binding, but only to bringing. Similarly, the word "bring" is associated with the cow and not with the horse. Nor may it be said that, since the word "cow" means "cow-ness" as associated with bringing and the word "bring" denotes the act of bringing as associated with the cow, there is the contingence of the two words being synonyms; for, neither of the words indicates by itself the relation to the other. When the word *gam* (cow, accusative singular) is uttered alone, no relation is seen to the act of bringing; and the mere word *ānaya* (bring) does not relate itself to the cow. It is only from the two words together that their reciprocal relation is cognized. Hence, there is not the said defect. It cannot be maintained that the difference in meaning between the two words is caused by the one being the earlier and the other the later; for, if that were so, there is the contingence of difference in meaning between the words *āhitāgni* and *agnyāhita* both of which signify one who has ceremoniously kindled the sacred fire. The fallacy of reciprocal dependence may be urged against the Anvitābhidhānavāda in this manner: when the word "cow" signifies "cow-ness", the other word indicates "bringing" which is related to that; and when the word "bring" denotes "bringing", the word cow makes known "cow-ness" which is associated therewith; and thus there is reciprocal dependence. But there is not this defect. At the time of hearing each word, its sense alone is cognized and when the last word is uttered, all the words, which are remembered, conjointly make known their own senses, which have already been indicated as mutually associated.

Nor is there confusion of the Anvitābhidhānavāda with the view of *abhihitānvaya*. In the view of *abhihitānvaya*, the words cease to function after indicating their senses; and then, there is the cognition of the sentence-sense from the word-senses. In the Anvitābhidhānavāda, however, words themselves make known the sentence-sense. This is the distinction.[42]

As thus reinterpreted, the Anvitābhidhānavāda serves the purpose of the Advaitin in an equal measure with the Abhihitānvayavāda of the Bhāṭṭas. Neither of the views comes into conflict with the Vedāntic interpretation of scripture. On considerations other than those which were relevant to Prakāśātman or Bhāratītīrtha, we find that the Bhāṭṭa view is more plausible than the theory of the Prābhākaras, though the latter serves to check the tendency to regard words as symbols of unrelated abstract universals and to indicate some truth from the standpoint of the speaker of the words.[43]

---

[42] *VPS*, p. 260: *abhihitānvaya-vāde hi padāni padārthān abhidhāyo 'pakṣīyante, padārthebhyo vākyārtha-pratipattih, anvitābhidhāna-vāde tu padānām eva vākyārtha-pratipādakatvam iti viśeṣaḥ* ।

[43] D.M. Datta, 1932, Six *Ways of Knowing*, pp. 289-99. Jñānaghanapāda in his *Tattvaśuddhi* favours the *Vivaraṇa* view, pp. 47-51: *abhihitānvaya-pakṣe aneka-śakti-kalpanā-prasaṅgat, saṅgati-grahaṇasya ca padānām anvitārtha-viṣyatvāt, vākyārthasya ca aśābdatva* । *prasaṅgāt, padārtha-nāmadheyāpūrvapramāṇa-parikalpanā-prasaṅgāt, vākyārtha-pratipatteḥ padānāṁ anvitābhidhāyakatve 'pi virodhābhāvāt, apagata-nikhila-doṣa-vrātaṁ anvitābhidhānam eva nyāyaṁ nyāyavido manyante* ।

A mere jumble of words cannot constitute a sentence. Words picked at random and put together do not make sense. A sentence is constructed under specific conditions. The words that go to form a sentence must stand in mutual need. The combination of words must be essential and not accidental. There must be *ākāṅkṣā* (expectancy) among the words of a sentence. The mention of the word "cow" makes the sense of the word hang in the air as it were, without any completion of meaning; similarly, from the isolated word "bring" no full sense is made out. Hence, each of the two words stands in need of some other word or words in order to convey some complete meaning. It is not enough that there are words which seek the aid of other words; there must also be available words which satisfy that want or seeking. The word "swine" added to the word "cow" cannot make sense. Though the word "cow" seeks the cooperation of some other word, the word "swine" is of no use for the purpose, for it is not capable of satisfying the demands of the word "cow". Only those words that are capable or compatible (*yogya*) can fulfil the *ākāṅkṣā* of other words. The word "bring", for example, is adequate to supply the want felt by the word "cow". Besides these two material conditions, *ākāṅksā* and *yogyatā*, there is a formal condition and that is *āsatti* (proximity). There is no use of pronouncing the word "cow" now, and the word "bring" after the lapse of an hour. The words that go to make up a sentence must be proximate or contiguous in time when they are spoken and in space when they are written. Thus, words which possess reciprocal expectancy, juxtaposition and competency constitute a sentence.[44]

A fourth factor which determines the cognition of the sentence-sense is the knowledge of purport (*tātparya jñāna*). The

---

[44] *Mānameyodaya*, p. 99:
atrā 'kāṅkṣā ca yogyatvaṁ sannidhiś ceti tat trayam ।
vākyā-'rthā-'vagame sarvaiḥ karaṇatvena kalpyate ॥

VPS, p. 212: *anyonyākāṅkṣā-sannidhi-yogyatāvanti padāni vākyam* ।

purport of the words which are used in the empirical discourse is settled with reference to the context. Though the word *saindhava* means both salt and horse, when a person who is taking his meal says, "Bring *saindhava*" the purport of the word is cognized to be salt and not horse.

The purport of the Vedic words is determined through six characteristic marks (*ṣaḍliṅga*). Only purportful scripture is authoritative.[45] The marks determinative of purport are: the harmony of the initial and concluding passages (*upakrama–upasaṁhāra*), repetition (*abhyāsa*), novelty (*apūrvatā*), fruitfulness (*phala*), glorification by eulogistic passages or condemnation by deprecatory passages (Arthavāda) and intelligibility in the light of reasoning (*upapatti*).[46] By applying these tests, the Advaitin discovers that the entire scripture has the non-dual *Brahman* for purport.

Vācaspati regards *śabda* (verbal testimony) as capable of generating only mediate knowledge. It is *prasaṅkhyāna* (continued meditation) and not *śravaṇa*, that is the cause of the intuitive experience of *Brahman*. According to the *Vivaraṇa* view, verbal testimony is capable of generating immediate as well as mediate knowledge (*PD* VII.58f.). A bare sentence yields only mediate knowledge. But the sentence whose purport has been inquired into causes immediate experience. When the full purport of the sentence, "This self is *Brahman*", is cognized after a thorough inquiry, *Brahman* becomes the content of immediate experience. In the illustration of the ten travellers who counted only nine after crossing a ferry, we find that there is the experience of the immediate presence of the tenth person, when a trustworthy man points to the traveller who forgot to

---

45 *Bhāmatī* (TPH), p. xiv:
tātparyavatī hi śrutiḥ pratyakṣād balavatī, na śrutimātram |

46 See Introduction to *Bhāmatī* (TPH), p. xiv:
upakramo-'pasaṁhārāv abhyāso, 'pūrvatā phalam |
arthavādo'papatti ca liṅgaṁ tātparya-nirṇaye ||

include himself in the counting and says, " You are the tenth". Similarly, in the case of *Brahman*, there is at first the mediate knowledge of its existence from the scriptural statements like "Existence alone, dear one, was this in the beginning, one only without a second" (*ChāUp* VI.ii.1), etc. and then, the major texts, "That thou art" (ChāUp VI.viii.7), etc. when their purport is known, reveal the immediacy of *Brahman*. That there is mediate knowledge from mere statement and immediate knowledge from the sentence whose meaning has been inquired into is illustrated in the episode of Bhṛgu (*TaitUp* III). Understanding *Brahman*, at first, mediately through its characteristic of being the cause of origination, sustentation and destruction of the world, Bhṛgu came to have immediate knowledge of *Brahman* through a searching inquiry into the purport of the definition of *Brahman* which his father imparted to him. The story of Indra in the *Chāndogya Upaniṣad* is a similar instance in point. Indra, after knowing mediately the nature of the self as indicated in the text, "That self which is devoid of defect, rid of ravaging effect of age, free from death and misery" (*ChāUp* VIII.vii.1), etc. approached his preceptor four times with a view to acquire the intuitive experience of the self. The *Aitareyopaniṣad* indicates *Brahman* mediately in the passage, "In the beginning, this was the one only self; nothing else existed" (I.i.1), etc. and later by the method of superimposition and subsequent withdrawal (Adhyāropāpavāda) it teaches the intuitive experience of *Brahman* which is of the nature of intelligence. The view that the major texts which are but sentences are capable of generating immediate knowledge is supported by Śaṅkara in his *Vākyavṛtti* where he declares that the *mahāvākyas* are for the sake of the establishment of the immediate experience of *Brahman* (*Mem. Ed.*, vol. 15, pp. 30-31).

Now, it may be argued that logic tells us that from a sentence only mediate cognition results; that, for example, from a statement about heaven only an inferential knowledge about heaven is obtained. The argument takes the following syllogistic form: the major text generates only mediate knowledge since, it is a sentence, like the sentence about heaven. But this mode of reasoning is not valid, for the *probans* is inconstant in the case of the tenth man in the parable of the travellers. From the statement, "You are the tenth man", there certainly results immediate knowledge of his being the tenth person for the one who lost himself in counting. Hence, it is not established that because the major text is a sentence, it generates only mediate knowledge. As for the non-immediacy of the knowledge of heaven, it is because heaven which is the object of knowledge is itself not immediate. In order that there may be immediate cognition of a thing, that thing must be immediate. And since *Brahman* is eminently immediate, the cognition thereof gained from the scriptural texts may intelligibly be immediate. If on hearing the *mahāvākya*s a person does not get an immediate intuition of *Brahman*, it is not because those *vākya*s are incapable of generating that experience, but because there is the obstruction caused by impossibilities and notions of the contrary (*VPS*, p. 100). What is called impossibility is the unfitness of the mind for one-pointedness which is the cause of a host of contemplations of the non-difference of the self from *Brahman*. And notions of the contrary are a host of the residual impressions of the superimposition of the body, etc. on the self. Hence, although *Brahman*-knowledge is the result of the *pramāṇa* of the sacred teaching, being obstructed by such mental defects as impossibility and notions of the contrary being true, it is in need of *tarka* (reasoning). Though reasoning is not independently an evidence in respect of *Brahman*-knowledge, it is helpful thereto by removing the said obstruction. A cause can originate its effect only when there is the absence of obstacles. When the obstacles, viz. impossibility and notions of the contrary, are removed by reasoning, from the Vedāntic texts there arises unshakable immediate experience of *Brahman*.

It is the conviction of the Advaitin that *Brahman* alone is real and that it is made known by verbal testimony. Now, is verbal testimony which is the evidence for *Brahman* real or unreal (*SLS*, p. 320)? If it be real, then as there is a reality which is other than *Brahman*, the latter's non-duality will be destroyed. If it be unreal, then, what is revealed by an unreal evidence should also be unreal. The words of an untrustworthy person which are untrue and misleading do not lead to the establishment of an empirically real fact. The statements about such sacrificial rites as Agnihotra, which have empirical validity, do not yield a fruit which is absolutely real. Words can establish a reality which is of the same grade as themselves. If the evidence of verbal testimony be illusory or unreal, *Brahman* which is its content cannot be real.

The Advaitin faces the dilemma by accepting the unreality of verbal testimony. There is no rule that an evidence establishes only what is of the same grade of reality as itself. Even the empirical and the unreal can be practically efficient; and there is no unintelligibility whatever in verbal testimony, which is empirical, being the cause of establishing the absolutely real *Brahman*. The Vedāntic texts teach *Brahman* by such terms as "real", and hence, *Brahman* is real. In respect of Agnihotra, etc. there is no teaching that they lead to a fruit which is real. And so, both the Agnihotra and its fruit are empirically, and not absolutely, real. Even if such words as "real" be used in connection with the Agnihotra, etc. the reality of the Agnihotra, etc. is sublated by the texts of non-duality which are of greater force. Thus, verbal testimony, though it is less than real, can be the evidence for the real *Brahman*. Even though *Brahman* be real, reality does not result for the validity present in the knowledge thereof, since there is not in that knowledge the attribute of being *Brahman* alone.[47] The illusoriness (*mithyātva*) of the validity present in the knowledge of the real *Brahman* is intelligible, since that knowledge contains also something other than *Brahman*,

47 *Kṛṣṇālaṁkāra*, commentary on *SLS*, p. 321 (ed. Harihara Sastri).

just as the validity present in the knowledge of pot contains something other than pot. The familiar example given by the Advaitins to show how the testimony of scripture, though it be illusory, can sublate the illusory world is that of the dream-cognition of a lion sublating the dream experience itself. The roaring of the lion cognized in a dream is no doubt illusory; but, nevertheless, it enables the dreamer to wake up from his dream.

To the Advaitin the final court of appeal is the testimony of the Vedānta. *Śruti* is superior in validity to the other *pramāṇa*s like perception and inference. In matters that are sensuous, however, perception, etc. may validly function. Even 1,000 scriptural injunctions cannot convert a pot into a piece of cloth. But in matters that are supersensuous, *śruti* is supreme. It is declared to be of greater value than the other *pramāṇa*s, since it is free from defect. And since the scriptural cognition of non-difference arises subsequently to the empirical *pramāṇa*s like perception and inference, it serves as the sublater with reference to them. The principle of the subsequent sublating the earlier is called the *apaccheda-nyāya.*[48] This principle is applied wherever there is the impossibility of the later arising except as sublating the earlier. The later cognition, "This is not silver", cannot come into being except as contradicting the earlier cognition: "This is silver". Where there is no such conflict between the earlier and the subsequent cognitions, there the initial cognition is predominant and with the sense of that everything that follows is syntactically united. This principle is known as the *upakrama-nyāya. Pramāṇa*s like perception are alleged to give us a knowledge of difference. Since the scriptural cognition of non-difference[49] is subsequent to them, the Advaitin decides, through the application of the *appaccheda-nyāya,* that the testimony of *śruti* which sublates the other *pramāṇa*s is supreme.

---

[48] *SLS,* vol. I, Introduction, p. 25.

[49] That non-difference is the purport of Vedānta is lucidly set forth by Śaṅkara in his commentary on the *Samanvayasūtra* (*VedSū* I.i.4).

There remains an important problem to be discussed before we conclude this chapter. If, for the Advaitin, the testimony of scripture be supreme, what is the place of reason in his scheme? If reason be but the handmaid of revelation, is not the Vedānta more a traditional theology than a rational philosophy? The reasons why the Advaitin regards *śruti* as the final authority in matters of the spirit we have given already. But all texts of scripture are not equally authoritative. It is only purportful scripture that is authoritative. We have seen above that in order to determine the purport of scripture six marks are laid down. One of these is *upapatti* (intelligibility) in the light of reasoning, and it is in no way the least important of the six marks. The light of reasoning is required even to determine which are the initial and which are the concluding passages. And the application of the other marks depends on the fixing of the initial and the concluding passages. Reason, it is true, is valid only insofar as it does not conflict with scripture; but even to judge when reason is in conflict with scripture and when it is not, reason is required. Hence, the alleged unphilosophical nature of the Vedānta is only apparent and not real. Far from being dogmatic and dictatorial, the philosophy of Vedānta is rational and yet in harmony with revelation. To quote Romain Rolland, one of the reputed thinkers of the West: "The only religion that can have any hold on intellectual people is the rationalistic religion of Advaita".

2

Truth and Error

Truth: Absolute and Relative

PRAMĀṆAS are avenues leading to valid knowledge. Valid knowledge (*pramā*) is truth; and what is opposed to it, viz. false knowledge (*apramā*), is error. Non-contradiction and novelty are usually stated to be the characteristics of truth. Anything that is contradicted or sublated cannot be true. Novelty, however, is not an invariable trait of truth. But in order to exclude memory which is not new knowledge, novelty is also included in the nature of truth.[1]

Judged by the test of unsublatability, nothing other than knowledge of *Brahman* can be true. The absolutely real is *Brahman*; and the absolutely true knowledge is the knowledge of *Brahman*. But so long as that supreme knowledge is not gained, we take the world to be real and the knowledge thereof to be true. Empirical knowledge is ultimately sublated only when there dawns the intuition of *Brahman*; hence, it possesses empirical validity. Less valid than the knowledge of the empirical world is the truth that pertains to such fanciful objects as those of dream,

---

1 *VP*, p. 15. When *pramātva* is subsumed under *yathārthatva*, memory-knowledge is said to be *yathārtha*, but not *pramā*. When, however, *pramātva* and *yathārthatva* are taken to be synonymous, memory-knowledge is also regarded as *pramā*.

etc. Unmixed truth or error is never had in this world. There is a soul of goodness in things evil.

> There will be no truth which is entirely true, just as there will be no error which is totally false. – Bradley 1908: 362

In the Absolute (*Brahman*), however, there can be no taint of error.

> The Absolute, considered as such, has of course no degrees; for it is perfect, and there can be no more or less in perfection.
> – Ibid.: 359

But such predicates hold good when applied to the world of appearance. While regarding *Brahman* alone as the absolutely real (*pāramārthika sattā*), the Advaitin concedes to ether, etc., empirical reality (*vyāvahārika sattā*), conditioned by *māyā* and to nacre-silver, etc., apparent reality (*prātibhāsika sattā*), conditioned by nescience (*VPS*, p. 36). The dreams, however incoherent they may be, are not cognized to be unreal so long as they last. Dream-cognition is true in its own sphere. Similarly, the experiences of waking life have a certain amount of truth which is greater than that of the dream-experience. It is only in *Brahman* and in the knowledge thereof that there is the perfection of reality and of truth.

Is Truth Intrinsic or Extrinsic?

Whether truth[2] is intrinsic or extrinsic is a disputed point. The Sāṁkhyas regard both truth and error as intrinsic. The Naiyāyikas consider both to be extrinsic. The Bauddhas say that error is intrinsic and truth extrinsic. The Advaitin's position, according to which truth alone is intrinsic, is quite the antithesis of the view of the Bauddhas (*VPS*, p. 100).[3]

---

2 Truth is used here as synonymous with validity, and error as synonymous with invalidity.

3 *Sarvadarśanasaṁgraha*, p. 279:
pramāṇatvā-'pramāṇatve svataḥ sāṅkhyāḥ samāśritāḥ
naiyāyikāste parataḥ saugatāścaramaṁ svataḥ

→

The view of the Sāṁkhyas – that both truth and error are intrinsic – is based on their theory of cause which is known as the Satkāryavāda or the doctrine that the effect is pre-existent in the cause. There is no production of anything *de novo.* What is called causation is the manifestation of what is in a latent condition. The effect exists potentially in the cause; and the causal operation (*kāraka-vyāpāra*) makes patent what is latent in the cause. It renders that manifest (*āvirbhūta*) which was previously in an unmanifested state (*tirohita*). This is how the Sāṁkhyas think (*MŚV*, pt I: 80f.): that which is of itself non-existent, like the horn of a hare, cannot be accomplished (ibid.: 89).[4] In the view that an effect is generated *de novo*, it is not possible to restrict the capacity to originate a particular effect to a particular cause. What restriction is there that a pot is produced out of clay alone and not out of water, since the non-existence of pot is common both in clay and in water? Thus, in the view that the effect is non-existent in the cause, it is impossible to determine the material cause of any product. Moreover, of the three kinds of cause, the instrumental or efficient cause (*nimitta kāraṇa*), the material cause (*upādāna* or *samavāyī kāraṇa*) and the non-inherent cause (*asamavāyī kāraṇa*), it is difficult to say which is the material cause. If it be said that where the effect exists there the material cause is to be found, then it amounts to the relinquishment of the Asatkāryavāda. The Sāṁkhyas also admit that the effect exists in a subtle form in the cause. It may be objected that if the effect is pre-existent in the cause, there results futility for causal operation. But it is not so. The causal operation has the fruit of manifesting what is unmanifest in the cause. The effects, though existent in their causes, are unmanifest prior to the operation of the causal-correlates. Hence, the operation of the causal-correlates is fruitful and not futile. If the causal-

---

← *prathamaṁ parataḥ prāhuḥ prāmāṇyaṁ veda-vādinaḥ*
pramāṇatvaṁ svataḥ prāhuḥ parataś cā 'pramāṇatā ॥

4 *Codanāsūtra, śi.* 47: *nahi svato 'satī śaktiḥ kartum anyena śakyate* ।

operation be for the sake of *manifesting* what is unmanifest, what is the significance, it may be asked, of such statements as: "The cause *produces* the effect", "The product *originates* from the cause", etc.? Is there no difference, it may be urged, between the *manifestation* of a pot by a lamp and the *origination* of a pot by the potter? Manifestation, reply the Sāṁkhyas, is of two kinds. When, in respect of an object whose form is not obstructed but whose cognition by a person is obstructed, there is the removal of that obstruction, then we have an instance of the first kind of manifestation. For a pot enshrouded in darkness there is no obstruction in respect of its shape. The removal of darkness manifests the pot, but it does not give it its shape. The second variety of manifestation is the removal of the obstacle which obstructs the form of the object from manifesting itself. In clay, the form of pot is obstructed by the form which is natural to clay. The removal of the form of clay which obstructs the form of pot from manifesting itself is what is popularly known as the production or the origination of pot. A change in the collocation of atoms in the cause is what is regarded as production of the effect (Das Gupta 1922, I: 257). Nothing new is added to the cause in order to produce an effect. The same atoms that constituted the cause appear in the effect in a different arrangement. The pot is not different from clay except in respect of its shape. Hence origination or production is only a mode of manifestation.[5] Another objection may here be raised against the Satkāryavādin. "Is manifestation pre-existent or not? If it is pre-existent, there is the futility of the causal-operation. If it is not pre-existent, there is the abandonment of the Satkāryavāda". The Sāṁkhyas reply, by admitting the prior non-existence of manifestation, that there is no futility for the causal-operation. As for the other

---

5 The Advaitin also subscribes to this view of causation. See *Iṣṭasiddhi*, p. 187:
tad eva kāraṇaṁ kāryam avyaktaṁ vyaktatāṁ gataṁ ।
kārya-kāraṇate na stāṁ tayor bhedā 'śva-meṣa-vat ॥

contingence, viz. the abandonment of one's theory, that, he says, is common to his opponent also. In the case of the manifestation of a pot which is enshrouded in darkness, the Naiyāyika admits that what was non-existent prior to the manifestation is the manifestation and not the pot. But if he is true to his principles, he must state that even the pot is originated like its manifestation. Or, he must accept that even the manifestation is pre-existent and not produced anew, in which case he will be relinquishing his own position. This contingence being common to both the adversaries and since the other defects which attend on the Asatkāryavāda are remedied in the Satkāryavāda, the Sāṁkhya holds that his theory is valid. When it is granted that nothing originates *de novo*, that every product is pre-existent in its cause, it follows that even validity (truth) and invalidity (error) exist by their own right, that they are intrinsic.

The Sāṁkhya view is not free from defect (*VPS*, p. 100). What do the Sāṁkhyas mean by stating that both validity and invalidity are intrinsic? Do they consider that in one and the same individual cognition there enter both validity and invalidity? Or, do they make a distinction between them through difference in the particular cognitions? The first alternative cannot bear reasoning, because it is manifest contradiction to say that in one and the same individual cognition there are present both validity and invalidity. Nor is the second alternative possible, for there is nothing to effect the distinction, "In this cognition there is validity and for this other invalidity". The nature of being cognition is common to both validity and invalidity, and anything else that effects distinction is not admitted by those who maintain the intrinsic nature of both.

Unlike the Sāṁkhyas, the Naiyāyikas consider both validity and invalidity to be extrinsic. The causal aggregate of validity is not the same as the causal aggregate of cognition. Cognition is generated by such causal aggregates as the senses, *probans*, etc. If even validity be generated by them, then, all cognitions must be valid and there can be no invalid cognition.[6] Hence, it must be admitted that the origination of validity is effected by something more than the causal aggregate which gives rise to cognition.[7] Where cognition arises through the senses, *probans*, etc. which are associated with some *guṇa* (excellence), there validity is generated. Where, however, cognition arises through the senses, *probans*, etc. which are devoid of any *guṇa*, there invalidity results. In the case of valid knowledge from perception, for example, what is called the *guṇa* is the contact of the senses with the major portion of the object. Thus, since in the origination of validity, there is the need of a *guṇa* over and above the causal aggregate responsible for the production of cognition, validity is said to be extrinsic. Like validity, even invalidity is extrinsic in respect of its origination. An invalid cognition is generated by defects (*doṣa*) which are other than the causal aggregate of cognition. Hence, the origination of invalidity is from factors which are external to the causal aggregate of cognition.

Validity is extrinsic even in respect of its apprehension. It is not apprehended by the causal aggregate which causes the apprehension of cognition. The apprehension of validity results from some cause which is other than that which yields the apprehension of cognition and cognitiveness. Through means of valid knowledge like perception there results the cognition of pot, etc. Through the relation of inherence of what is in contact with mind there arises the cognition of the cognition of pot, etc. The former cognition takes on the form, "This is pot"; and the latter which is known as reflective cognition (*anuvyavasāya-jñāna*) is of the form, "I know this pot". The reflective cognition manifests the original cognition (*vyavasāya-jñāna*), the pot which

---

6 See Udayana's *Kusumāñjali*, p. 59: *yadi ca tāvanmātrā 'dhīnā bhavet, apramā 'pi pramaiva bhavet, asti ca tatra jñāna-hetuḥ, anyathā jñānam api sā na syāt* ।

7 Ibid., p. 59: *pramā jñāna-hetv-atirikta-hetv-adhīnā, kāryatve sati tad viśeṣatvāt, apramāvat* ।

is the content of that cognition and the self which is the locus of that cognition. Hence, that cognition whose sphere is the triple form (*tripuṭī*), viz. the cognizer, cognition and the object cognized, is called reflective cognition. Mind is the instrument of reflective cognition; and the original cognition which is the content of that reflective cognition is itself the relation of mind with the object. Thus, the causal aggregate of reflective cognition, which gives rise to the apprehension of cognition and cognitiveness, is the contact of mind, etc. and from that there does not arise the apprehension of validity. Validity, however, is inferred from fruitful activity. The cognition of water, for example, is ascertained to be valid only when it has resulted in fruitful activity.[8] Since the causal aggregate which causes the apprehension of validity is different from the causal aggregate of reflective cognition, validity is extrinsic. Similarly, the apprehension of invalidity is also extrinsic. Invalidity is not apprehended merely by the help of the causal aggregate of cognition.

It is only when there is the apprehension of the causal aggregate as associated with defects that the apprehension of invalidity results. The superimposition of silver on nacre, for example, is recognized to be invalid, not from the causal aggregate which has given rise to that perception of nacre-silver, but from the apprehension of such defects as similarity, etc. Hence, the apprehension of invalidity is caused by the recognition of something over and above the causal aggregate of cognition and so it is extrinsic.

This view of the Naiyāyikas is defective. Their theory that a cognition is made manifest by the reflective cognition will not stand the test of reasoning. There can be no unknown-ness in a cognition. To state that the manifestation of an object does not

---

[8] See Nīlakaṇṭha's *Dipikā* on *Tarkasaṁgraha*, p. 39: *pūrvotpannaṁ jala-jñānaṁ pramā, saphala-pravṛtti-janakatvāt, yannaivaṁ tannaivaṁ, yathā apramā* ।

require the manifestation of the manifesting cognition is absurd. No lamplight which is itself not luminous illumines an object. Nowhere is the manifestation of an object by an uncognized cognition experienced. Cognition can never be the object of cognition. Even for the reflective cognition it is not the original cognition that is the content. What it cognizes is the knownness (*jñātatā*) of the pot, not the cognition of the pot. The causal aggregate of the apprehension of cognition is not the reflective cognition, but it is the activity of the senses, etc. And from this causal aggregate itself the origination and apprehension of validity is possible. Of this, later.

The Naiyāyika says that both validity and invalidity are extrinsic (*VPS*, p. 1000). Then, it would have to be stated that the cognition which has barely arisen rests for a while devoid of validity or invalidity. But this is not in the scope of what is well established in experience.

The Bauddhas declare that validity is extrinsic and invalidity intrinsic. Invalidity is natural to cognitions; validity is dependent on extrinsic factors.[9] It is a matter of experience that a cognition as soon as it arises does not give rise to flawless activity. So long as there is not the instrumentality of the senses, etc. possessing excellence, and so long as there is not accord with practical efficiency, there is no validity for cognitions. Validity is the fruit of empirical usage; hence, by nature there is only invalidity for cognitions; validity, however, is other-dependent.

This is the reasoning for the intrinsic nature of invalidity. Invalidity is devoid of a cause, because it is not an entity. Whatever is not an entity is devoid of a cause, like the horn of a hare. As for what is said that invalidity is generated by defects, that is unsound. A non-entity can have no cause. The reasoning for the extrinsic nature of validity is this: validity has a cause, since it is an existent, like a pot. The cause of validity is some

9 Commentary on *Śloka-Vārttika*, pp. 85f.

guṇa (excellence) present in the cause of cognition. In the case of perception, it is the purity present in the senses. It is intelligible that validity is generated by such excellence, because it is of the nature of an existent. Thus, all cognitions when they arise are certainly invalid, being of the nature of incertitude. When, however, there is the origination of some excellence or accord with practical efficiency, then, on the strength of that there is generated validity for cognitions.

The view of the Bauddhas is also unintelligible (*VPS*, pp. 100-101). What is meant by saying that validity is extrinsic? Is validity extrinsic in respect of its origination or in respect of its cognition? The extrinsic nature of validity cannot possibly be in respect of its origination; for in the case of the momentary cognition which arises from causes like the sense of sight, continuance till the rise of the attribute of validity is impossible. It may be stated that the extrinsic nature of validity in respect of origination consists in this, that in a cognition, which has arisen from the cause of cognition, validity rises subsequently from the excellence present in the cause. But it is not sound. Over and above the non-existence of defect, there is nothing as excellence which is alleged to be the cause of validity. The non-existence of defect which is an obstacle to validity is itself an excellence. Nor may it be said that the non-existence of defect is the cause of validity, for defect is an obstacle the non-existence of which cannot be the cause. An obstacle is that which obstructs the origination of the effect when the full cause is present; and so, the non-existence of defect cannot be the cause of anything. Thus, it is impossible to establish that validity is extrinsic in respect of origination. Validity is not extrinsic even in respect of cognition. What is called validity is the capacity of cognition to determine an object.[10] The Bauddha asserts that this capacity is known either through the cognition of being originated by an excellence

---

10 *VPS*, p. 101: *prāmāṇyam nāma jñānasyā 'rtha-pariccheda-sāmarthyam* ।

or from the cognition of accord with practical efficiency. But neither of his alternatives is sound. If it be admitted that the capacity of cognition to determine an object is known through the cognition of being originated by an excellence, then, even when a pot is cognized, so long as there is not apprehended the generation of that cognition by an excellence, the capacity to determine the pot not being cognized, there is the contingence of the non-origination of empirical usage relating to the pot. Nor is it possible to say that subsequent to the cognition of being generated by an excellence, there is empirical usage; for, even for the cognition of origination by an excellence, another cognition is required in order to ascertain its own validity and for this other cognition there is the need of a fourth cognition and so on ad infinitum. Thus, there is the contingence of infinite regress. This line of argument applies equally to the second alternative, namely, that the capacity of cognition to determine an object is from the cognition of accord with practical efficiency. There is also the contingence of reciprocal dependence as between the ascertainment of validity and the cognition of accord with practical efficiency; for, it must be stated that the ascertainment of validity is from the cognition of accord with practical efficiency in the case of a person who is active and that there is activity when there is ascertainment of validity. It is indeed legitimate to say that in cases where there is doubt there is activity for the sake of ascertainment of validity. But in the case of things about which there is no doubt whatever it is not proper to maintain that activity is for the sake of the ascertainment of validity. Therefore, in respect of both origination and cognition validity cannot be extrinsic in nature.

The Bauddha asserts that invalidity is natural to cognitions. He argues that it can have no cause because it is a non-entity.[11]

---

11 *VPS* formulates the inference thus: invalidity is not originated extrinsically, since it is of the nature of non-existence of validity, like the prior non-existence of validity, p. 102.

But the *probans*, viz. that invalidity is of the nature of non-existence, is not established. Ignorance, doubt and error are what are called invalid cognitions. "Invalidity is divided into three kinds, in respect of illusoriness, ignorance and doubt", says Bhaṭṭapāda.[12] None of these three kinds of invalidity is of the nature of non-existence. Hence, it is quite intelligible that invalidity has a cause and that it is extrinsic.

The Advaitin's position is that validity is intrinsic in nature and invalidity extrinsic. The intrinsic nature of validity consists in the non-requirement of anything other than that which originates or reveals cognition.[13] Invalidity, however, is extrinsic in nature, since the origination is by a defect present in the cause of cognition and the cognition of it is by sublation.[14]

He who upholds the view that validity is extrinsic in nature objects to the final position of the Advaitin thus:[15] what is the intrinsic nature of validity? The generation of validity cannot be from itself, for a thing cannot be its own cause. Nor is its generation possible from cognition, since cognition which is a *quality* (of the self) cannot be the *material cause* of its validity. Nor

---

12 *Śloka-Vārttika*, p. 92: *aprāmāṇyam tridhā bhinnaṁ mithyātvā- 'jñāna-saṁśayaiḥ* ।

13 *VPS*, p. 102: *prāmāṇyasya utpattau jñāptau ca jñānotpādaka-jñāpa-kātiriktā-'napekṣatva-lakṣaṇam svatastvam* । *yāvat-svāśraya-grāhaka-grāhyatvaṁ svato-grāhyatvam* ।

The Mīmāṁsakas, with whom the Advaitin agrees in this respect, infer the intrinsic nature of validity thus:

vimatā pramā vijñāna-sāmagrī-janyatve sati tad-atirikta- janyā na bhavati, apramātvā-'nadhikaraṇatvāt, ghaṭādi- pramāvat ।

– *Sarvadarśanasaṁgraha*, p. 283.

14 *VPS*, p. 182: *aprāmāṇyasya tu jñāna-kāraṇa-gata-doṣād utpattir bādhācca jñaptir iti paratastvam* ।

svāśraya-grāhakā-'tirikta-sāmagrī-grāhyatvaṁ parato-grāhyatvam ॥

15 The arguments that follow are from Citsukha's *Tattva-Pradīpikā*, pp. 115-26.

is it possible to say that validity is generated from the causal aggregate of cognition. Whether validity be regarded as an undefined attribute (*upādhi*) or as a generality (*jāti*) its origination is an impossibility. It is thus on the assumption that validity is an undefined attribute, what is called validity is the absolute non-existence of the sublation of a cognition which is not a case of memory. And for that no origination is possible, since it is of the nature of absolute non-existence. Even on the assumption that validity is a generality, its generation is unintelligible, since generality, which is eternal, cannot be generated. Nor may it be said that, being dependent on the cognition generated by the causal aggregate of cognition is the intrinsic nature of validity; for, in that case there is the contingence of intrinsicality even for invalidity which is equally the product of the causal aggregate of cognition. It may be said that the intrinsic nature of validity consists in its being generated by the causal aggregate of cognition alone, whereas, invalidity is generated by the causal aggregate of cognition assisted by defects. But this statement will not bear the test of reasoning. Whether validity be regarded as the product of the causal aggregate of cognition which is assisted by the non-existence of defect or as the product of the cause of cognition which is not assisted by defect, there results the contingence of the view that validity is extrinsic in nature. In either case, it is impossible to deny that in respect of validity the non-existence of defect is a cause. Nor may it be urged that because the non-existence of defect is of the nature of non-existence, it cannot be a cause; for that is intelligible even as it is intelligible that the non-existence of specific cognition of shell as shell is the cause of a delusion.

Not only is there the impossibility of defining the intrinsicality of validity. There is no evidence for it. Two inferences may be given as evidence for estabfishing the intrinsic nature of validity:

1. Validity is generated by the bare cause of cognition, since, while being other than invalidity, it is the attribute of cognition alone, like cognitiveness.
2. Validity is generated by the bare cause of cognition, since, while being other than invalidity, it exists in a sphere which is less than that of cognitiveness, like perceptualness.

These two inferences are infested by defects. In the first inference, the example is devoid of *probandum,* since it is not admitted that all cognitiveness is not generated by defects over and above the cause of cognition. Cognitiveness exists even in invalidity which is the product of defects. In the second inference there is inconstancy in respect of incertitude, etc. Incertitude is certainly other than invalidity and it exists in a sphere which is less than that of cognitiveness; but at the same time it is not generated by the bare cause of cognition. Further, the example is devoid of the *probandum,* since for him who advocates the extrinsic nature of validity there is not established even of perceptualness that it is generated by the bare cause of cognition. Thus, there is no evidence for validity being intrinsic. That validity depends on a cause which is other than the cause of cognition is proved on the ground that it is a product like pot. Thus, in respect of origination, validity is not intrinsic.

Nor is validity intrinsic, says the opponent of Advaita, in respect of its cognition. What is called the intrinsic nature of validity: is it the apprehension of the validity of the cognition of blue from the cognition of blue itself? Or is it the apprehension of that validity from the bare cause of that cognition? Not the first, since the cognition of blue cannot be a valid means of knowledge in respect of itself. The perception which manifests blue is capable of doing that because there is sense-contact with blue. But, as for manifesting its own validity, it is incapable, because sense-contact is impossible with itself. Further, does that perception apprehend the validity of cognition alone, or of its fruit also? Not the first: since cognition is inferred from its fruit, it is not perceptible; and hence its validity is also imperceptible. Nor the second: since the fruit of cognition is self-luminous, it cannot be an object of the external senses; and so validity which is of the nature of truth inherent therein cannot intelligibly be the object of the external senses. Nor does the intrinsic nature of validity consist in the cognition of validity from the bare cause of cognition. If validity be apprehended from the bare cause of cognition, then, there is the contingence of the absence of doubt whether in a cognition there is validity or not. And further if it be admitted that validity is apprehended from the bare cause of cognition, there is the contingence of the apprehension of validity even in the cognition of nacre-silver. It may be thought that this is a contingence of the acceptable in that though validity is apprehended in the nacre-silver, it is later on removed through sublation. But in that case, there is the contingence of the extrinsic nature of validity, since the ascertainment of validity is bound up with the non-existence of a sublating cognition.

There is no evidence for validity being intrinsic in respect of its cognition. It is sought to establish the intrinsic nature of validity thus:

1. truth is known of its own accord, since its origination is not other-dependent, like cognition;
2. similarly, validity is known of its own accord, since, while being other than invalidity, it is the attribute of cognition alone, like cognitiveness. In the first of these inferences, the *probans* is not established for him who advocates the theory that validity is extrinsic, and there is no example also. In the second inference, there is inconstancy in the case of the attribute of the bare cognition which is self-luminous, according to the Prābhākara and in the case of the attribute which, according to the Bhāṭṭa, is of the nature of being inferred from known-ness. In these cases, though there be the nature of being the attribute of bare cognition,

there is not the character of being apprehended by the bare causal aggregate which apprehends cognition. That validity is extrinsic in respect of cognition is established by Udayana in his *Nyāyakusumāñjali* through syllogistic reasoning: validity is extrinsically known, since at the stage of non-recognition it is doubted, like invalidity.[16] Thus, the doctrine that validity is intrinsic is objected to by those who believe in the extrinsic nature of validity.

As against the objections detailed above, the Advaitin defends his position by defining what he means by the intrinsic nature of validity. While being generated by the cause of cognition, not being generated by anything other than that is the intrinsic nature of validity.[17] The evidence which establishes the validity of this position is the inference: truth, while being generated by the cause of cognition, is not generated by anything other than that, since it is other than invalidity, like cloth, etc.[18] That the absence of defect is not a cause of validity we have seen above; and how the view that validity is extrinsic is defective we have observed in the refutation of the Naiyāyika and the Bauddha theories. Invalidity, however, is extrinsic, we have said, since it is prompted by defects. Thus, the Advaitin's position is stable and safe, that validity is intrinsic and invalidity extrinsic.

Ignorance as the Material Cause of Error

Apramā (error) has its root in nescience (*avidyā*). The material

---

16 See Udayana's *Kusumāñjali*, p. 7: *prāmāṇyam parato jñāyate, anabhyāsa-daśāyāṁ sāṁśayikatvāt, aprāmāṇyavat, yadi ca svato jñāyeta, kadācid api prāmāṇya-saṁśayo na syāt* ।

17 *Tattva-Pradīpikā*, p. 122:
āhur vijñāna-sāmagrī-janyatve saty ajanyatā ।
tadanyataḥ pramāyās tat-svatastvam iti tad-vidaḥ ॥

18 Ibid., p. 122.
pramā vijñāna-sāmagrī-janyatve sati nānyataḥ ।
jāyate vyatiriktatvād āpramātaḥ paṭādivat ॥

cause of error, which consists in the reciprocal superimposition of two things of unequal reality whether in respect of their existences (*svarūpa*), relations (*saṁsarga*) or cognitions (*jñāna*), is ignorance which is of the nature of an existent, beginningless and indeterminable (*VPS*, p. 14). The evidence for ignorance which is of the nature of an existent is the perceptual experience "I am ignorant", etc. This experience does not relate to non-existence of knowledge, since it is experienced immediately as "I am happy", etc. whereas non-existence is known through *anupalabdhi* (non-cognition) (*VPS*, p. 16). That ignorance is an existent can be established even through the following argument. Any valid cognition must be preceded by something other than its antecedent non-existence, which obscures the content of that cognition, which is removed by it and which is present in its own locus, because it manifests some object which was not manifest already, like the lamp-light which arises for the first time in darkness. Just as the lamp-light is preceded by darkness which is an existent (in the view of the Advaitin), valid cognition is preceded by ignorance which is of the nature of an existent (*VPS*, p. 17). The negative particle (*nañ*) in *ajñāna* cannot have as its sense either non-existence or the sense of an opposite or any other sense, in which case non-existence of knowledge, delusive cognition and its residual impression would alone be the denotation of *ajñāna* (*VPS*, p. 21). An analysis of the experience of sleep reveals that there is in that experience ignorance which is not non-existence of knowledge, nor delusive cognition, nor its residual impression. Non-existence is impossible for knowledge which is eternal. The true nature of *Brahman* is non-manifest in sleep. But *Brahman* cannot be non-manifest of its own accord, because it is self-luminous. Delusive cognition cannot be the cause of its non-manifestation, since there is no delusion in sleep. Nor can the residual impression of delusive cognition be the cause, for it is not an obstruction to the manifestation of the true nature of the self. Hence in sleep, there must be admitted the experience of ignorance which is of the nature of an existent.

Ignorance is admitted to be beginningless, for otherwise the inquiry into causes will lead to infinite regress. It is indeterminable because it bears within itself a contradiction, and yet it cannot be characterized as non-existent.[19] As we shall see later in this chapter, error which is a product of ignorance is indeterminable (*anirvacanīya*). For an effect which is indeterminable, there cannot be a real cause. If the cause be real, the effect must also be real and it must be known through means of valid knowledge. Hence, it must be admitted that ignorance is indeterminable.[20] Thus, it is established that ignorance, which is of the nature of an existent, beginningless and indeterminable, is the cause of erroneous knowledge which consists in coupling the true with the untrue, superimposing the nature and the attributes of the one on the other through non-discrimination.[21]

Erroneous cognition is knowledge that is sublated by a subsequent cognition. In fact, it is no knowledge at all, but only a semblance thereof (*jñānābhāsa*). The sting of error lies in its passing for right knowledge.

> Error is that form of ignorance which poses, to itself and to others, as indubitable knowledge; or that form of false thinking which unhesitatingly claims to be true, and *in so claiming* substantiates and completes its falsity. – Joachim 1906: 14

Were error not an appearance of knowledge, it would never be sublated. Since it is removable by right knowledge (*jñāna-nivarttya*),[22] it is necessarily an illusory appearance which can be characterized neither as real nor as unreal (*sadasad-vilakṣaṇa*).

---

19 Joachim 1906; 138: "So long as I am genuinely in error, it is essential that I should believe myself to be thinking truly. As soon as I recognize that I am in error, I have passed beyond error itself and am on the road to truth. This is somewhat paradoxical."

20 Vimuktātman's *Iṣṭasiddhi*, p. 48.

21 See Śaṅkara's *Adhyāsa-Bhāṣya*.

22 This interpretation of *mithyātva* is attributed to the author of the *Pañcapādikā-Vivaraṇa*, p. 34.

Theories of Error

Delusion and sublation are explained by the adherents of the different schools of Indian thought in different ways. The Advaitin's view of delusion or error is that it is indeterminable (*anirvacanīya*); and this he demonstrates by a criticism of rival theories.[23] Those theories can be grouped under two classes, (i) *asat-khyāti*, and (ii) *sat-khyāti* (see *Iṣṭasiddhi*, p. 39). According to the theory of *asat-khyāti*, which is advocated by the Mādhyamikas, in error there is cognition of the unreal. The doctrines that go under the class of *sat-khyāti* hold that in error there is cognition of the real; and they are three:

(a) *ātma-khyāti*, the view of the Vijñānavādins who are subjectivists,

(b) *akhyāti*, the doctrine of the Prābhākaras who regard all knowledge as true, and

(c) *anyathā-khyāti*, the theory of the Bhāṭṭas and others who hold that what is given in erroneous knowledge is otherwise than in the mode in which it is presented.

ASAT-KHYĀTI

In the view of the Mādhyamika to whom unreality is ultimate, error consists in the cognition of the unreal as real. There is no substrate whatever for the delusive cognition as for other valid cognitions and the sublation of that delusion is without any limit. Substrateless delusion is possible as in the case of *keśoṇḍraka*[24] and the *fata morgana*; and limitless sublation is also possible as in the case of the statement of the trustworthy person

---

23 There are five theories of error including the one maintained by the Advaitin:

ātma-khyātir asat-khyātir akhyātiḥ khyātir-anyathā ।
tathā 'nirvacna-khyātir ity etat khyāti-pañcakam ॥

24 *Keśoṇḍraka* is the appearance of a bright woolly mass when the closed eye is pressed with the finger-tip.

"not snake" which sublates the delusive cognition of rope as snake (*VPS*, p. 41).

The statement of *śūnya-khyāti* (as *asat-khyāti* is otherwise known), which is stated above as found in the *Vivaraṇa-Prameya-Saṁgraha,* is elaborated in the *Iṣṭasiddhi* (pp. 154-60) as also is its refutation. It is only silver which is nullity (*tuccha*), says the Mādhyamika, that appears in delusion, since its *tuccha*-nature is understood from its sublation in, "This is not silver".[25] The sublation makes known the silver which was manifest in delusion to be unreal. Were silver real, there would be no sublation thereof. And since there is observed sublation of the illusory silver, silver must be unreal. Sublation, which as cognition is an intimation of real nature, cannot destroy a real thing. Hence, it can sublate only what is unreal. When there is the sublating cognition, there is neither the appearance nor the existence of silver. On the contrary, it appears as not existing. This would be unintelligible if silver be regarded as real. Therefore, the sublating cognition makes known only the nullity nature of silver; not otherwise could it be a sublating cognition. If it has a real content like the cognition of pot, etc. then it would not be a sublating cognition. Hence, in delusion, the unreal silver alone appears.

It may be argued that in delusion and in the sublating cognition the *tuccha* is not cognized, on the ground that cognition of the *tuccha* is an impossibility. The Śūnyavādin replies that, if the delusion and the sublating cognition make known what is real, there would be no delusion because of the impossibility of the sublater and what is sublated. If delusion be the cognition of the real, then, it cannot be sublated whether by a cognition of the real or by a cognition of the unreal. And if the sublating cognition be a cognition of the real, then, it can sublate neither a cognition of the real nor a cognition of the unreal. Thus, the relation of sublater and sublated as between cognitions

---

25 *Iṣṭasiddhi*, p. 154: *tuccham eva rūpyaṁ bhāti, tasya nedaṁ rajatam iti bādhāt tucchatā 'vagamāt* ।

of the real being made impossible, there is the contingence of the cognition of silver being not a delusion. Since this is not a contingence of the acceptable, it must be admitted that delusion consists in the cognition of the unreal as of the nature of the real and that sublation makes known its unreality.

It may be said that since the *tuccha*, because it is non-existent, is not cognized even in respect of its existence, it cannot be cognized as of the nature of the real. But this statement is contradicted by the sublating cognition which makes known the *tuccha* nature of silver, as also by the cognition of *tuccha*. The cognition in the form "This is not silver" does make known the *tuccha*-ness of silver. Nor may it be said that the sublating cognition, if it be the cognition of non-existence, cannot be the sublater of a perceptual delusion; for what is called the perceptual delusion is nonetheless a delusion. On the assumption that the delusion is a case of perception, it is urged that cognition of non-existence which is weaker cannot sublate it. But even if it were perception, another perception could not be the sublater, being only of equal strength. Further, it was pointed out above that a cognition, whose content is an existent, could not be a sublater; and so, how could perception, whose content is an existent, sublate the earlier cognition of silver. Nor may it be said that because of conflict, the later perception is a sublater; for there can be no conflict as between cognitions of existents either with different contents or with an identical content. Even the Māyāvādin who admits the non-existence of the reality of silver should recognize sublation as the evidence therefore. Otherwise, the reality of silver would remain unsublated. Hence, it must be accepted that the *tuccha*-ness of silver is made known by the sublating cognition. Further, it is a contradiction to say that the *tuccha* does not appear; for if the *tuccha* does not appear, it is not even possible to say that the *tuccha* does not appear, which statement would be on a par with the absurd assertion, "My mother is barren". The very word *tuccha* in the sentence, "The *tuccha* does not appear", presumptively implies the cognizedness of the *tuccha* and hence contradicts the validity of the statement. Even if the cognition of *tuccha* be regarded as delusive, as is done by the Māyāvādin, the denial of the cognition of *tuccha* does not stand to reason, for the cognition of *tuccha* should, then, be recognized in the delusion of *tuccha,* as of silver in the delusion of silver. Hence, since the cognition of what is unreal is intelligible, it is not correct to say that the unreal cannot be cognized. It may be urged that it is the cognition of the real nacre that sublates the delusion and not the cognition of the unreal; but since even the Advaitin recognizes the cognition of the non-existence of silver in saying that silver does not exist anywhere, sublatership legitimately belongs to that cognition alone, because of being well known. The Advaitin holds that silver, etc. which are the content of delusion, are products of ignorance. But, since ignorance is the absence of knowledge, the product thereof can only be non-existence and not the indeterminable; for, according to the Advaita theory of causation, what is generated by the unreal cannot be other than unreal, if the unreal could generate anything at all. Another important argument urged by the Mādhyamika is based on the law of excluded middle. The counter-correlate of the real is the unreal, and there is no middle ground between the two. When the sublating cognition reveals the unreality of silver, there is no doubt in the form: "Is silver indeterminable? Or is it unreal?" And people determine without any doubt that it is certainly unreal. The crux of the Śūnyavādin's argument is this: the silver that appears in delusion is unreal, since it is sublated and sublation is not possible of what is real.[26] This is what is meant by the statement of *asat-khyāti* in the *Vivaraṇa-Prameya-Saṁgraha* that delusion is substrateless.

The Mādhyamika view comes in for a thorough logical criticism in the *Iṣṭasiddhi.* We shall here summarize the main

---

26 *Iṣṭasiddhi*, p. 39: *bādhāyogād asat sataḥ* ।

argument of that great work so that what is declared in the *Vivaraṇa-Prameya-Saṁgraha*, that substrateless delusion and limitless sublation are impossible,[27] may become intelligible. Vimuktātman begins by stating that without the postulation of an indeterminable *māyā*, cognition of the unreal cannot be established. Without granting the existence of *māyā* which is indeterminable, the *asat* will not be established, much less its cognition. What is this which is called *asat*? Does it *exist* as different from the real? Or does it not? If it does exist, then, there is no *tuccha*-ness for it, even because of its *existence.* If it does not, then, there can be no cognition thereof. Hence, it must be admitted that what is called *asat* is *māyā*-generated and indeterminable (*Iṣṭasiddhi*, p. 161). The concept of *asat* as meaning nullity is impossible. The *asat* must either be real or other than real. If it be real, then, it is not unreal; and if it be other than real, even then, there must be reality for it as for another real. Thus, the *asat* is non-established (ibid., p. 167).

That the *asat* is not *tuccha* may be proved even on the principles of the Asatvādin. According to him, even silver cannot appear in delusion, because it is non-silver. Hence, non-silver alone appears as silver. In the same way, it must be admitted that the *atuccha* (i.e. what is not nullity) alone appears in delusion as *tuccha.* If the *tuccha* should appear in delusion, there should be recognized *tuccha*-ness for that too, as for silver; and this will lead to infinite regress (ibid., p. 163). That the *asat* is not *tuccha* is evident even because it is expressed by a word. If it be expressible by a word, then, it should be different from that word and *atuccha,* as otherwise there could not be between them the relation of the expressed and the expression (ibid., p. 169). The view of the Vaiyākaraṇa (Grammarian) that the word

[27] "Error is thinking the thing which is not. False thinking is the thinking of nothing. But this sounds like not thinking. And if we are to put it, we must certainly agree with Plato that the man who judges falsely, undoubtedly thinks, and thinks something".
– Joachim 1906: 127

is itself the expressed is incorrect; for both expressiveness and expressedness cannot belong to one and the same thing. The expression and the expressed, sound and object, must be posited only as reciprocally different; otherwise, the empirical usage of words as denoting things would be impossible. There being no non-difference between word and object, what is expressed by the word *asat* must be different from that word and hence, also real. If the *asat* be non-existent, there can be no expression thereof; if it be word-denoted, it cannot be a void. Since the void is what is non-cognized, there can be no apprehension of the relation of sound therewith. There can be no cognition of the void because of its non-existence; and what is non-existent and non-cognized cannot be expressed by a word (ibid., p. 176).

Here, a possible objection may be raised:

> Expressing the void even by that word, how is it possible to declare that it is not expressed? Even for condemning a thing there must be assumed its existence. Therefore, even by him who condemns the void, there should be admitted its cognizability and denotability by a name.

The Advaitin's reply to this objection is that what he means by such words as *asat* and *śūnya* is not the void. Those words are resorted to only as established by *māyā*, as indeterminable. Further, in order that a thing may be criticized, it is not necessary that it must be real. Condemnation is possible only of what is established by delusion, not of what is established by a means of valid knowledge, nor of what is non-established, because of the impossibility and futility of such criticism. In condemning the Śūnyavāda, however, the words *asat* "void", etc. are used by the Advaitin as denoting the *tuccha* too. But this is only for the purpose of refuting *tuccha*-ness recognized by the Śūnyavādin. Hence, there is not the contingence of admitting either the cognizedness or the expressedness of the void (ibid., pp. 162-63, 177).

If the void should be regarded as cognized through a cognition, then, it must be either real or indeterminable. It cannot be the cognition itself, for cognition cannot be the object of cognition. If the cognition be cognized by the cognized cognition, there is self-dependence. And if it be cognized by some other uncognized cognition, there is infinite regress. There should be some *ālambana* (basis for cognition). This basis cannot be cognition itself, for, if the subsequent cognition be based on the antecedent cognition, since that antecedent too would require another antecedent to rest upon, it would have to be admitted that no cognition that has arisen perishes. Were cognition to perish, there would be no cognition at all. The void cannot be the basis of cognition; for that which is the basis of anything should either be real or indeterminable and not non-existence.

Thus, the existence of the void, even because of voidness, is non-established; need it then be said that the cognition of the void either in its nature or as of the nature of the real is an impossibility?

The Śūnyavādin thinks that error consists in the cognition of the void as of the form of the real silver. But the silver-nature which appears for the void can neither be from itself nor from another. If the silver-nature be natural to the void, then, the silver-cognition would not be false and no subsequent cognition would sublate it. If the silver-nature be adventitious to the void, then, it would have to be admitted that the silver present elsewhere appears adventitiously in the void. If the cognition of the real in relation to the void be acceptable to the Śūnyavādin, why should he not accept the cognition of the real in relation to nacre alone? When it has been shown that the cognition of the void as of the nature of silver is unintelligible, it is needless to demonstrate how the origination of the void in the form of silver is impossible. There can be no origination for the void which is partless. And if the void had parts, there would be for it non-eternality and non-voidness as for a pot.

The crux of the argument is that cognition of non-existence is an impossibility. Of the non-existent, since its very nature is not established, there is no cognition whether in its own nature or in the nature of the existent (ibid., p. 185). There can be no cognition without a substrate. The Śūnyavādin quotes the cognition of the *keśoṇḍraka* and the appearance of the *fata morgana* as examples of substrateless cognition (*VPS*, p. 41). But he is wrong in his citation. The rays of light are the substrate of the *keśoṇḍraka* and ether is the substrate of the *fata morgana.* The nerve of the Mādhyamika's argument is based on the fact of sublation. He regards the sublation as having no limit. But he fails to see that there can be no bare negation. All negation is significant negation. The sublation in the form "not snake" culminates in the cognition "but a rope". Subsequent to sublation, there is, of course, unreality for the superimposed snake; but prior to that there must be admitted, even by the Śūnyavādin, the presentation of an illusory object on a real substrate.

Sat-khyāti

The Satkhyātivādins, who are dissatisfied with the view of error as the cognition of the unreal as of the nature of the real, base their theories on the positive import of delusive cognition. Of the unreal, there can be no cognition.[28] In delusion, however, there is the cognition of the content, e.g. silver. Hence, silver must be real.

Ātma-khyāti

Ātma-khyāti (self-apprehension), the first mode of *sat-khyāti* we shall examinc, is held by the Vijnānavādins according to whom reality consists in a series of momentary cognitions, particular perishing psychical presentations. There is no difference whatever between an object and the cognition thereof. There is no reality over and above cognitions. *Esse est percipi.* Because of the invariability of the simultaneous presentation of blue and its

[28] *Iṣṭasiddhi*, p. 39: *asataḥ khyāty ayogāt sat* ।

cognition, say the Vijnānavādins, there is non-difference between the two.[29] If blue were different from the cognition of blue, then it would not be manifest in the cognition. Or, if it be said that it is manifest in the cognition, then, what restriction is there that all things should not be manifest in a single cognition? It may be said that in the experience "I know this" the cognizer, the object and the cognition are experienced as of distinct natures and as reciprocally related. But that is not intelligible, for, how can there be relation among the momentary? Therefore, it should be assumed that first three separate cognitions "I", "this" and "know" associated with the respective forms arise. Thence, from the third cognition coloured by the *vāsanā*s (residual impressions) called the first and the second cognitions, there is generated another cognition which is of a nature similar to the third cognition and is associated with the three forms. And thus, it must be admitted that the momentary cognitions alone are objects. That cognition is momentary is established by perception. Just as the cognition of blue makes known also the exclusion of other colours, similarly, the cognition which appears as present intimates also its non-relation to the times past and future. Thus, the Vijñānavādin reduces what appears to the man-in-the-street as the block universe into a series of momentary cognitions.

The Vijñānavādin's theory of error is rooted in his subjectivistic metaphysics. The silver which appears in delusion is real, he admits (*Iṣṭasiddhi*, pp. 40-41); but it is real not as existing outside in space, but as a mode of the mind. Error consists in regarding what is mental as material. When cognitions are mistaken to be facts in the external world, error results. What is negated by the sublating cognition "This is not silver" is not silver but only its externality. When delusion and sublation are

---

[29] *VPS*, p. 75: *sahopalaṁbha-niyamād abhedo nīla-tad-dhiyoḥ* ı

Bhāmatī, p. 544. *yad yena saha niyata-sahopalaṁbhanaṁ tat tato na bhidyate* ı

intelligible by the sublation of externality alone, it is prolix to assume the sublation of silver also; and prolixity of assumptions is a serious fallacy. To avoid this defect it may be said that silver alone is sublated, not its externality. But this is absurd on the very face of it; for, when the substrate is sublated, its attribute, viz. externality, cannot remain unsublated; and hence there is the contingence of the sublation of both. In this manner, the Vijñānavādin maintains that externality alone is sublated, not silver. The real nature of silver, however, is cognition and that too is a product of *vāsanā*.

Postponing the criticism of the metaphysical theory of the Vijñānavādin to a later stage, we shall here consider critically his doctrine of error alone. The Saugata divides the world of reality into two categories, the intellect (*citta*) and its products (*caitya*) and regards them as originating in dependence on four kinds of causes: the auxiliary causes (*sahakārī-pratyaya*) like light, etc. the *adhipati-pratyaya* such as the sense of sight, etc. the immediately antecedent cause (*samanantara-pratyaya*) which is the prior cognition and the substrate cause (*ālambana-pratyaya*), viz. the external thing (*VPS*, p. 34). Of these four kinds of causes none will explain the origination of cognition in the form of silver which is fundamental to the position of the Vijnānavādin.[30] Since an auxiliary cause like light is responsible for clearness alone, it cannot originate the form of silver. Nor is the rise of the form of silver possible from the sense of sight, etc. called the *adhipati-pratyaya*, since that is the cause only of the restriction of the content to a particular cause as visible, audible, etc. If a thing is apprehended through the sense of sight, we do not regard that thing as the product of the sense of sight. The sense of sight characterizes that object as a visible thing and does not generate it. What is called the immediately antecedent cause (*samanantara-pratyaya*) which is the prior cognition cannot originate the form of silver; for immediately antecedent to the rise of the delusion

30 Who belongs to one of the four main Saugata schools.

of silver there might have been the cognition of some object, say, a pot, which belongs to quite a different class and which cannot possibly be the cause of the origination of silver. Nor is the rise of the form of silver possible from the external thing called the substrate cause (*ālambana-pratyaya*), since the Vijñānavādin does not acknowledge any extra-mental object. When cornered thus, the Vijñānavādin tries to escape by stating that cognition comes to have the form of silver because of the capacity of *saṁskāra* or *vāsanā*. But the acceptance of this statement falsifies his own position. The *saṁskāra* which is alleged to be the cause of the form of silver must either be permanent or momentary. If it be permanent, there is the abandonment of the doctrine that everything is momentary. If it be momentary, there is relinquishment of the view that there exist cognitions alone.

The Vijñānavādin may restate his position thus: in the beginninglessly established stream of cognition there occurs at some time or other the cognition of silver. This cognition itself serves as the *saṁskāra* which brings about later on the delusive cognition of silver. No doubt the two cognitions are separated by many other cognitions of a different class; but still that is intelligible even as paddy yielding paddy after a long time. Thus, the silver which appears in delusion is brought about by beginningless *vāsanā*. Being real as a form of cognition alone, it delusively appears as if outside.

Even the above restatement does not make the position of the Vijñānavādin clear. Is the silver which appears in delusion originated or not? If it be not originated, it cannot be of the nature of cognition which is originated. If it be generated like the silver of ordinary experience, even then an external thing cannot generate it, since the Vijñānavādin does not accept an extra-mental reality. Nor can the origination of the illusory silver be from pure cognition which is of the form of release. If it be said that the origination of silver is from cognition generated by a defective cause, even then, does the generating cognition apprehend the silver, or is the apprehension of silver by another cognition? The generating cognition cannot apprehend the form of silver, for, since the generator and the generated which are momentary belong to different times, there is the contingence of the non-existence of immediate cognition of silver. Even if the form of silver be apprehended by some other cognition, that cognition cannot be one not generated by a defective cause, because of undue extension. Nor may that cognition be one generated by a defective cause; for, if it be generated by silver, then silver, which is proved to be practically efficient insofar as it is the generator of cognition, must be acknowledged to be real and external; and if it be not generated by silver, then silver cannot be its content, since it is admitted that the content is the cause which contributes the form to the cognition. Thus, in the view of *ātma-khyāti* even silver would not appear.

When it is proved that in the view of *ātmā-khyāti* even the cognition of silver is unintelligible, it is not necessary to demonstrate how the silver cannot appear as if outside. The statement that the silver which appears in delusion is not external conflicts with the cognition of silver as external (*Iṣṭasiddhi*, p. 41). If there could be the cognition of externality in what is non-external, then, there is the possibility of the cognition of intellect in what is non-intellect. But such an admission would be cutting at the very root of the Vijñānavāda according to which there is no real other than the intellect or its product.

Delusion and sublation are unintelligible in the view of *ātma-khyāti* (ibid., pp. 113-15). The silver which is the content of delusion is said to be of the nature of cognition. Now, by what is that cognition known? It cannot be apprehended by itself, for one and the same cognition cannot be the apprehended as well as the apprehender. Nor can it be the content of another cognition, for both the cognitions are on a par and momentary. As between two momentary cognitions which are not simultaneous, there cannot be the relation of the apprehended and the apprehender.

Further, if a cognition be the content of another cognition, there would result non-self-manifestness for all cognitions. And if cognition be self-manifest, it cannot be the content either of itself or of another cognition. Hence, the delusive cognition of silver is an impossibility on the theory that the silver is of the nature of cognition. The sublation of silver is also unintelligible on the subjectivist assumption. The silver-form of the cognition and the externality are asserted to be self-cognized. Now, are these the only forms of cognition? Or are there other forms too? If they alone constitute the forms of cognition, and if they be illusory, then, there can be no valid cognition at all. If there be some other forms of cognition which are non-illusory, then, even like them, the cognition-forms of silver and externality may also be non-illusory. Therefore, all cognitions whatsoever should be illusory, or all of them non-illusory. In either case there can be no sublation. Admitting that there is an illusory form of cognition, is it self-cognized or other-cognized? If it be self-cognized, it cannot be illusory, since it is apprehended as it is. If it be other-cognized, there is the abandonment of the theory of self-apprehension as well as the contingence of it not being the form of cognition. And for a single cognition contradictory natures – self-cognizedness and non-self-cognizedness – are not possible. In this manner, the doctrine of *ātma-khyāti* leads to a blind alley and instead of explaining delusion and sublation it makes them unintelligible.

Akhyāti

The theory of *akhyāti* (non-apprehension)[31] is advocated by the Prābhākaras according to whom there is no invalid cognition.[32] A cognition may be less than true, but it can never be untrue. Hence, in this view of the nature of cognitions, which is quite the antithesis of the theory held by the Mādhyamikas, there is no

---

31 See *VPS*, pp. 26f.; *Iṣṭasiddhi*, pp. 41-42.

32 *yathārthaṁ sarva-vijnānam* ।

room for logical error. The Prābhākara recognizes only a twofold classification of cognition into valid cognition and memory. He does not acknowledge delusive cognition as a third class. Instead of regarding delusion as a single cognition, he considers it to be a composite of two cognitions. In the case of "This is silver", the "this" is perceptually cognized and the "silver" is remembered. The cognition of the "this" is perceptual, because there is sense-contact with what is in front. The cognition of the silver, however, is a memory being generated by a sense-impression called up by similarity, etc. Neither of these cognitions is untrue. But because of a defect in the instrument, the conceit of memory-ness is lost and the two cognitions and their respective contents are not discriminated. There is the non-apprehension of their non-relation (*asaṁsargāgraha*), and consequently, what is usually called error results.[33] The element of untruth lies in the empirical usage of the "this" and "silver" as being appositional and not in the cognitions themselves. Truth and error depend on practical efficiency. What is useful is true. From the point of view of cognitions there is no error at all. This is in keeping with the Mīmāṁsaka doctrine of the self-validity of knowledge. The validity of a cognition cannot be doubted. Hence, non-discrimination (*aviveka*) alone is the cause of error. Because of the loss of the conceit of memory, through such defects as desire present in the agent, the that-element does not figure in the memory of silver. Similarly, through those same defects, the nacre-ness of what is in front is not perceived. The peculiarities of the "this" such as its having a dark exterior, etc. are obscured. And thus, there results non-discrimination as between apprehension and memory. As a consequence of such non-apprehension of non-relation as between the "this" and "silver", he who seeks silver comes to be active in respect of what is in front. The sublation "This is not silver", which results from the discrimination of nacre from

---

33 *TC*, p. 475: *evaṁ svarūpato visayataś cā 'gr̥hīta-bhedaṁ jñāna-dvayam eva visaṁvādi-pravr̥tti-hetuḥ* ।

silver, destroys non-apprehension of non-relation and removes wrong empirical usage.

In the view of *akhyāti*, delusion and sublation cannot intelligibly be explained (*VPS*, pp. 26-33). The Akhyātivādin regards the silver which is presented in delusion as the remembered. But just as in the case of the cognition of real silver, the illusory silver is presented as existing in front. The delusive cognition is in no way inferior to the cases of right cognition. Nor may it be said that the non-existence of silver in front made known by the sublating cognition makes the delusive cognition inferior; for the sublating cognition negates only the silver known to the world as real and not the illusory silver which appeared in the delusion. The Prābhākara considers delusion to be a composite of two cognitions. But just as in the case of right cognition, in delusion also the general and the particular are immediately presented as in reciprocal relation. Even of the delusive cognition the content is a "this-what"; and hence the characterization of delusion as a succession of two cognitions mistaken for one is not sound. If delusion consists of two cognitions, the activity to which it prompts cannot be explained. Further, since, in the view of the Prābhākara, *saṁvit* is self-revealing, the cognitions, if they be two, must be recognized as two, in which case there would be no delusion at all.

The Prābhākara identifies the true with the practically efficient. Since the silver seen in delusion gives rise to activity which is not fruitful, the cognition of that silver is decided to be not valid. But practical efficiency is not the criterion of truth. The Pragmatist who regards truth as "a class-name for all sorts of definite working-values in experience" (James 1922: 68), fails to see the distinction between the saying, "It is useful because it is true", and the assertion, "It is true because it is useful" (ibid.: 204).[34] What is true may be useful, but it does not follow that what

[34] You can say of it then either that "it is useful because it is true" or that "it is true because it is useful".

is useful must be true. The fruit of a *pramāṇa* is ascertainment of the object, not practical efficiency (*Iṣṭasiddhi*, p. 45).

Further, the Prābhākara, who does not accept the category of non-existence, cannot validly maintain the view of *akhyāti*. What does he mean by non-apprehension or *akhyāti* (*VPS*, p. 28)? Non-apprehension cannot be mere absence of cognition; for, if that were so, there should be delusion only in sleep where there is non-existence of cognition and not in waking and dreaming. Nor can non-apprehension be a cognition which prompts a man, who wants one thing, to activity in respect of another; for it is possible that a person who sees nacre-silver in front is not active in respect thereof either because of quick sublation or because of laziness. In such a case, since there is no activity for the man who seeks one thing in respect of another, it would have to be said that his cognition of nacre-silver is not a delusion. Nor can non-apprehension mean the cognition of many undiscriminated things. The Prābhākara holds that non-discrimination is non-apprehension of non-relation, that delusion is the result of not cognizing "this" and "silver" to be non-related. But non-apprehension of non-relation cannot be as between apprehension and memory. In the cognition "I am a man" which is a delusion, there is non-apprehension of non-relation as between two apprehensions and not as between apprehension and memory. Nor can non-apprehension of non-relation be as between any two whatsoever. In such cognitions as, "The cow is a *khaṇḍa*" (one with broken horns), "The cloth is white", etc. there is non-apprehension of non-relation, but they are not delusions. Nor can non-apprehension of non-relation be as between two devoid of the cognition of relation, because of the same defect. Therefore, it makes the position of the Akhyātivādin no better by defining non-discrimination as non-apprehension of non-relation.

Nor is it possible to determine what the conceit of remembrance is, because of the loss of which delusion is said to be caused. The conceit of remembrance cannot be memory itself; for in that case, since in delusion memory itself would be lost, there is the contingence of the non-existence of the cognition of silver. Nor can the conceit of remembrance be something other than memory; for it would have to be said that when something other than memory is lost, there is non-discriminated-ness for memory; and thus there is the contingence of the absence of a common locus. Nor is the conceit of remembrance an attribute present in memory; for no such attribute is cognized. Nor is it the apprehension of a thing as qualified by prior experience; for in the case of a delusive recognition, "This is that Devadatta", while there is the apprehension of relation to prior experience, there is seen non-discrimination even without the loss of that apprehension. Nor is the conceit of remembrance some particular memory present in itself; for without such external adjuncts as the cause and content, nowhere is a distinction among cognitions observed. The conceit of memory is neither a particularity which is the cause of the object of knowledge as distinguished from the sphere of prior experience nor being the generator of a different fruit; for in memory there is no object of knowledge and fruit over and above those that are present in experience. Nor is the conceit of remembrance the experience "I remember"; for, if elsewhere discriminatedness is established for the experience "I remember", it is possible in the case of delusion to say that there is no discrimination because of the loss somehow of that experience. But that itself is not established. Thus, the conceit of remembrance, which is to be lost, is difficult to explain.

The presentation of silver as existing in front is said to be effected by non-discrimination. But non-discrimination is not the cause in respect of delusion. The non-discrimination cannot be between two things apprehended; for in the dream-state, which is a delusion, nothing other than the self is apprehended. Since there do not exist two apprehended things, there is the contingence of the dream-experience being not a delusion. Nor can the non-discrimination be between the apprehended and the remembered; for in dream, when there is non-discrimination of the remembered blue, etc. from the apprehended self, there is the contingence of the presentation of the dream cognition in the form "I am blue", etc. Nor can the non-discrimination be between the remembered; for, then, everything would be presented only as mediate and not as immediate in delusion. Since the conceit of remembrance which is to be lost in order that there may be non-discrimination is not determined and since non-discrimination itself is not proved either as between apprehension and memory or as between the apprehended and the remembered, the theory of *akhyāti* (non-apprehension) stands condemned.

Anyathā-khyāti

The Bhāṭṭas in particular urge the theory of error known as *anyathā-khyāti* according to which delusion is apprehension otherwise. Otherwiseness implies change. In delusion, is there a change in the object? Or does the cognition alone change? A change in the object with its implication of Pariṇāmavāda (the theory that causation is transformation) is unacceptable to the Advaitin. And there can be no change in cognition without a change in the object. Hence, it must be admitted that the delusive cognition presents the object as other than what it is. This is what the Bhāṭṭa means by saying that error is apprehension otherwise. Nacre which is real appears as of the nature of another real, silver (*Iṣṭasiddhi*, p. 46). Nor is there the contingence of the apprehension of silver not being a delusion; for it is an apprehension of a thing as what it is not. Nacre is certainly not silver; and in delusion it is silver that appears and not nacre. Silver is apprehended in the place of nacre by the sense organ that is in contact with nacre and affected by a defect (*VPS*, p. 33). Hence, the cognition of silver is a delusion. By stating that error is the cognition of a thing as what it is not there is not the contingence of the apprehension of the unreal. The mode is not a void, the silver being real. Though non-existent in the place in which it appears, silver is present at another place, e.g. the treasury. Nor may it be asked how, if nacre and the mode be real, it is possible to say that nacre is not as it appears; for silver is of the nature of the non-existence of nacre. Silver indeed is the non-existence of nacre. In the view of the Bhāṭṭas as in the view of all Mīmāṁsakas, there is no non-existence in the sense of bare negation. *Abhāva* is *bhāvantara.* Non-existence is but another existent.[35] Hence, it is said that nacre is not of the nature of silver which is another existent. Though both nacre and silver are real, nacre in its own nature is the content of true cognition and when it appears as of the nature of its non-existence, silver, it is the content of delusive cognition. As for sublation, it is intelligible even with the removal of delusively occasioned silver-nature in nacre. It is evident that on this view error is traced to a subjective element. Neither of the two terms in an erroneous judgement, "this" and "silver", is unreal. It is the relation of identity (*tādātmya*) in which they are perceived to be that is unreal. Though silver is real as existing in the treasury, its presentation as "here and now" and in apposition with nacre is what constitutes error.

The criticism of this theory rests on proving the unintelligibility of the concept of otherwiseness (*VPS*, p. 33). Wherein does otherwiseness lie? Is it in respect of the cognition, in respect of the fruit, viz. manifestation, or in respect of the thing?

1. Otherwiseness cannot be in respect of the cognition. If it were in respect of the cognition, it should be stated in the form that the cognition with the form of silver abides in nacre. Now, if nacre were to serve as the abode, it must either offer its own form in respect of the cognition, or be the content of empirical usage prompted by the cognition.

[35] *bhāvāntaram abhāvo nyo na kiñcid anirūpaṇāt* ।

The first alternative is not possible; for in respect of the cognition which is possessed of the form of silver, the offering of the form of nacre is impossible. Nor is the second alternative intelligible. Though the nacre may be the content of empirical usage prompted by the cognition of silver, it cannot be the abode of the cognition of silver. The perception of tiger, etc. gives rise to the empirical usage of sword, spear, bow, etc.; but on that account sword, etc. are not the abode of the cognition of tiger, etc.

2. Otherwiseness cannot be in respect of the fruit. The fruit of cognition is manifestation. Whether in delusion or in valid cognition there is no difference whatever in respect of the nature of the fruit, manifestation.
3. Nor is there otherwiseness in respect of the thing. What is otherwiseness in respect of the thing? Is it the identity of nacre with silver? Or is it that nacre transforms itself in the form of silver? Even on the first alternative, is there absolute difference between nacre and silver? Or is there difference-cum-non-difference?

There can be no identity as between what are absolutely different. Nor is there the cognition of identity which is a nullity; for, as that is possible even in respect of quality and the possessor of quality, there is the contingence of delusiveness for the cognition thereof. In the view that there is the relation of difference-cum-non-difference as between nacre and silver, the perception of silver would be no delusion even as the cognition "The cow is a *khaṇḍa*". The second alternative, viz. that nacre transforms itself in the form of silver, is also unsound. If silver be a transformation of nacre, it can never be sublated. The cognition of silver which is in dispute is unsublatable, since it is the cognition of a transformation, like the cognition of curd, which is a modification of milk. Hence also, even like the milk, nacre would never again be cognized. There is another reason why the view of transformation is defective. If silver were a transformation of nacre, even those who are not affected by defects ought to cognize silver. Indeed it is not observed that the same milk is transformed in the form of curd in respect of some persons, but not in respect of others. Therefore, the theory of *anyathā-khyāti* which does not stand the test of investigation is not the correct view of error.

ANIRVACANĪYA-KHYĀTI

The Advaitin's theory of error results as a logical consequence from the refutation of rival theories (*Iṣṭasiddhi*, p. 47). We have seen how both the *sat-khyāti* and the *asat-khyāti* are at fault. If nacre-silver were real, its cognition could not be delusive; nor could there be sublation for it. If silver even as it appears be but absolutely real, it would be apprehended even by those that are free from defect (*VPS*, p. 38). Further, there is the sublating cognition "This is not silver", which makes known the non-existence of silver in all three times in the locus where it was cognized. Therefore, because nacre-silver is not apprehended by those without defect and because it is sublated by the cognition of nacre, the silver that appears in delusion cannot be real. Nor can it be unreal, since it is cognized. If it were unreal, then, as in the case of human-horn, there would be no cognition thereof. Hence, there would be neither delusion nor sublation. Delusion and sublation are, however, established in experience. If any one asserts that he does not admit delusion and consequently its sublation, then, he will be contradicting himself. To establish that what is well known in the world, delusion, is unacceptable to him, he must state that it itself is a delusion and he must also frame a sublating argument; but in so doing he would himself be establishing delusion and sublation. Hence, error is an incontrovertible fact of experience. Neither the theories which regard the object of error as real nor the doctrine which considers it to be unreal can adequately explain error. Because of cognition, the silver which is seen in delusion is not unreal;

because of sublation it is not real. And it cannot be both real and unreal, because of contradiction. Hence, it must be stated that nacre-silver is indeterminable (*anirvacanīya*) either as real or as unreal.[36] Since the cognized silver is indeterminable, the cognition cannot legitimately be determinate. Therefore, erroneous cognition is also indeterminable. The material cause of error, we have seen, is nescience. For an effect which is either unreal or indeterminable there cannot be a cause which is real. If the real were the material cause of error, then the object of error must be real and there would be cognizability for it by means of valid knowledge. Hence, nescience which is the material cause of error must be admitted to be indeterminable.

Superimposition

The Advaitin explains the process of the appearance of illusory silver in this manner (*VPS*, p. 35). First, there is sense-contact with what is in front, viz. nacre. But since the sense organ which apprehends it is associated with a defect, the psychosis of the internal organ generated thereby has this-ness alone for content, not the specific nature of nacre. Then, there is the manifestation of intelligence in the this-ness and in the psychosis that apprehends it; and the nescience present in that intelligence is agitated because of a defect. Then, owing to the defect-prompted agitation, the nescience present in the intelligence defined by the this-element is transformed in the form of silver. The transformation in the form of silver is, however, the result of association with the residual impression of silver, which is called up because of similarity. Even as the nescience present in the intelligence defined by the this-element is transformed in the form of silver, the nescience present in the intelligence defined by the psychosis is transformed into the form of a

---

36 *Iṣṭasiddhi*, p. 47:
sattve na bhrānti-bādhau stāṁ nāsattve khyāti-bādhakau ।
sad-asadbhyām anirvācyā 'vidyā vedyais saha bhramāḥ ॥

psychosis, being associated with the residual impression of the psychosis apprehending silver. And that which manifests both of them, viz. the transformation into silver and the transformation into the psychosis, is their common substrate, i.e. the witness-intelligence. Thus, there is the presentation of silver.

It will be evident from the foregoing description of the process of delusion that there are involved in that process two cognitions, the psychosis of the internal organ which apprehends the "this", and the psychosis of nescience which apprehends the "this" to be silver. Though there are two cognitions here, they come to have a single content, because each of the two, the "this" and the "silver", is of the nature of the other. Since the content is one, the fruit defined thereby is also one; and so the delusive cognition is figuratively spoken of as single. This is the view of the author of the *Vivaraṇa* as set forth in the *Vivaraṇa-Prameya-Saṁgraha*. But Kavitārkika-cakravartī Nṛsiṁha Bhaṭṭopādhyāya directs his invective against such a view of delusive cognition (*SLS* II, p. 52). Prior to the origination of the illusory silver there is no experience of the psychosis of "this" as distinct from the psychosis in the form, "This is silver". The perception of a bare "here" and "now", of the substrate as a mere "this", is never within the scope of the seen. Even the evidence of modern psychological knowledge is against the assumption of a psychosis apprehending the characterless substrate (ibid. I, p. 31). Any cognition, however crude it may be, presents a "that-what" and not a mere "that" as severed from the "what". It is truer to say that later reflection discriminates the "what" from the "that", both of which are at first presented in an indistinguishable whole, than to maintain that the "that" is presented at first to which a "what" is later super-added. Though it may appear plausible to admit in the case of delusions involving similarity, as in "This is silver", an initial cognition of the bare substrate, it is not possible in the case of other delusions like "The shell is yellow" to admit any such cognition. But in all cases of delusion without any exception whatever we find that some defect present either in the sense organ or in the percipient is the cause. It is defect that sets up an agitation in nescience, the material cause of delusion; and as was explained above, agitated by defect, nescience transforms itself into silver and the psychosis which apprehends that silver. Thus, when it is in keeping with parsimony to explain delusion as a single cognition, it is profix to assume an initial psychosis apprehending the characterless substrate.

In explaining delusions due to external adjuncts (*sopādhikā-bhrama*) Advaitins come very close to the view of *anyathā-khyāti*. Vācaspati's description of such delusions like "The conch-shell is yellow" (*Bhāmatī*, pp. 18-19) resembles the doctrine of *anyathā-khyāti* so much that his commentator, Amalānanda, feels compelled to defend him against the charge of upholding *anyathā-khyāti* (*SLS* I, p. 28). The difference between *anyathā-khyāti* and *anirvacanīya-khyāti*, however, is this. While the former view regards the object of delusion as belonging to another place and another time, the latter theory maintains that it is originated by nescience at the time and at the place it is perceived. Hence, what is cognized in delusion is not the remembered. Nor is delusive cognition identical with memory.

Superimposition which constitutes error may be defined in two ways. From the point of view of the thing which is superimposed, superimposition may be defined as "that thing which is similar to what is remembered and appears as of the nature of a different thing", and from the point of view of the cognition, superimposition is that "cognition similar to memory, which is the presentation of one thing as of the nature of another" (*VPS*, p. 26).

Thus, error in the view of the Advaitin is inexplicable. While others attempt the impossible in defining the content of error either as real or as unreal, the Advaitin frankly admits the futility of the task. He shows how the opposite theories are barren. The content of error cannot be unreal, because it is cognized. It cannot be real, because it is sublated. And it cannot be both real and unreal, because there would then be violation of the law of contradiction. Since there is no other alternative left, it is indeterminable, *anirvacanīya*. Though it is not possible to determine the content of error either as real or as unreal, it is *jñāna-nivarttya*, removable by right cognition. True knowledge (*samyag-jhāna*) destroys ignorance and its product, delusion.

3

Reality as Existence

HAVING passed through the portals of philosophy, we come now to its central court, viz. ontology. We have found that there are six gateways of knowledge. While *pramāṇa*s like perception and inference give us relative truth, that which takes us to the absolutely real and the absolutely true is only the testimony of *śruti*. The quest of knowledge is the search for truth; and the aim of philosophy is to discover truth in its totality. The sages of the Vedic age were inspired by the true philosophic spirit when they began their inquiry by asking: "What is that by knowing which everything else becomes known?" Since the avenues of knowledge like perception and inference belong to the realm of the sensuous they cannot transcend their own limitations and lead us to the supersensuous. *Śruti*, however, can yield the intuition of the Infinite, since it is free from defect and since the cognition to which it gives rise is subsequent (and hence superior) to perception, inference, etc. And we observed in the first chapter that through the application of the *apaccheda-nyāya śruti* can well be the sublater of the *pramāṇa*s which precede it.

Nature of Reality

"Metaphysics", it is said, "sets itself more systematically than any other science, to ask what after all is meant by being real" (Taylor 1920: 4). It is defined as an inquiry into the meaning of reality. Aristotle calls it a science of being *qua* being. Now, what, according to the Vedānta, is the nature of Reality? What is its ontology or the general doctrine of Being? A thing may be defined in two ways. We may state its essential nature; or we may distinguish it from the rest by mentioning its accidental attributes. A house may be defined in terms of its essential character; or it may be demarcated from the rest by the accidental qualification of a crow perching on its roof. That is the essential nature (*svarūpa-lakṣaṇa*) of a thing which is present in that thing so long as it lasts and distinguishes it from the rest.[1] And that is the qualification *per accidens* (*taṭastha-lakṣaṇa*) of a thing which remains in that thing only for a time and distinguishes it from the rest.[2]

Brahman, the absolutely real, according to the Vedānta, is defined in both the ways. The causality of the world is the qualification *per accidens* of *Brahman*. *Brahman* is the cause of the origination, sustentation and destruction of the universe.[3] Of this nature of *Brahman* we shall take note in a later chapter. Our present concern is with the essential nature of *Brahman*. The Vedāntic texts define its essential nature as "Being", "Intelligence" and "Bliss". Existence, intelligence, infinitude is *Brahman*; and that which is infinite is bliss.[4] The threefold nature of *Brahman* given by scripture is essential to it because it constitutes its essence and serves to distinguish it from the name- and form-world which is unreal (*anṛta*), non-intelligent (*jaḍa*) and of the nature of misery (*duḥkha*). Being (*sat*), intelligence

---

1 *svarūpaṁ sad vyāvartakaṁ svarūpa-lakṣaṇam* ı

2 *kādācitkatve sati vyāvartakaṁ taṭastha-lakṣaṇam* ı

3 *yato vā imāni bhūtāni jāyante, yena jātāni jīvanti, yat prayanty abhisaṁviśanti* ı *tad brahma* ı – *TaiUp* III.i.1.
janmādy asya yataḥ ı – *VedSū* I.i.2

4 *VPS*, p. 195:
satyam jñānaṁ anantaṁ brahma ı – *TaitUp* IIi.1
yo vai bhūmā tat sukham ı – *ChāUp* VII.xxiii.1.

(*cit*) and bliss (*ānanda*) are neither parts of *Brahman* nor its properties. The real is devoid of internal differentiations and external relations. Being, intelligence and bliss constitute the very nature of *Brahman*, and not its attributes. Though they are not different from *Brahman* they appear as if different. Even though happiness, experience of objects, eternality, etc. constitute the very nature of the self, they are metaphorically called attributes, since they appear to be distinct in the external adjunct, the psychosis of the internal organ.[5]

In this and the succeeding two chapters we shall consider the essential nature of *Brahman*. The *Pañcadaśī* which derives its name from the fact of its containing fifteen *prakaraṇa*s (chapters) is divided into three sections of five chapters each. The first section (*viveka-pañcaka*) gives an exposition of the existence or Being (*sat*) aspect of *Brahman*; the second (*dīpa-pañcaka*) is devoted to the characterization of the real mainly as intelligence (*cit*) and the last (*ānanda-pañcaka*) expounds the Absolute as *ānanda* (unsurpassable and unalloyed bliss). In the present chapter we shall be concerned primarily with the existence-nature of *Brahman*, reserving the consideration of the other two aspects to the next two chapters.

The Synthetic Method of the Upaniṣads

In setting forth the nature of *Brahman*, Bhāratītīrtha adopts what may be called the synthetic method which is wielded in an exquisite manner by the Upaniṣadic thinkers. The nature of any system of philosophy is largely determined by its methodology. The results of a metaphysical inquiry depend not a little on the method that a philosopher adopts. Method and material are interdependent. The former without the latter is barren, and the latter without the former is blind. Descartes is hailed as the father

---

5 *VPS*, p. 12 and *Pañcapādikā*, p. 4:
ānando viṣayā-'nubhavo nityatvaṁ ce 'ti santi dharmāḥ ।
apṛthaktve 'pi caitanyāt pṛthag ivā 'vabhāsante ॥

of modern philosophy because of his innovation in the field of metaphysical methodology. Immanuel Kant is known as the Copernicus of philosophy because of the unique epistemology he gave to the world.

"The diversity of our opinions", says Descartes, "is not because some are more reasonable than others, but only because we conduct our thought by different ways, and do not all consider the same things" (1901: 2). Of all the different ways of approach, the most important are the objective and subjective methods. Those metaphysical systems which pursue the objective path land themselves mostly in materialism and atheism. Though Descartes began with the method of "universal doubt", and started his metaphysics with the postulate *cogito ergo sum*, he relinquished this position while actually building the superstructure of his system. The mathematical method of the Cartesian philosophers is mainly an objective method. It is because of this method that even Spinozism lends itself to a materialist interpretation. In the East, the Vaiśeṣika system makes use, for the most part, of the objective approach. With its analytic skill in classifying the various phenomena of the universe, it leaves us with an infinite number of finite particulars. But particulars cannot be the ultimate realia. A billiard-ball universe will satisfy no thorough seeker of truth. Of late this objective method has invaded even the realm of psychology. The Behaviourist materializes the mind, makes it a shadow of the flesh and explains its functions in terms of physics and physiology.

The subjective method is equally one-sided and, if pursued to its logical consequence, would lead to subjectivism and scepticism. The history of the English empiricist school bears witness to this fact. The psychological method which Locke inaugurated led logically to the phenomenalistic pluralism and scepticism of David Hume. The Buddha's way, in the East, was to a great extent subjective and psychological. Though he was launched upon his career of philosophic thought by an objective observation of human misery, insofar as his aim was to discover the cause and the cure of sorrow, the Buddha had to choose the subjective method of introversion and psychological analysis. And a thoroughgoing method of this kind involved him naturally in the position of an agnostic.

There are certain systems which employ both the objective and subjective methods, but in an unsynthesized fashion. The Sāṁkhya pursuing the objective method traces all the manifold of sense-perception to the primal source, *pradhāna* or *prakṛti*, the *prius* of creation; and through the subjective method of inquiry he arrives at a plurality of *puruṣa*s (selves). But because of a lack of synthesis, he is left with an irreconcilable dualism as between *prakṛti* and *puruṣa*, and a plurality of spirits.

The Upaniṣadic method is a synthesis of the objective and subjective ways of approach to Truth. The terms *adhyātma* and *adhidaivata* occur frequently and in a successive order in the Upaniṣads. The cosmic ether is spoken of as identical with the ether of the heart. "He who is in the *puruṣa* and he who is in the sun, he is one", says *Taittirīya Upaniṣad* II.viii.1 and III.x.4. Uddālaka in the *Chāndogya Upaniṣad* instructs his son how from the *sat*, one only without a second, the world sprang forth. After describing in detail the process of the objective manifestation of the self of the universe, Uddālaka turns with a dramatic swiftness and says, that the universal Self is identical with the self of Śvetaketu, his son. This is a typical instance of the synthetic method of the Upaniṣads and of the system of Vedānta which is based thereon. It is through this method that the Advaitins reach the non-dual Absolute which can be characterized neither as objective nor as subjective. And Bhāratītīrtha, who is one of the ablest expositors of the post-Śaṅkara Advaita, wields this weapon of synthesis in an eminent way. In the second chapter of the *Pañcadaśī* entitled the Pañca-Mahābhūta-Viveka, he shows how *Brahman* is to be discriminated from the external world through the objective method of approach; and in the third chapter called the Pañca-Kośa-Viveka, he makes use of the subjective method of analysing the sheaths that seem to encase the self and of divesting it of them just as we remove the chaff from a *kodrava* grain (*MemEd*, vol. 6, p. 75).

Existence and Reality

"Existence is not reality, and reality must exist. … Existence is, in other words, a form of the appearance of the Real", says Bradley (1908: 400). McTaggart regards existence as prima facie a species of the Real. While it is universally admitted that all that exists must be real, he says, there is a view which maintains that there is reality which does not exist. And he sets himself to refute that theory and prove that there is nothing real which is not existent.[6] "There is nothing which compels us to believe in non-existent reality."[7] The Vedānta regards existence neither as the appearance of reality nor as a species of the real, but as the characteristic nature of the Absolute. "Of the real there is no non-existence, and of the unreal, no existence".[8] There is no non-existent reality. Nor is there unreal existence. The objects of the name- and form-world which are appearances are no doubt regarded as existent. But "existence" is not their nature; it is the essential nature of the Absolute. We wrongly attribute the nature of the absolute *Brahman*, existence, etc. to the objects of the world which are illusory, couple the true with the untrue and indulge in such empirical usage born of ignorance as that "The pot is real", "The cloth is real".

Almost the first task that a seeker after truth has to undertake is to discriminate the real from the unreal, the truly existent from the apparent things of the universe. The principle that guides him in this undertaking is that of non-contradiction.

---

6 J.M.E. McTaggart, 1921, *The Nature of Existence*, vol. I, chaps I and II.

7 Ibid., p. 33.

8 *BhG* II.16: *nā 'sato vidyate bhāvo nā 'bhāvo vidyate sataḥ* ।

"Ultimate reality is such that it does not contradict itself; here is an absolute criterion" (Bradley 1908: 136). Unsublatability is the test of truth.[9] This is not a mere negative standard. While denying inconsistency, it asserts consistency. "If we can be sure that the inconsistent is unreal, we must, logically, be just as sure that the reality is consistent" (Bradley 1908: 139). That is real (*satyam*) whose nature by which it is cognized, remains constant; and that is unreal (*anṛtam*), whose nature by which it is determined, varies.[10] "That which is constant in whatever is variable, that is different from the latter, as a string from the flowers (strung thereon)."[11] Real existence is never sublated. Through the application of the principle of *anvaya-vyatireka* (co-presence and co-absence), the author of the *Pañcadaśī* shows how existence is the essential nature of the Absolute and not of the things of the world, external or internal.

The Nature of Existence: Objective Approach

Dissatisfaction with the first view of things is the mother of all metaphysics. One who refuses to think can never get behind the shifting scenes of the world. The theories of the First Look do not satisfy those who are in quest of truth. The common-sense point of view regards the world of names and forms as real. Existence is thought to pertain to the objects of the universe. Five characteristics are discernible in every object of experience: existence (*asti*), manifestation (*bhāti*), lovability (*priyam*), name (*nāma*) and form (*rūpa*). Of these, the last two vary from object to object. They are inconstant and are products of *māyā*. They are the stuff of the world and are unreal. The first three constitute the essential nature of *Brahman* which is existence–intelligence–

[9] See Chapter 2.

[10] Śaṅkara's commentary on the *TaiUp, MemEd* vol. 6, p. 62: *satyam iti yad rūpeṇa yan niścitaṁ tad rūpaṁ na vyabhicarati tat satyam, yad rūpeṇa yan niścitaṁ tad rūpaṁ vyabhicarati tad anṛtam ity ucyate* ।

[11] *Bhāmatī* (TPH): *yeṣu vyāvartamāneṣu yad anuvartate tat tebhyo bhinnam, yathā kusumebhyaḥ sūtram.* See Commentary on *PD* I.41.

bliss.[12] We speak of the elements and the elementals as existing (*asti*), as manifest (*bhāti*) and as being attractive (*priyam*). These characteristics which are common to all products really belong to *Brahman*. Ether, for example, the first product of *māyā*, exhibits the essential nature of *Brahman* insofar as it exists (*asti*), is manifest (*bhāti*) and is attractive (*priyam*). But spatiality (*avakāśa*) which is its distinctive feature is a mode of *māyā* (*PD* XIII.67). When the Advaitin says that ether is unreal, he does not mean that its existence, manifestation and attractiveness are unreal; what he maintains is that its spatiality is illusory. Spatiality is a product of delusion because prior to the manifestation of ether, it did not exist and when ether is destroyed, it will cease to exist. What is unreal at the beginning and unreal at the end cannot be real in the middle (*PD* XIII.68). Beings are unmanifest in the beginning, manifest in the middle and unmanifest again in the end (*BhG* II.28). But the real nature of *Brahman* persists for all time. We defined reality as that which is permanent in things that perish, constant in entities that change. Existence is constant in objects that are variable; hence it is different from the latter and constitutes the essential nature of Reality. The existence that is persistent in such cognitions as "The pot exists", etc. is the substrate, *Brahman*, while only the particulars, pot, etc. are illusory (*VPS*, p. 200).

"Existence alone, dear one, was this in the beginning, one only without a second," declares scripture (*PD* II.19; *ChāUp* VI.ii.1). The five elements with their distinctive properties, the cognitive and conative senses with their respective functions, the *antaḥkaraṇa* with its power of direction and control – all these which are modifications of *māyā*, products of *prakṛti*, are illusory imputations on the secondless *sat*. Prior to the origination of this unreal superimposition, there was only existence (*sat*), one without a second.

12 *Dṛg-Dṛśya-Viveka*, 20:
asti bhāti priyaṁ rūpaṁ nāma ce 'ty aṁśa-pahcakam ।
ādya-trayaṁ brahma-rūpaṁ jagad-rūpaṁ tato dvayam ॥

Existence, which is the essential constitution of Reality, has neither external relations nor internal differentiations. It is unrelated to anything, for there is nothing else with which it can be related. The Real which is the most perfect Being cannot be delimited by determinations and relations. To limit it is to finitize it. It has nothing of a like kind or of a different kind, and it has no internal variety. A tree, for instance, has internal variety of foliage, flowers and fruits, it has the relation of similarity to other trees and of dissimilarity to objects of a different kind like stones. The *sat* has no other thing which is similar to it or dissimilar to it, and it has no internal differentiations (*PD* II.20-21).

The *sat* has no internal modes, since it is not a whole-of-parts. Parts can be attributed only to inert matter. The *sat* is pure intelligence, single and indivisible. It is infinite and partless. Assuming that it is a whole-of-parts, we must inquire whether the parts are intelligent or inert. If they be intelligent, are they different or non-different from the *sat*? They cannot be different, for the scriptural texts declarative of non-difference would then be contradicted. If they be non-different from *Brahman*, they cannot be related to it as parts to the whole. If the parts be inert, then, the *sat* must also be inert. What is inert is subject to origination and destruction, and hence cannot be real (*sat*). This leads us to the absurd position of stating that the real is not real – a glaring case of self-contradiction. If *Brahman* have parts, is there self-luminosity for both the parts and the whole, or only for either? If both be self-luminous, then, since either is not the content of the other, the possession of parts will not be cognized. If either be self-luminous, there will not be established the relation of part and whole between them, any more than between pot and the self (*VPS*, p. 206). The real is not a one-in-many, an identity-in-difference. It cannot even be said that name and form are the constitutents of the *sat*. The name *sat* which is attributed to the real is for empirical purposes, for instruction which is through mortal words. *Sattā* (Supreme Being) is the highest category that human mind can cognize. All that the finite intellect can say of the real is that it *is*. *Brahman* can have no form, since it is immutable, eternal. *Sat, cit* and *ānanda* (being, intelligence and bliss) are not parts of *Brahman*. They constitute its nature. If they be parts, they must be mutually exclusive. If *sat* be sundered from *cit* and *ānanda,* it would be inert and of the nature of misery, and hence also unreal (*asat*). If intelligence were different from being and bliss, it would be non-being accompanied by misery and so *acit* (insentient). Excluded from *sat* and *cit, ānanda* would not be bliss but misery. *Sat, cit* and *ānanda* are neither parts of *Brahman* nor its properties. Names and forms cannot be the limbs of *sat,* since prior to creation they were non-existent. The real is devoid of parts. It has no modification (*PD* II.22-23).

If particulars be the only realia, there would be many reals of the same kind. But a plurality of reals is an impossibility. What is real cannot be many. If there were other reals of the same class as the *sat,* then, the *sat* would be limited. But a limited real cannot be *sat* (existence). And an unlimited real can be only one. With determinations the *sat* cannot be; without them a plurality of reals cannot exist. Hence, there is nothing akin to the *sat* (*PD* II.24).

Nor is there anything which is of a different class than the *sat*. What is not *sat* (existence) must be *asat* (non-existence). But the *asat* cannot be the counter-correlate of the *sat,* since it is non-existent and unreal. Hence, there can be no entity different from and opposed to the *sat*. Real existence is one without a second. It has no genus; it possesses no properties, and it is unrelated to anything else (*PD* II.25).

The Mādhyamikas regard non-existence as the stuff of reality (*PD* II.26). Non-being is the source and solace of this world. The cosmic process is like an illusory wheel of fire. Incapable of grasping the supersensuous and the supra-rational, dependent solely on inferential reasoning and discarding the intuitions of scripture, the Nihilists conclude that everything is void (*PD* II.26). They fail to recognize that there can be a real beyond the reach of speech and mind. To make confusion worse confounded, they quote the scriptural text, "Non-existence alone this was in the beginning" (*ChāUp* III.xix.1, VI.ii.1) in support of their doctrine. But, unfortunately, scripture is not in their favour. What the *Chāndogya Upaniṣad* declares is not that non-existence is the parent of the world but that the world of names and forms was non-existent, i.e. undifferentiated, before creation.

When the Mādhyamika says that non-existence was in the beginning, does he mean that non-existence is related to the real or that it is itself real? In either case he would be contradicting himself. Non-existence which is unreal cannot be associated with reality, nor can it be itself real. Light can be neither dark nor coordinated with darkness. The *sat* and *śūnya* are diametrically opposed to each other. The world of names and forms is a superimposition on the *sat*. If the Nihilist assert that non-existence is also a superimposition on the real, then he falsifies his own theory that nullity is the ultimate category. He may turn round and say that like non-existence the name and form of the *sat* are also superimpositions thereon. But this objection of his is unintelligible. The *sat* has neither name nor form. Assuming that they are superimpositions, on what are they superimposed? Are the name and form of the *sat* superimposed on the *sat*, or on the *asat*, or on the world? Not the first, since the name and form of a thing are not superimposed on itself. The name and form of silver are superimposed not on itself but on nacre. Nor can the *asat* be the substrate of superimposition, for how can non-existence be the substrate of anything? Nor can the world be the substrate of superimposition, for the world is the product and not the parent of the *sat*. Nor can it be maintained that the name and form of the real need no substrate whereon they can be superimposed, since substrateless delusion is impossible (*PD* II.32-35).

A series of objections may be raised against the Advaitin's doctrine that existence was in the beginning. It may be asked whether the senses of the two words "existence" and "was" are different or identical. If there be difference between them, non-difference will be destroyed. If there be no difference, there is idle repetition. Hence, says the opponent of Advaita, the doctrine that existence was in the beginning is unintelligible. The Advaitin replies to this contention by rejecting the first alternative and pointing out that repetition is not a fallacy in this case. Our empirical usage abounds in repetition. We speak of a man as doing his deed, of wearing the daily wear, etc. To us who are accustomed to this kind of repetitive language, it is no fallacy on the part of scripture to instruct us in the same manner as we talk (*PD* II.36-37).

The next objection that the opponent urges is about the tense of the verb used in the scriptural passage: "Existence alone *was* this in the beginning". Since in the non-dual reality there is no past time, it is unintelligible, he says, to declare that it *was* in the beginning. The Absolute is, no doubt, beyond the measures of time. But for the sake of instructing the disciple who is limited by temporal conditions, the *sat* is spoken of as having existed prior to creation without any differentiations of the name and form. Both questions and answers belong to empirical language whose sphere is the realm of duality. In the language of the non-dual spirit there is no query, nor is there any reply. The real is too deep for the mind to fathom, too great for words to describe (*PD* II.38-39).

Accepting the unreality of the earth and other objects because they are generated and are observed to change and perish, the opponent asks the Advaitin how ether also can be declared to be unreal. According to the Vaiśeṣika, the four elements, earth, water, fire and air, are atomic; but ether is eternal, indivisible and homogeneous. The rejoinder of the Advaitin is that, however subtle ether may be, it is material and hence perishable. He asks: if it be possible to cognize the existence of ether without the earth, etc. why cannot the *sat* be cognized without ether? Further, pure ether unrelated to the other four elements is not an object of experience. The *sat*, on the other hand, is the most intimately experienced by the enlightened and the ignorant alike. None doubts his own existence. The man-in-the-street may not realize that the real is intelligence and bliss, but self-existence is experienced by all. The Supreme Reality is intuited with the utmost certitude in the serenity of silence. The experience of quietude cannot be a night of nothing-ness, for there one does not perceive non-existence or non-being. As the *ātman* is realized in its native purity in the state of silence, so also the *sat* is intuited to be non-dual existence when the encumbrances of the name- and form-world are discarded (*PD* II.41-46).

Existence which is the substrate of the five elements and their products is Reality. Whatever is distinctive in the elements and the elementals are a product of *māyā*; and whatever is common and constant in them constitutes the nature of reality. Ether which is the primary mode of *māyā* is of the nature of space. Spatiality is its distinctive feature. It is not present in the other elements and hence it is unreal. Existence persists in ether as in other things; and so it is the nature of Reality (*PD* II.60). In air, fire, water and earth we find attributes which are not common and constant. They are non-real superimpositions of *māyā*. But existence is fundamental to them all. Nor may it be said that existence is an attribute of the elements. Just as substance which is persistent in colour, taste, etc. is the substrate and not attribute, the *sat* which is persistent in ether, air, etc. is the substrate and not attribute. And in the same way as for colour which excludes taste, etc. there is for ether which excludes air, etc. attributeness and not substrateness. It may be said that, just as there is reality for colour as distinct from pot, there may be reality even for ether which is different from existence. But this objection is groundless, since ether as distinct from existence is indemonstrable. Sundered from existence, ether, etc. would be non-existent and therefore unreal (*PD* II.68). *Sattā* is the *summum genus* which is present in all things. It is not a mere concept as with the Naiyāyikas. It constitutes the very essence of Reality.

The Nature of Existence: Subjective Approach

By an analysis of the external world we found the nature of reality to be existence. We shall now see how the substrate of the internal world is also existence. Bhāratītīrtha in the first *prakaraṇa* of the *Pañcadaśī* examines the three states of consciousness and shows how pure intelligence (*saṁvit*) alone is real, non-contradicted by any experience. In the state of waking the objects of experience vary and vanish; but the intelligence which cognizes them is single and the same throughout (*PD* I.3). The objects of sense such as a tuning-fork and a bright light, and the stimuli that we receive from them are different from one another because of their mutual exclusion and particularity. But the knowledge of the sensory objects which is other than the sensations is identical and undivided and hence not differentiated and dissipated. Pure intelligence is not a series of sensations. It is not a collection of particular perishing psychical presentations. Presentations by themselves yield no knowledge. But for the unitary principle that connects and controls them, they would be a chaotic mass akin to that which constitutes an idiot's lore. In dreams the objects of waking life are not present. There exists only the impressions of the waking experience. More evanescent and fleeting than the world of our waking life is the dream-world. But the pure intelligence which witnesses the dreams does not undergo change. If it were one consciousness that was awake and another that dreamt, then there would be no case of identity at all. But, in actual experience, we find that it is the same *saṁvit* which remains as the witness of both the states of consciousness (*PD* I.4). In the experience of deep sleep undisturbed by dreams there is neither the play of the external world nor the cinema of internal objects. But this *abhāva* (absence) of the world does not affect the witness-intelligence, since that intelligence is the witness even of the nescience of sleep. Pure intelligence which persists in sleep is different from its object, viz. ignorance, but not from the *saṁvit* which experiences the other two states. Thus, in the three states of experience, what is constantly present is intelligence (*PD* I.5-6). True existence belongs only thereto. This single, self-luminous intelligence neither rises nor sets.[13] It is an ever-existent eternal light.

Five sheaths (*kośa*s): These are which cover the empirical self and obscure its real nature. They are not of the nature of reality, because they are fleeting and not permanent. In dream-experience the gross body or the sheath of food is sublated, but not the self. The subtle body which consists of three sheaths, viz. vital air, mind and intellect, is not manifest in sleep. But the self does never cease to shine even in the experience of sleep. It is not affected by the presence or absence of body and mind. That it is imperishable, ever existent, is shown by the fact that it remains constant when the gross and subtle bodies change and perish. The gross body which plays its chief role in waking disappears in dream and the subtle body which is manifest in dream ceases to exist in sleep. But there is never a time when the self is not. It is the silent witness, eternal and everlasting. The causal body, which is attendant on the self in waking, dream and sleep, vanishes in *samādhi* (state of superconsciousness). In the state of superconsciousness, there is the manifestation of the self but not that of nescience. The causal body or the sheath of *ānanda*, viz. nescience, which persists even in sleep perishes in *samādhi*. While the sheaths are finite and particular, the self is infinite and eternal. Though sustaining the sheaths in the relative plane of existence, it is never identical with them. It is like a thread which courses through and holds together a collection

13 *PD* I7: *no 'deti nā 'stam ety ekā saṁvid esā svayaṁprabhā* ।

of pearls (*PD* I.38-41). The three bodies are not co-present with the self; and the self is not co-absent with them. It is contradicted by no experience, since it is of the very nature even of him who contradicts.[14]

The five sheaths have been characterized as unreal. The sheath of food is not the self, because it is a modification of matter. It has only a modal existence. Nor is the sheath of *prāṇa* (vital air) the self, since it is unintelligent and inert. It is a blind force, a mere strife and striving. Nor is the sheath of mind the self, for it is also a mode of *māyā*, subject to ceaseless change. The mind is a victim to changing passions and passing moods; and so it cannot be the self. That which is a slave of modifications cannot be the changeless *ātman*. Change implies imperfection and inherent want. The self is immutable and perfect. It is not only metaphysical, but also metapsychical. Nor is the sheath of *vijñāna* (intellect) the self, because it stops functioning in sleep and in other abnormal states. In waking it pervades the body up to the finger-ends, but in sleep it is resolved in nescience. Nor is the sheath of bliss (*ānandamaya-kośa*) the self, since it is inconstant and exists only at certain times. In the sheath of bliss there is only a reflection of the self which is supreme happiness. That bliss which is the prototype of the reflection in the *ānandamaya-kośa* is the self, because it is ever existent (*sarvadā sthiteḥ*) (*PD* III.3-10).

"Now, let there not be for the five sheaths the nature of being the self. But they are facts of experience, whereas the self is never experienced". If this be said, true. All the sheaths are experienced and nothing else is so experienced. But there must be something which itself being unexperienced makes all other experiences possible; and that is the self. Since it is itself experience, it is not an object of experience. The self is not an object of cognition, since there is neither a cognizer nor a cognition apart from it (*PD* III.11-13). The witness-self is always the seer and never the

[14] *ya eva hi nirākartā tad eva tasya svarūpam* । See Śaṅkara's commentary on *VedSū* II.iii.7.

object of sight.[15] Scripture declares:

> Where there is duality, there one perceives another, one smells another, one tastes another, one contacts another, knows another; but where all this is the self, who is there to be heard by whom, who is there to think, touch and know whom? Who can know him by whom all this is known? Who can know the knower?
> – *BṛUp* IV.v.15

Since the self is not an object of experience, it is not proper to say that it is non-existent. It is not a non-object of experience like the horns of a hare or the son of a barren woman. It is a self-resplendent experience and hence not an experienced object. It is existence and not an existent.

Since we have shown the five sheaths to be unreal, it may be said that only nullity remains when the sheaths are discarded. But this is unsound (*PD* III.22). Even for nullity there must be a witness. Self-existence cannot become a matter of controversy. Nobody doubts his own existence. Descartes who began doubting everything could not doubt his own existence. *Cogito ergo sum* is the first postulate of his philosophy. The dictum is not at the fag end of a syllogistic process.

> Self-knowledge is far too primitive and simple to admit of an *ergo*. If the "I am" depends on an "I think", the "I think" must also depend on another *ergo* and so on, and it will land us in infinite regress.
> – Radhakrishnan 1932: 140

"The man who calls this syllogism", says Hegel, "must know little more about a syllogism, save that the word *ergo* occurs in it. Where shall we look for the middle term? It was as a self-evident or immediate truth that the *cogito ergo sum*, the maxim on which the whole history of modern philosophy was built, was started by its author." In self-consciousness, thought and existence cannot be separated. As for our own existence, says Locke, we perceive it so plainly and so certainly that it neither

---

15 *Dṛg-Dṛśya-Viveka*, 1. *sākṣī dṛg eva na tu dṛśyate.*

needs nor is capable of proof. For Kant, the transcendental unity of apperception is the central postulate. Self-existence is the basic fact on which all knowledge and logic are grounded. Self-knowledge is inseparable from self-existence. Śaṅkara says that self-knowledge which is neither logical nor sensory is the presupposition of every other kind of cognition. It is beyond proof, since it is the basis of all proof. If a person asserts that the self is unreal, then he is predicating his own unreality; for he is no other than the self.

They reckon ill who leave me out;
When me they fly, I am the wings;
I am the doubter and the doubt,
And I the hymn the Brahmin sings.[16]

[16] *Brahma*, a poem by Ralph Waldo Emerson.

4

Reality as Intelligence[1]

"*Brahman* is consciousness (*prajñāna*)" (*AitUp* III.3). "Here this self is self-luminous" (*BṛUp* IV.iii.9, 14). "The self alone is its light" (*BṛUp* IV.iii.6). Reality is not bare existence. It is intelligence as well. It is self-effulgent; by its light everything else shines. It neither rises, nor sets. It knows neither growth nor decay. Being self-luminous, it illumines all other things without depending on any external aid (*Dṛg-Dṛśya-Viveka* 5). "Who can cognize that by which everything is cognized? By whom can the knower be known?" asks Yājñavalkya. The self knows all; but it is not apprehended by any means of knowledge (*PD* III.18). It is neither the manifest world of name and form which is presented to sense; nor is it the unmanifest *māyā* unrevealed to sense-perception. It is neither the modes of *māyā* nor *māyā* itself. The experience of self-consciousness is an undeniable fact. The self is not known, because it is more than known. It is knowledge itself, the light of intelligence but for whose manifestation the entire world will be blind.

The Self Is Self-luminous Experience

The Prābhākaras hold egoity to be the self, and cognition to

---

1 In this chapter we shall be mainly concerned with the objective approach to Reality as intelligence, reserving the consideration of the subjective approach to the chapter on the witness-intelligence.

be an attribute thereof. In a cognitive process of the form "I know the pot", the cognition which is self-luminous manifests pot, etc. as content and the self as the locus. Hence, luminosity belongs to cognition and not to the self which is egoity. The self is the substance of which cognition is an attribute. Since substance is not attribute, the self is not cognition and hence not self-luminous. It is cognition that manifests it. The self is not self-revelatory. The self is not intelligence. Nor is intelligence the only attribute of the self, since there are other qualities like desire, aversion, activity, etc. They are not inherent in the self. They come into being as a result of the conjunction of the self with the mind caused by its unseen potency (*adṛṣṭa*) in the form of *karma*s which have begun to bear fruit. When in sleep the unseen potency is resolved, the attributes quit the self, which then remains qualityless, non-intelligent (*PD* VI.88-91). The Vedānta view that the self is self-luminous is not acceptable to the Prābhākara. When empirical usage results even with the self-luminosity of cognition which is admitted even by the Advaitin, there is prolixity in assuming that in respect of the self also. Therefore, the Prābhākara maintains that the three aspects (*tripuṭī*) are immediately experienced in an act of cognition. The non-intelligent egoity, which shines as the locus of the self-luminous cognition of the object like the wick which is the locus of the flame, is the self. Apart from egoity there is not the cognition of the self anywhere. There is no distinction between egoity and the self. Therefore, egoity alone is the self (*VPS*, pp. 54, 56).

The Logician agrees with the Prābhākara in regarding the self as non-intelligence. Cognition is an attribute of the self inherent therein. But the Logician does not subscribe to the view of the Prābhākara that cognition is self-luminous. Cognition which is inherent in the self conjoined to mind is immediately experienced by another cognition (*anuvyavasāya*) through the relation of inherence in the conjoined (*saṁyukta-samavāya*).

Hence, according to the Logician, neither the self nor cognition is self-luminous (*VPS*, p. 55).

The Bhāṭṭa view is that the self is a composite of intelligence and non-intelligence. Like the glow-worm, the self is a mixture of light and darkness, of intelligence and inertness (*PD* VI.17). There are two elements in the self, the substance-element and the knowledge-element. To the former belongs cognizedness and to the latter belongs cognizership. Since it may easily be said that the cognized-element is the principal and the cognizer-element is the subsidiary, there is no conflict between the status of subsidiary and principal (*VPS*, p. 54). Both inertness and intelligence are experienced in the state of sleep. One who has woken up from slumber says that he knew nothing in sleep. This implies that inertness belonged to the self. But there was also the *experience* of inertness which is impossible without an element of intelligence. Hence, says the Bhāṭṭa, the nature of the self is intelligence-cum-non-intelligence (*PD* VI.15-16).

The self which is without parts cannot be a composite entity. Therefore, the Sāṁkhyas assert that the self is intelligence. A double nature is unintelligible in the case of the homogeneous self. The element of inertness belongs to the nature of *prakṛti* which is "a string of three strands" and which creates the whole universe for the sake of the bondage and release of the intelligence-self. *Puruṣa*, though by himself non-active, is lured by the activity of *prakṛti*. Bondage and release do not really belong to the self. They are due to the want of discrimination between the intelligent *puruṣa* and the non-intelligent *prakṛti*. In order to account for the distinction of bondage and release the Sāṁkhyas admit of a plurality of *puruṣa*s. So long as the *puruṣa* is ignorant of his real nature he plays into the hands of *prakṛti*. He identifies himself with *prakṛti* and its products and tastes, and the sweets and bitters of life (*PD* VI.98-100). The pure nature of *puruṣa*, however, is intelligence alone. That the self is intelligence can be inferred in the form:

> The reflection of intelligence in the inert internal organ must be preceded by a prototype of that nature, since it is a reflection like the reflection of the face.
>
> – *VPS*, p. 54 and *Pañcapādikā-Vivaraṇa*

According to the Advaitin, the self is of the nature of experience. If a distinction be made between the self and experience, it must be asked: is the self alone the light of intelligence, or is experience too that light, or experience alone? If the self alone be the light of intelligence, what about experience? How does it, which is an inert light, manifest the universe? Does it manifest the universe, while remaining itself unmanifest, in the same way as the sense of sight, etc.? Or does it manifest objects while being itself manifest, like light, without depending on some other light of the same class? Experience which is an inert light cannot manifest objects in the same manner as the sense of sight, etc. The sense of sight generates experience which is other than itself, while experience is not thus. Hence, experience cannot manifest the universe, while being itself unmanifest. If it illumines objects while being itself manifest, then, since there exists the characteristic of the light of intelligence, viz. manifestation without depending on an experience other than itself, experience would certainly be the light of intelligence. If this be not admitted and if experience be regarded as an inert light, then, there is the contingence of the blindness (unconsciousness) of the world. Nor may it be said that the self which is the light of intelligence makes manifest everything on the strength of inert experience; for, in the case of what is of the nature of intelligence, manifestation in dependence on the inert is unintelligible. If it be said that the objects are manifested by another experience, as distinct from the self's intelligence, generated by the inert experience, then, since a third experience is needed even for this second experience which is inert, there would be infinite regress. Hence, experience cannot be regarded as an inert light (*VPS*, pp. 56-57).

Nor may it be said that both the self and experience are the light of intelligence, for, if that were so, they would be independent of each other and the establishment of each would not be dependent on the other. If the self and experience be independent of each other, how could the relation between cognition and the self be known? Neither the self nor experience would be capable of apprehending the relation. It may then be thought that the self, though of the nature of intelligence, does not shine of itself, like another person's consciousness, and that therefore the self is established only in dependence on experience. But this line of argument can well be advanced in respect of experience too; for, there is no disparity between the self and experience in being of the nature of intelligence. If it be said that the self-luminosity of experience is because of its non-remoteness, then that is common to the self too. Therefore it is not possible to make a distinction between the self and experience both of which are the light of intelligence and say that the self does not shine of itself. It may with equal justification be said that the self shines of itself, since, while being of the nature of intelligence, it is non-remote, like experience (*VPS*, p. 57).

Nor is it proper to say that experience alone is the light of intelligence. The self cannot be an inert light. The self and experience are not different. The Logicians and the Prābhākaras consider experience to be a quality of the self. The Sāṁkhyas, who regard it as of the nature of the self, call it a substance by presumption. The Bhāṭṭas call it an act, since, according to them, it is the fruit of an act of transformation, and act and fruit are identical. Thus, experience has been regarded variously by the followers of the different schools. We shall now take these views in the reverse order and see how they are not intelligible. The Bhāṭṭas consider experience to be an act. If it be an act, like the act of going, etc. it would not be luminous, nor would it be the fruit. The Sāṁkhyas say that experience is a substance. If experience be a substance, and if it be of atomic size, it would be incapable of manifesting an object in its entirety. It would, like a glow-worm, manifest only a limited part of the thing. If it be extensive in size, there is the contingence of the manifestation everywhere even of the self, whether the self be regarded as of the nature of that experience or as the locus thereof. If experience be of medium size, then it would be dependent on its parts and not on the self. Just as between lamp-light and luminosity, there is no difference between the self and experience.

The Logicians and the Prābhākaras maintain that experience is a quality of the self. Even if experience be a quality, it must be admitted that it is not originated in the absence of the origination of the locus as in the case of the brightness present in the lamp-light. Since the self is eternal, experience must also be eternal; and since experience is non-inconstant in respect of the self, it follows by presumption that the self itself is experience. It cannot be said that the establishment of the self is dependent on experience; for, if that were so, there is the contingence of non-selfhood for the self. Nor may it be said that because the experiences of blue, yellow, etc. are diverse, they cannot be of the nature of the self. The experiences are not diverse in their own nature. Difference is due to adjuncts. Nor is it possible to assert that the experiences are not of the nature of the self because they are originated and destroyed. Origination and destruction are dependent on the establishment of difference; and for the assumption of difference, there is no evidence. Difference of consciousness need not be assumed in order to explain the different cognitions of different objects or of the same object at different instants. It is not necessary to admit that the origination of a subsequent experience is preceded by the destruction of the earlier experience. Since this is established even through the origination and destruction of the relations of one consciousness with several objects or with the same object at different moments, there is prolixity in the assumption of the origination and destruction of consciousness too (*VPS*, pp. 57-58).

The Saugatas point out on the analogy of the different successive flames that difference even while existing in the cognitions is not manifested in the absence of an external cause. But that does not stand to reason. Since the flames are cognized by another, there can possibly be the non-manifestation of difference. In the case of the self-luminous consciousness, however, it is not possible that difference should exist and yet be not manifest. Therefore, consciousness is one alone and beginningless. It is beginningless because there is no prior non-existence for it. Thus, there is no unintelligibility whatever in the eternal self-luminous experience being of the nature of the self. When the self is conditioned by objects, it is spoken of as experience; and when the adjuncts are not intended, it is called the self.[2]

Ānandabodha on Self-luminosity

The importance of the present topic, viz. the self-luminosity of the self, is evident from its treatment by almost all the preceptors of Advaita. Ānandabodha Bhaṭṭārakācārya, on whose *Nyāya-Makaranda* Bhāratītīrtha depends very much for his arguments in this connection, says that the self-luminosity of the self follows from the fact that it cannot be manifested by anything else. Men recede from objects which are hurtful and approach those which are helpful. The knowledge that a particular object is either helpful or hurtful is dependent on its determinant, the luminosity of the self, because it is a determinate light. And this luminosity of the self is dependent on nothing else, because, while manifesting everything, it is not manifested by any other thing (*Nyāya-Makaranda*, pp. 130-45).

The Logician's view that the self is mentally perceived is unsound; for, if that were so, it would have to be stated that the self is the object of its own cognitive operation. Agency and

---

2 *VPS*, p. 58: *ātmaiva viṣayo-'pādhiko 'nubhava iti vyapadīśyate* ।
avivakṣito-'pādhiś cā'tme 'ti ॥

objectness cannot belong to a thing at the same time and with reference to the same act. Cognition is a function of the self. Hence, the self cannot be an object of cognition.

While admitting that the self is not the object of mental perception, the Prābhākara denies self-luminosity to the self. The luminosity of the self is dependent not on itself, since the self is manifest in all object-cognitions which are dependent on the senses, etc. Cognition reveals the object as its content and the self as its locus. Though the self in this manner comes to be the fruit of an act, there is not the contingence of objectness for it, in which case there would be conflict with its own operation. Hence, the cognition of blue, etc. manifests the self, its locus, as "not-this", and the object as "this". Because the cognition is self-luminous, nothing else is required to manifest it. The Advaitin refutes the Prābhākara view by saying that if the self be different from cognition and if it be not the object thereof, then, its luminosity too would not depend on cognition. That which is different from cognition and yet not its object, cannot be in need of cognition for its manifestation. What is manifested by cognition must of necessity be an object of cognition and, therefore, if the self be not an object of cognition, it cannot be manifested by cognition. "Being manifested by cognition" is pervaded by "being an object of cognition", even as "*śiṁśapa*-ness" is pervaded by "tree-ness" When a thing is declared to be not a tree, it follows necessarily that it is not a *śiṁśapa*. Similarly, if the self be not an object of cognition, it is necessarily not manifested by cognition. Hence, the self is self-luminous; and it is non-different from cognition.

As for what the Logician says that cognition itself is non-self-luminous, he must be asked: does cognition, while being itself unmanifest, manifest objects? Or does it manifest them, while being itself manifest? If cognition were to manifest objects, while being itself unknown, then, in the instant immediately subsequent to the cognition of pot, there would be the doubt whether the pot was cognized or not. If *A* has seen *B*, and if he is questioned whether he *has seen B* or not, he never doubts about his *having seen B*. On the contrary, he is sure about his cognition of *B*. This is impossible if *A*'s cognition of *B* is not self-manifest. Hence, knowledge at the time of manifesting an object manifests itself, since subsequently there is not seen any doubt as to that cognition. If it be argued that cognition manifests an object, while being itself manifested by another cognition, then, since for the manifestation of that second cognition a third cognition is needed, there is the contingence of infinite regress. Nor may it be held that there is some other mental cognition which has for its content the awareness of the awareness of the object. Here, it must be asked whether the cognition whose content is cognition is generated by the same mind-contact which generates the cognition of object, or by some other contact. Not the first, since by a single mind-contact two cognitions cannot be generated and since simultaneity is not possible for them. Nor does the second alternative stand to reason; for, how can the mind-contact occurring at a subsequent moment have for its content the cognition of the object-cognition which has already ceased to exist? Simultaneously with the origination of pot-cognition there is mind-activity; then, there is the cessation of that activity and consequent destruction of the prior contact; and then there is the generation of the latter mind-contact followed by another cognition. Thus, the subsequent cognition is separated from the first very much in time; and, hence, it cannot have the original pot-cognition as its object. Even if this be somehow possible, the empirical usage "I know the pot" as having reference to present time, would be unintelligible. Hence, it must be admitted that cognition is self-luminous, that while manifesting objects it reveals itself also.

Nor is there for the inert self, which is of the nature of existence, the capacity to illumine objects, as for the sense of sight, etc. Is the luminosity, which is generated by cognition and which belongs to the object, while being different from cognition, non-different from the object? Or, is it different therefrom? It cannot be the nature of the object, since what is inert and what is luminous cannot be identical and since there could be no identity between the momentary luminosity and what is illumined thereby. Nor is the illumination of the object something other than the object, which is an attribute of the object, brought about by cognition; for, if that were so, it would not illumine past and future things, whereas their manifestation is seen. If it be said that the luminosity which illumines the object is internal, then, it is only cognition that is called by another name. And if it be inert, it would not shine. Nor would the objects be manifested, for the self itself is not luminous. Thus, there is the contingence of the blindness of the entire world. Hence, it must be admitted that cognition alone, while being self-luminous, manifests objects.

The next objection that is raised is that since a thing cannot be the object of its own operation, the self or cognition cannot know itself. The reply is that the self does not need any operation to manifest itself. Just as light removes darkness, helps the sense of sight in its operation and illumines itself and the object without requiring any other light, the self manifests itself and the objects without the need of any intervening activity.

The Vijñānavādin holds cognitions to be momentary on the ground that the cognition of blue is different from the cognition of yellow. But there is an underlying identity of all cognitions insofar as they are cognitions. Blue may be different from yellow; but the cognition of blue is not fundamentally different from the cognition of yellow. If there were only particular cognitions, then even their differences would not be perceived. But for a basic consciousness which strings together all the particular cognitions the differences of the latter would not be apprehended. Even to say that there is a series of cognitions there must be a permanent consciousness which persists in and through all the particular cognitions. Movement is inconceivable without a reference to a thing which does not move. The concept of momentariness is unintelligible without a reference to a principle which is immutable and eternal. The self, which is of the nature of consciousness or intelligence, is self-luminous and eternal. But for its luminosity, the world will be blind. The sun that warms us during the day, the moon that cools our eyes and pleases our hearts, and the stars of the milky way – all these shine after the light of the self.

Citsukha on Self-luminosity

Citsukhācārya defines self-luminosity as the capability of being called immediate in empirical usage, while remaining at the same time a non-object of knowledge.[3] That is self-luminous, which, while not being an object of cognition, is fit to be called immediate. "Now, at the time of release, there is not in the self the attribute known as fitness for empirical usage. Hence, if fitness be regarded as an attribute, the definition which states that it is an attribute would be non-pervasive. And further, there would be conflict with the final position of the Advaitin who considers the Absolute to be attributeless." If this be said, the reply is: the admission of the attribute of fitness in the self does not imply its constant presence in the latter. What it means is that the self is the non-locus of the absolute non-existence of fitness, just as substance is the non-locus of the absolute non-existence of quality. Hence, there is no non-pervasion of the definition simply because the self is free from attributes at the time of release. Nor is there conflict with the final view, since in the state of transmigration assumptive attributes are admitted in the self. Sureśvara asks: why should you be impatient if in the case of the non-dual self-*sadhakatvu* (nature of being the accomplisher) is assumed? Do you not see that *saṁsāra* itself is superimposed by nescience thereon (*BṛVārt* I.iv.1279)? The author of the *Pañcapādikā* says that there are in the self such attributes as happiness, experience of objects, eternality, etc.

[3] *Tattva-Pradīpikā*, p. 9: *avedyatve saty aparokṣa-vyayahāra-yogyatāyās tal-lakṣaṇatvāt* ।

And at the time of release, though the intended attributes are not present, since they are present at some time or other (i.e. in the state of transmigration), the self is established to be the non-locus of the absolute non-existence of attributes. Hence, the definition of self-luminosity as the possession of the attribute of fitness to be called immediate is not non-pervasive. And in order to remedy the definition being over-pervasive in respect of pot, etc. which are capable of being called immediate, it is said that the self's self-luminosity consists also in not being an object of knowledge. Nor is it enough to define self-luminosity as the trait of not being an object of cognition; for, if that were so, the definition would be over-pervasive in the case of things which are past and which are yet to be and in the case of merit, etc. which are ever to be inferred. "Now, even in their case there is not the character of not being objects of cognition, since they are known by scripture, tradition, etc." If this be said, no. What is intended by *vedyatva* (being an object of knowledge), is being pervaded by the fruit. The fruit is, according to the Advaitin, the object-defined-intelligence which is manifested; and manifestation is a particular transformation of the mind through the channel of the senses in the proximity of an object. Hence, *vedyatva* here means being an object of perceptual cognition. This is not present even in the case of merit, etc. which are to be inferred. Nor are merit, etc. immediate through being apprehended by Yogic perception; for they are to be known only through the *pramāṇa* of Vedic injunctions. With this much there is not the destruction of omniscience for the *yogins*. What is meant by omniscience is only the knowledge of those things which are capable of being known. Merit, etc. are not capable of being known; and hence, in order to exclude them, there is in the definition the qualification, "while being capable of the empirical usage of being immediate".

"Now, in the case of ignorance, internal organ and its attributes, desire, etc. and in the case of nacre-silver, etc. the over-pervasion of the definition remains in the same condition. They too are not objects of cognition, since they are not pervaded by the fruit. At the same time they are capable of the empirical usage of being immediate in the form "I am ignorant", etc. If this be said, true. But although they are not objects of cognition, they are not capable of the empirical usage of being immediate; for they are established only as superimpositions. "Even then, since there is seen the empirical usage of their being immediate, fitness therefor must be assumed." If this be said, not so. A piece of nacre is not entitled to be called silver. But still there is observed the empirical usage of silver in respect thereof.

"Now, even thus, the qualification of not being an object of cognition is of no use; for, in your view, even pot, etc. are not fit to be called immediate as they are superimpositions." If thus it be objected, not so. At the stage of empirical usage, for them, which are objects of the *pramāṇa* of perception, the capacity for being called immediate is admitted. Then it may be thought that it is sufficient to define self-luminosity as the character of being immediate, while not being an object of cognition. True; but since the word "immediate" is used even in respect of objects of immediate cognition, in order to avoid confusion with them, self-luminosity is defined as the capacity to be called immediate, while not being an object of cognition. The objects of sense appear to be immediate; but, in truth, they are not fit to be called immediate, since they are superimpositions. It is the self alone that is really capable of being called immediate while not being an object of cognition.

The evidence for self-luminosity is this: experience is self-luminous, because it is experience. What is not experience is not self-luminous, e.g. a pot. If experience were not self-luminous, there should be some other experience to illumine it and this will lead to infinite regress. And further, if experience were itself not manifest at the time of manifesting the object, then at the immediately subsequent moment the person who experienced the object would either doubt or deny his own experience. But no one doubts or denies in this manner. When he is questioned whether the object was seen by him or not, he replies without a shadow of doubt, "This, surely, I have seen". Hence, experience, while being itself manifest alone, generates empirical usage in respect of objects. It may be said that even if experience were dependent for its own manifestation on something else, there would be no room for either doubt or denial. But the defect of infinite regress would still remain unremedied.

The Logician says that an experience is manifested by a subsequent experience which has that (former) for content. Now, is the reflective experience generated by the same mind-contact which is the generator of the experience of the object, say, pot, or is it generated by another mind-contact? Even on the first alternative, does that mind-contact generate the two cognitions at the same time, or in sequence? Not the first, since simultaneity of origination is not possible for what generates and what is generated. The original cognition and the reflective cognition are indeed in the relation of generator and generated, since the former is the object-causal-correlate of the latter. Nor is it possible for the same mind-contact to generate the two cognitions in sequence; for difference in cognitions is admitted only on the basis of difference in non-inherent causes. Mind-contact is the non-inherent cause of cognition. Hence, the same mind-contact cannot generate two different cognitions. Nor is the second alternative, that the reflective experience is generated by another mind-contact, intelligible. The reason which Citsukha gives for rejecting this alternative is the same as that afforded by Ānandabodha. When a person perceives a pot, there is generated in him a knowledge of pot and at that time there is the conjunction of his mind with the pot. Subsequently the mind gets separated from pot and there is the consequent destruction of the first contact. Thence, there is the origination of the later contact and of another cognition. Now, how can the second cognition which comes into being many moments later apprehend the first cognition which has ceased to exist? Immediate cognition is possible only of present things and not of objects which are past. It may be said that there is no rule that cognition manifests objects, only while being itself manifest; and the example of the sense of sight, which apprehends objects without itself being apprehended, may be cited. But this is not sound. If experience or cognition were to manifest objects without being itself manifest, then there would be for it, as for the sense of sight, etc. the capacity to manifest objects and not luminosity. But luminosity is established for experience; and so, there is no parity with the sense of sight, etc. And further, if luminosity be not inherent in cognition, no cognition would be able to illumine an object. The inert, even because of their inertness, cannot manifest either themselves or one another. Thus, the result of denying self-luminosity to experience is the contingence of the world being blind or unconscious.

If it be said that since experience is cognized by such perception as "I am endowed with the knowledge of pot", "The pot is known", etc. it is not a non-object of knowledge; no. That empirical usage is intelligible in respect of the self-luminous experience even without its being an object of knowledge. And further, in "The pot is known", it is the pot that is cognized through the reflective cognition and not knowledge, since the attribute of being known is a qualification of the pot. If the prior cognition be made the object of the subsequent cognition, then, the self would be capable of knowing itself (as an object of knowledge) – a view which is consistent not with the Vedānta but with the Saugata doctrine. Experience, no doubt, is pervaded by the psychosis of the internal organ generated by *pramāṇa*; and hence, in a sense it may be called the object of such a psychosis. But with this much there is no conflict with its self-luminosity; for it is not an object, like pot, etc. either as the locus of the manifestation generated by *pramāṇa* or as the object of such manifestation. Experience, though an object of psychosis, is not non-luminous. On the contrary, it is self-luminous, since it is not manifested by any extraneous light.[4] Psychosis is of use only insofar as it manifests the light which is inherent in experience. Hence, there is not the contingence of experience being an object of knowledge. Just because a thing is known by a *pramāṇa*, it does not necessarily follow that that thing is non-self-luminous. Though the knowledge of another person is the object of inference having as its *probans* the activity, etc. of the person, it may intelligibly be self-luminous, since it is not in need of any other knowledge for generating in its own locus the empirical usage of itself being immediate. Hence, self-luminosity does not consist in not being known by a *prāmāṇa*; but it consists in not being dependent on any other light for generating the empirical usage of immediacy in respect of itself. It is in this sense that the self or experience is self-luminous.

That experience or intelligence is the self, Citsukha next proceeds to establish. The self is self-luminous, because it is of the nature of intelligence, it is not an object of knowledge and there is the declaration of scripture that it is its own light.[5] The self is of the nature of intelligence, since it is immediate without being an object of intelligence. If the self were not of the nature of intelligence, there would be either doubt or denial in respect of itself. But self-existence cannot be doubted; nor can it be denied. And self-certainty would not be possible, if the self were not self-luminous. There is no relation between the self and cognition; for relation implies difference between the relata and there is no difference between the self and cognition. That the self is self-luminous follows also from the fact that it is not an object

---

4 *prakāśa-prakāśyatvā-'bhāvāt*, p. 9. See *Tattva-Pradīpikā*, p. 19, Pratyag-bhagavān's *Nayanaprasādinī.*

5 *Tattvapradīpikā*, p. 21:
cid-rūpatvād akarmatvāt svayam-jyotir iti śruteḥ ।
ātmanaḥ sva-prakāśatvaṁ ko nivārayituṁ ksamaḥ ॥

of cognition. If it were an object, we have seen, there would be the conflict of agency and objectness in the same locus. What is other than intelligence is immediate only by being an object of knowledge; and so, it is non-self-luminous. But intelligence is immediate without being an object of knowledge; hence, it is self-luminous. There is also the testimony of scripture for the self-luminosity of the self. Scripture declares: "Here, this self is self-luminous" (*BṛVārt* IV.iii.9, 14). The self is referred to as *jyotis* (light) because it illumines the universe illusorily superimposed by ignorance and it also removes the darkness of ignorance.

Vimuktātman on the Relation between Self and Objects

Vimuktātman begins his *Iṣṭasiddhi* with an invocation to the beginningless, uncognizable experience which is infinite and of the nature of bliss and which is the canvas whereon the illusory world-picture has been sketched.[6] Experience is self-established and self-revelatory, since if it be revealed by another, there would not be for it, as for pot, etc. the nature of being experience. And for what is self-established there can be no antecedent non-existence, etc. and hence experience is unborn, beginningless. It is also uncognizable and infinite. The atoms are ordinarily regarded as beginningless and as having no magnitude. But this is unsound. There is no beginninglessness for atoms, as for pot, etc. since they also, like the latter, are endowed with colour, etc. Nor are they partless, since if they had no parts, conjunction of atoms would be impossible. Hence, beginninglessness and partlessness can be predicated only of the self which is of the nature of pure experience.

The objects of knowledge are held to be different from intelligence in that while the former are cognized as "this", the latter is manifest as "not this". The objects of knowledge are

---

6 *Iṣṭasiddhi*, p. 1:
yā 'nubhūtir ajā-'meyā-'nanta-'tmānanda-vighrahā ।
mahad-ādi-jagan-māyā-citra-bhittiṁ namāmi tām ॥

neither of the nature of intelligence, nor are they its attributes. If there were no difference between the objects and intelligence, then, there would be no difference even among the objects. But difference among objects is clearly manifest. Hence, the opponent of Advaita maintains that difference between intelligence and what are illumined thereby cannot be denied.

The Advaitin, while admitting that there is empirical usage of difference, replies that there is no logical ground on which such usage may be based. Difference between the seer (*dṛk*) and the seen (*dṛśya*) is not possible, since the seer is not the seen. Difference either of what is not seen from what is seen or of what is seen from what is not seen cannot be cognized, for, cognition of difference requires cognition of the substrate and the counter-correlate. Therefore, it is only as between what are seen that cognition of difference is possible, not between what is seen and what is not seen, nor between the unseen.

Vimuktātman next proceeds to show how the very concept of difference is unintelligible. What is called difference, is it the nature of the differents, or is it their attribute? If it be their nature, then, the cognition of difference would not be in need of the counter-correlate. The cognition of the nature of a thing, verily, is not dependent on the counter-correlate. But the cognition of difference cannot arise without the counter-correlate. Hence, difference is not the nature of the differents. Nor is it their attribute. If it be non-different from the differents, there results the aforementioned defect. If it be different from them, then it must be cognized by another knowledge of difference as between the first difference and the differents, and then for the cognition of the second difference there must be a third and so on *ad infinitum*. Thus, there would be a vicious infinite. The same reasoning applies to reciprocal non-existence also. Such being the case, difference between the seer and the seen is not possible to be cognized, nor their reciprocal non-existence. In order that the difference between the seer and the seen may be cognized, there must be another cognition; but in that case the seership of the seer would be destroyed. And further, the seer is self-cognized; and if there be another cognition which cognizes it, self-luminosity would have to be denied for it. The seer, however, is self-luminous. It is ever-present and shines without depending on any other light. If difference and non-existence be objects of cognition, they cannot be the attributes of the seer. If they be not objects of cognition, they are not even established. Hence, difference and non-existence are not the attributes of the seer. Nor are they its nature; for if they were so, there is the contingence of their not depending on the cognition of the correlate and the counter-correlate. Since difference and non-existence are neither the nature nor the attributes of the seer, it follows that they cannot be either the nature or the attributes of the seen as well.

The seer cannot be the counter-correlate of difference and of non-existence, since if it were the counter-correlate, there would be no seership for it, as for pot, etc. If difference and non-existence have the seer for counter-correlate, what is the evidence therefor? Neither the senses nor the mind can be the evidence, since the seer is not cognized by them.

Knowledge of non-existence is defined as the non-cognition of what is capable of being cognized. But there is no cognition other than the seer. Hence, there cannot be knowledge of the non-existence of the seer. Assuming that there is the non-existence of the seer, how could that be cognized, since the seer is of the nature of cognition? The non-existence of an object of cognition whose existence is doubted is known through non-cognition. But the seer is not an object of cognition and its existence is never doubted even because of its self-luminosity. Thus, there can be no non-existence of the seer; much less can it be cognized. Since difference is unintelligible without reciprocal non-existence and since non-existence cannot be proved, there is no cognizable difference between the seer and the seen.

From the foregoing arguments, it is possible to conclude that the seer and the seen are non-different. But if the seer were non-different from the seen, there would result for it all the limitations of the latter and the seer would cease to be the infinite self-luminous intelligence. The demonstration of the unintelligibility of the difference between the seer and the seen is not the same as the assertion of non-difference between them. There is not even a trace of non-difference between the seer and the seen. The Advaitin does not say that they are non-different. Nor does he deny difference between them which is well established in the world. What he wants to show is that there is no evidence for difference. Non-difference between the seer and the seen is not manifest; nor is it intelligible in the light of reason. As between what are opposed to each other like light and darkness no non-difference is possible. If the seen were non-different from the seer, it would be the seer and not the seen. If the seer were non-different from the seen, it would be the seen and not the seer. If the seen were cognized as of the nature of the seer, then it would be cognized by the knowledge which has the seer for its sphere, there would be for it seership and it would not be an inert light. If the seer were cognized as of the nature of the seen, then, it would be cognized by the knowledge which has the seen for its sphere, there would be the seen nature for it and there would be no knowledge of the seer. Hence, as between the seer and the seen, there is neither difference nor non-difference.

The Vijñānavādin thinks that the seer and the seen are non-different, since they are invariably apprehended together. Without the seer, the seen, verily, is not manifest; nor is the seer manifest without the seen. Hence, because of simultaneous manifestation, the seer and the seen are identical, says the subjectivist. But his view is not sound. If there were non-difference, simultaneous manifestation would not be possible. Togetherness is possible only for two or more objects. We do not say that the seer is manifest along with the seer; nor do we maintain that the seen is manifest along with the seen. But what the Vijñānavādin himself expressly states is that the seer and the seen appear together. Hence, their difference must also be manifest. Otherwise, it is not possible to say that they are cognized together. Nor is non-difference the sense of the cognition of difference, since there is the contingence of the non-existence of difference everywhere. Hence, because of the contingence of the loss of all empirical usage, there is no non-difference between the seer and the seen. Further, the alleged rule that the seer and the seen are apprehended together is not true. The seer is not an object of apprehension. It cannot even be said that the seer and the seen are manifest together alone; for while it is intelligible that the seer is ever manifest, since it is eternal and self-luminous, the seen is not so manifest, since it is non-eternal and non-self-luminous. Hence, how can it be said that both of them are manifest together alone? Although the seen is not manifest without the seer, the seer is manifest even without the seen. Therefore, there is not the rule that both of them always appear together.

When a particular object is made manifest by consciousness, the other objects are not illumined. But there is never a time when consciousness is not manifest. Intelligence is not always qualified by a particular objective content; for, if it were so, then, even that object would be self-luminous and it would be constantly manifest. Moreover, since consciousness is self-luminous, it cannot be the object of cognition. If it were a cognized object, then there would be for it, as for pot, non-self-luminosity and inertness. Nor are pot, etc. of the nature of cognition; for there is no evidence which can prove them to be so. If they were cognitions, then, they would not be objects. Indeed, a cognition of pot is not manifest at the same time as an object either of the pot or of something else. Nor is it manifest as an object of itself; for a thing cannot be at the same time both an object and a subject. If a particular cognition be the object of another cognition, then, that cognition would be manifest as an object alone and not as a subject. But it shines as the subject, whereas pot, etc. are ever manifest as objects. Hence, because of the disparity between consciousness and objects, they are not identical.

It has been shown that there is no evidence either for difference or for non-difference between the seer and the seen. There is yet another alternative, viz. that there may be the relation of difference-cum-non-difference between the seer and the seen. Vimuktātman tries to point out that even this alternative is impossible. The upholder of the view of difference-cum-non-difference says that, though the seer and the seen are not identical in their own nature, yet there is non-difference between them in their nature as *Brahman*. But this view cannot rationally be maintained. If the seer and the seen be non-different from the single *Brahman*, then even between themselves there cannot be difference. If it be said that their identity with *Brahman* is in another form than the one in which they differ from each other, then also, is that form different from their form as the seer and the seen? Or is it non-different therefrom? If it be different from their form as the seer and the seen, then, there would be no non-difference between them, since their forms are different. If the form in which they are non-different be identical with their own forms, then, they must either be different in their form as *Brahman*, or there must be non-difference between them even in their own nature. And further, we do not find a double nature either for the seer or for the seen. There is no seen-form for the seer; nor is there for the seen the seer-form. And since a double nature is not possible, there is no difference-cum-non-difference. Therefore, if *Brahman* be single, then, it must be either the seer or the seen; it cannot be both. Hence, the statement that the seer and the seen are non-different in their nature as *Brahman* is illegitimate.

It may be thought that there is no conflict with what is seen if a thing is said to have many forms. But, how is this, intelligible? Are the forms observed to be non-different from the thing? Or are they different, or different and non-different therefrom? If they be non-different from the thing, then, since the thing is one, the forms cannot be many. If it be said that many forms alone are seen and that the thing is observed to be non-different from them, even then, the thing which is seen to be identical with one form cannot be observed to be identical with the other forms. Otherwise, since even that form is seen to be identical with the other forms, there is the contingence of all the forms being seen as identical. If, then, the forms be different from the thing, how can there be the relation of form and content between what are absolutely different? If the forms be both different and non-different from the thing, then, for each form two forms must be admitted and thus there would be infinite regress. The crux of the entire argument is that two contradictory attributes like difference and non-difference cannot belong to anything at one and the same time. Since the seer and the seen, each of them, cannot possess more than one form, it is absurd to say that in their nature as *Brahman* they are non-different and that in their own nature they are different.

If the seer and the seen were not of the form of *Brahman*, then *Brahman* would be different from them. And if different, there would result for them defects like origination, destruction, non-*Brahman*-hood, etc. as for pot, etc. If, to remedy these defects, it be said that the seer and the seen are non-different from *Brahman*, even then, both of them cannot be non-different therefrom. The seen cannot be identical with *Brahman*, because it is inert and perishable. As for the non-difference of the seer from *Brahman*, that is acceptable; and there is no defect whatever in this. Hence, it follows that there is not even a trace of identity between the seer and the seen. The seer is the self and is non-different from *Brahman*. The seen which is a product of *māyā* is indeterminable.

Summary of Results

The doctrine of the self-luminosity or the intelligence-nature of Reality is one of the foundational tenets on which the entire edifice of Advaita is built. Hence, not being content with setting forth how Bhāratītīrtha establishes the intelligence-nature of Reality, we have given above the relevant arguments advanced by some of the other great preceptors of Advaita. The Advaitin has to meet opponents generally drawn from the ranks of four different schools. As against the Prābhākara who maintains that the self is manifested by cognition as the locus thereof, he says that there is no difference between the self and cognition. As against the Logician who holds that one cognition is revealed by another cognition, he says that cognition cannot be an object of cognition. As against the Bhāṭṭa, according to whom the self is a composite of inertness and intelligence, he says that the self which is homogeneous and partless cannot be the substrate of contradictory attributes. And as against the Vijñānavādin who identifies objects with cognition and splits reality into a cognitional series, he shows how the seer and the seen cannot be identical and how a series of cognitions cannot even be known but for the existence of an eternal, unchanging consciousness. This consciousness is *Brahman*. The self is intelligence. Scripture declares, "*Brahman* is *prajñāna*".

5

Reality as Bliss

"BRAHMAN is intelligence-bliss." Reality is not only the pure intelligence which is the witness-consciousness of this world-drama. It is also unexcellable bliss. We delude ourselves by thinking that happiness rests in external objects, in the world without. But the real seat and centre of happiness is the self. "This which is of the nature of the impartite essence is the supreme bliss; of that all other beings enjoy but a fraction" (*PD* XV.2). The bliss of *Brahman*, as contrasted with material happiness, is unsurpassable. In the Ānandavallī of the *Taittirīya Upaniṣad* the calculus of happiness is made to culminate in *Brahman*-bliss which is declared to be unexcellable.

Happiness and Its Manifestation

The intelligence-nature of Reality is ordinarily manifest, whereas its bliss-nature is generally obscured. "Knowledge" refers to the general nature of Reality; its particularization is bliss; that alone is *Brahman* (*VPS*, p. 217).

The happiness that we find in objects of sense is a reflection of *Brahman*-bliss; and it is revealed by psychoses of the internal organ. Psychoses are of three kinds: the pure, the virile and the dull, answering to the three *guṇas*: *sattva*, *rajas* and *tamas*. The pure psychoses are characterized by such elevating and ennobling qualities as renunciation, restraint, generosity, etc. The virile psychoses are marked by violent passions like thirst, intense attachment, aversion, anger, etc. The dull psychoses have the attributes of delusion, fear, etc. In all these psychoses there is a reflection of the intelligence-nature of *Brahman*; but the bliss-nature is reflected only in the pure psychoses (*PD* XV. 3-5). Just as the reflection of the moon is dim in impure and muddy water, and bright and clear in pure and undisturbed water, even so, the reflection of the self is entire in pure psychoses while it is dull and disturbed in impure psychoses. This is the reason why the virile and dull psychoses reflect the intelligence-nature of the self, while the pure psychoses reflect the happiness nature also. Reality is unobscured as intelligence, but as bliss, it is obscured. In the virile and dull psychoses the happiness-nature is obscured by impurity; and since there is a little purity in them the intelligence-nature is revealed. Water receives from fire the latter's heat and not its luminosity. Similarly, while the pure psychoses reflect the intelligence- and happiness-aspect of Reality, the psychoses which are impure reflect the intelligence-nature alone (*PD* XV.8-11).

Just as the lamp, which is of the nature of both light and heat, spreads only light and not heat, even so the self, which is of the nature of both happiness and intelligence, reveals only its intelligence-nature in all the psychoses. Nor may it be asked why, if intelligence and happiness be non-different, both of them are not manifest in one and the same psychosis; for there is no invariable rule that where intelligence is revealed, happiness should also be revealed. In a flower, though fragrance, colour, etc. reside, a single sense organ is able to apprehend only a single quality and not the rest. Similarly, it is intelligible that in a psychosis wherein the intelligence-nature is revealed, the bliss-aspect need not necessarily be manifested. It cannot be said that in the example of the flower, fragrance is different from colour, whereas in the case of what is illustrated, viz. the self, there is no difference between intelligence and bliss; for, although in reality there is no difference between intelligence and bliss, there is admitted apparent and adventitious difference. Even in the flower we do not recognize any inherent difference between its fragrance and colour. They appear to be different only because they are apprehended through different sense organs. In the same way, happiness and intelligence which constitute the essential nature of the self appear to be different because they are manifest in different psychoses. In that psychosis of the intellect which is of the nature of the transformation of the *sattva*-constituent brought about by meritorious deeds there is revealed the identity of intelligence and happiness, because that psychosis is flawless and pure. And in the psychosis of the nature of the *rajas*-constituent because of its impurity, there is manifest only the intelligence-aspect, the bliss-nature being veiled. This is analogous to the sourness of the tamarind being concealed when it is seasoned with salt (*PD* XII.73-79).

Even among the pure psychoses there are different grades in the matter of manifesting happiness. Advaita-vidyācārya gives the analogy of the reflection in mirrors of different degrees of purity. In truth, there are no grades in happiness per se. Superiority and inferiority in happiness are superimposed because of the purity or impurity of the reflecting intellect (*SLS*, vol. II, p. 48). The purer a psychosis, the intenser is the manifestation of happiness. When the *rajas* and *tamas* overbalance the *sattva*, then, the happiness-nature is obscured totally and there is the cognition of misery and pain.

Desire for external objects brings misery along with it. There is the anxiety whether the desired object will be obtained or not. If it is not obtained, misery increases and there arises aversion to those things that stand in the way. If the obstructions be difficult to be removed, then, there is misery again; thus in those activities of the mind which are prompted by *rajas* and *tamas* there is not even a suspicion of happiness. When what is longed for is achieved, there is the feeling of pleasure and satisfaction. When it is enjoyed, there is still greater happiness. But the greatest happiness, however, is not in the objects of sense. They appear to be the sources of pleasure. But they manifest only a fraction of *Brahman*-bliss. Of the threefold nature of *Brahman*, the inert things reveal only existence, intelligence and happiness being obscured; the impure psychoses manifest, besides existence, intelligence also; and the pure psychoses reflect all the three, existence, intelligence and bliss (*PD* XV.12-21).

The Self as the Seat of Love

Sage Yājñavalkya taught Maitreyī that the self alone is the seat of supreme love. The love that one bears to other objects is not really for their sake; but it is for the sake of the one who loves (*PD* XII.5). "This self is dearer than the son, dearer than wealth, dearer than everything else, and is innermost" (*BṛUp* I.iv.8). The love for other objects is secondary, since they contribute to the pleasure of the self; and the love for the self alone is primary (commentary on *BṛUp* II.iv.5). Husband, wife, progeny, wealth, cattle, caste, the worlds, gods, the Vedas, elements and all the rest have no intrinsic value in themselves. They are dear for the sake of the self (*PD* XII.6). "Not for the sake of the husband is the husband dear, but for the sake of the self is the husband dear" (*BṛUp* I.iv.5; IV.v.6). A woman loves her husband only when she likes him and that too for her own pleasure.[1] If the

[1] This is how Bhāratītīrtha interprets the *Bṛhadāraṇyaka Upaniṣad* passages in question. But it would be more in keeping with the spirit of the Upanisadic teaching if the love be said to be not for the sake of the empirical self that loves but for the sake of the Supreme Self that is the substrate not only of the lover but also of the loved. It is, perhaps, for the sake of easy understanding even by the dull-witted, as Bhāratītīrtha says, that he interprets the *Bṛhadāraṇyaka Upaniṣad* texts in the way he does. It is to be feared, however, that this line of interpretation has found much favour with the adherents of that type of Advaita which upholds solipsism and abstractionism. To this extent, the doctrine presented here is degenerate.

husband were the object of her absolute love, she ought not at any time and under any circumstances be displeased with him. But this is not in the scope of what is generally observed (*PD* XII.7). "Nor for the sake of the wife is the wife dear, but for the sake of the self is the wife dear." Even when husband and wife are attracted towards each other at the same time, each loves the other for his or her own sake (*PD* XII.9). Similar is the case with the love that one bears towards one's children. "Not for the sake of the sons are the sons dear, but for the sake of the self are the sons dear." Sometimes, a child may cry when fondled by its parent; but the parent derives pleasure and does not weep with the child. It is clearly evident from this that he loves the child for his own pleasure and not for the sake of the child (*PD* XII.10). If this be the case with beings which are endowed with intelligence, need it then be said that inert things like wealth, caste and the worlds and the inferior animals like cattle, etc. are loved not for their own sake but for the sake of the self? "Not for the sake of wealth is wealth dear, but for the sake of the self is wealth dear. Not for the sake of brāhmaṇahood is brāhmaṇahood dear, but for the sake of the self is brāhmaṇhood dear. Not for the sake of kṣatriyahood is kṣatriyahood dear, but for the sake of the self is it dear. It is not for the sake of the worlds that they are dear, but for the sake of the self that they are dear." The gods like Viṣṇu are worshipped not without any ulterior motive. The devotee worships them for the removal of his sins and not for the sake of the gods themselves who are devoid of sin. "Not for the sake of the gods are the gods dear, but for the sake of the self are the gods dear." The brāhmaṇas study the Vedas in order to preserve their brāhmaṇahood. The members of the three higher castes take to Vedic study so that they may not become *vrātya*s (outcastes). Hence, even the study of the Veda is not intrinsic. "Not for the sake of the Vedas are the Vedas dear, but for the sake of the self are the Vedas dear." In short, everything subserves the purposes of the self. The self is the centre and the seat of love (*PD* XII.11-20).

"Now, what is this love which is said to be for the sake of one's own self? Is it attachment (*rāga*), faith (*śraddhā*), devotion (*bhakti*) or desire (*icchā*)? There is attachment to objects like women, etc.; there is faith in such rites and rituals as the sacrifice, etc.; there is devotion to the preceptor, the deity, etc.; and there is desire for things which we long to have. But all these four forms of love are not found for one and the same object. Hence, love as such cannot have everything for its object. If love be regarded as devotion, then, as there is no devotion (*bhakti*) to one's wife, it would result that there is no love for her. Thus, it is with love taken in any of its forms." If this be said, the reply is that this is true only when the nature of love is understood in the above manner. But, in all the varied manifestations of love, there is a constant character which does not change. That psychosis of the internal organ we call love has for its object pure pleasure or happiness (*PD* XII.21-22).

The self is the seat of love, not because of the non-existence of misery therein, for love is of the nature of an existent. Nor is the self supremely lovable because of being the locus of the non-existence of misery, for even at the time of misery there is seen love for the self. Nor is the self the centre of love because of being instrumental to the non-existence of misery, for if it were merely a means, then, there would not be for it unconditioned love. For the same reason the self is not a means to happiness (*Tattva-Pradīpikā*, p. 359). It may be said that since love is seen for food, etc. which are instruments of happiness, there may be love for the self, not because it is an end in itself, but because it is a means to happiness; and it may be inferred that the self is competent to be a means to happiness, because it is dear, like food, etc. But this reasoning is unsound. Food, etc. possess the characteristic of being enjoyed (*bhogyatva*); but the self is not what is enjoyed. It is the enjoyer, the subject of all experience. And to say that the self is its own object is a contradiction, for one and the same thing cannot be at the same time both the helper and the helped, the subject and the object (*PD* XII.23-24).

The love for material happiness is not sublime. The objects of sense excite in us inconstant love. But the self is the most lovable, the locus of supreme happiness. The pleasure that accrues from objects of sense is not constant, whereas the happiness that is centred in the self is ever present without any inconstancy. When a person gets disgusted with a particular object which for some time has pleased him, he puts it by and takes to another object in the hope of finding happiness there. Thus, the pleasure which the objects yield is not constant. That the self is the seat of supreme love is shown by the fact that never does a person get a desire to destroy himself. The self can neither be abandoned nor be accepted, neither be renounced nor be received. Nor is the self an object of indifference; for, even of indifference, since the self is the subject, it cannot be the object thereof (*PD* XII.25-27). It may be said that since, when a man gets disgusted with himself owing to excessive attachment or aversion, he desires to put an end to his life, what was said before that nobody desires to destroy himself is wrong. But this does not stand to reason; for what the man who is tired of his life wants to do is to destroy his body; and the body, verily, is not the self. It is the body that is sought to be destroyed and not the self (*PD* XII.28-29; *Tattva-Pradīpikā*, p. 358).

We have seen above the evidence of scripture for the fact that the self is the locus of absolute and unconditioned love. It is possible to arrive at the same conclusion through reasoning. In the world it is observed that the parent, Viṣṇudatta, loves his son, Devadatta, more than his son's friend, Yajñadatta. His son is dearer to him than his son's friend who is remote in relation. Similarly, since the self is dearer than all other things, it is the locus of supreme love. Further, the experience of the desire "Let me not go out of existence; let me live for ever" proves that the love for the self is direct, immediate and unconditioned. Thus, it is established from scriptural statement, reasoning and experience that the self is the home of happiness and the locus of love (*PD* XII.30-31).

The Three Notions of Selfhood

There is a view which holds the self to be secondary to son, wife, etc.; and it cites in its favour such scriptural texts as: "Thou art thyself under the name of the son", etc. (*KauṣīUp* II.11). That the son, etc. are primary is alleged to be evident from the declarations of the *Aitareya Upaniṣad*. The birth of a son is considered to be supremely valuable to a father; and it is said that "there is no world for him who has no son". The *Bṛhadāraṇyaka Upaniṣad* states the same idea in the positive way in the passage: "They speak of an educated son as being conducive to (the attainment of) the (other) world" (*BṛUp* I.v.17). Not only is the attainment of the other world made possible through the son; even this world is to be won through him. "This world of men is to be won through a son alone and by no other rite" (*BṛUp* I.v.16). In describing the *sampratti-karma* (the entrusting rite),[2] the Upaniṣad states how the worlds are to be won by a parent through his son. Even the derivation of the word *putra* points out that, should anything, any duty, be left undone by the father, through any slip or slight omission in the middle, the son exonerates him from all that unfulfilled duty of his standing as an obstacle to his attainment of the world, by fulfilling it himself. Because he saves his father by fulfilling his duties, he is called a son. The father although dead, is immortal and lives in this world through such a son. Thus, it is that he wins this world of men through his son.[3] From all this it is argued that scripture is evidence for the fact that the self is subsidiary to son, wife, etc. (*PD* XII.32-37).

Those who uphold this view do not rest content with quoting scripture in their favour. They show how even empirical usage testifies to the correctness of their position. The son is regarded as the principal member of his family. Through sweat and toil

---

2 The rite is so called because a father, when he is about to die, is to entrust his own duties to his son in the prescribed manner.

3 See *Śaṅkara's Commentary, Mem Ed*, vol. 8, pp. 194-95.

the father hoards money for the sake of his son. Hence, the son, etc. are more important and primary than the self (*PD* XII.38).

The arguments set forth above do not prove that the self is subsidiary to other things. The self can be characterized in three ways as the secondary self, the illusory self and the principal self. The selfhood of son is secondary, since difference is seen of son, etc. from the self. There is difference between the psychophysical organism which consists of five sheaths and the witness-self; but still that difference is not manifest. The mind–body combination is mistaken to be the self. Hence, there is for it illusory selfhood. There is neither the existence nor the manifestation of difference between the witness-self and anything else, since there is nothing apart from the self to be the counter-correlate thereof. And because the immutable witness is the self, of all, it is called the principal self. Thus, there are three notions of selfhood: secondary, illusory and principal; and according to the difference in empirical usage, the conception of selfhood also varies. In an empirical usage concerning any one of the three, that one assumes primacy and the other two take on a subsidiary significance. For example, in the act of protecting the family of a dying person what is useful is the secondary self in the form of son, etc. In the empirical usage, "I am lean, I am fair", etc. it is the body-self (i.e. the illusory self) that is meant. What is adequate as the subject of such assertions as "Through austerities I shall attain heaven" is the agent-self and not the body-self; for the man who desires heaven performs sacrifices even at the risk of neglecting the care of his body. Of the usagc "I shall be liberated from the bonds of transmigration" the subject is the intelligence-self. Thus, it is patent that the concept of selfhood differs according to the difference in the mode of empirical usage. It is analogous to the distinctions made in respect of eligibility to particular rites. The performance of sacrifices like the Bṛhaspati-sava is prescribed for the brāhmaṇa and not for the members of the other castes; kings are asked to perform the Rājasūya sacrifice; and for the merchant-class the Vaiśyastoma is enjoined. In the same way, it is to be understood that each empirical usage has for its content a particular notion of selfhood as the primary one to which the rest are subsidiary. Whatever notion of selfhood is primary in a particular usage, that exacts supreme love; and there is love of a lower degree for such of those things of the class of not-self which subserve the purpose of the self. For what is neither the self nor a subsidiary thereto, there is not even a fraction of love. Thus, it is seen that the self, whatever may be the conception thereof, is the centre and seat of love. If there be love for any other object, it is for the sake of the self to which that is a subsidiary (*PD* XII.39-50).

What is neither the self nor a subsidiary thereto is the object either of disregard or of disdain. For tilings like a blade of grass on the wayside we have no regard, while we look with horror on such harmful beings like the beasts of the wild. The self, we have said, is the seat of supreme love, while what is helpful thereto is the object of moderate love. There is no rule, however, by which we can characterize certain things to be helpful all the time and certain other things to be harmful. The tiger, for example, is hated when it pounces upon us; when it is indifferent to us we take no notice of it; and when it is in a playful mood with us, we love it. And so we cannot give as a fixed rule which things are lovable, which are hateful and which we can disregard. But we can formulate general definitions. Those things are lovable which are helpful to us; those are hated which are hurtful to us; and those are objects of indifference which are neither helpful nor hurtful. But the case with the self is unalterable. It is always the locus of supreme love. This is what Yājñavalkya had in view when he said that for the sake of the self everything is dear.

That the self is the most lovable of all is declared by the scriptural text, "This self is dearer than the son, dearer than wealth, dearer than everything else, and innermost" (*BṛUp* I.iv.8). While commenting on this passage Viśvarūpācārya

(Sureśvara) observes:

> Dearer than wealth is the son; dearer than the son is the body; dearer than the body are the organs; dearer than the organs is the vital air; much dearer than the vital air is the self.
>
> – *PD* XII.60; *VPS*, p. 92

The nearer a thing is to the self, the dearer it is than the rest. The intensity of love that an object merits is dependent on its proximity to the self.

Those who do not realize this fundamental fact and consider things other than the self to be dearer than the self meet with disappointment and final disillusionment. They find themselves in "a vale of tears" and what they regard as dear turns out to be the cause of their misery. That things other than the self are sources of misery becomes very clear when we examine, for instance, the life-history of a son. The parent is worried so long as a son is not born to him; when a son is about to be born there are the dangers of delivery; after the child is ushered into existence, anxiety continues to sit on the brow of the parent who is in constant fear of his darling being badly influenced by malevolent stars; when the child grows up into a boy, there is the risk of its turning to bad ways; even after the boy is invested with the sacred thread there is the contingence of his continuing to be illiterate; or if he becomes proficient in learning, the anxiety for getting him properly married haunts the parent; when the boy is married, there is the fear whether he would be faithful to his wife or not; if he begets children and becomes the father of a large family, there is the difficulty of finding means to provide him and his offspring with money; and when the son is provided with enormous wealth, there is the contingence of his passing away. Thus, there is no end to the misery which things other than the self bring in their train. Hence, a man of discrimination should discern the defects that lie deep-seated in things other than the self and cease to be attached to them. He should realize that the witness-self alone is the locus of supreme love (*PD* XII.61-68).

When it is settled that the self is the locus of supreme love, it is easy to deduce that it is also the seat of the highest happiness. The self is of the nature of supreme happiness, since it is the object of unexcellable love. What is not of the nature of supreme happiness is not the object of unexcellable love, just as pot, etc. which are neither of the nature of supreme happiness nor the objects of the highest love. In the *Taittirīya* and the *Bṛhadāraṇyaka Upaniṣad* we find it declared that according to the increase or decrease in love there is a corresponding increase or decrease in happiness. From the post of an emperor to the position of Hiraṇyagarbha, wherever there is an increase in love, there is also a proportionate increase in happiness. Since the self is the apex of this pyramid, it is the locus of supreme love and the seat of the highest happiness (*PD* XII.72).

Brahman-Bliss and the Evidence of Sleep

The objects of sense reflect but a fragment of *Brahman*-bliss. They are lovable only insofar as they serve as auxiliaries to the self. We have seen how Yājñavalkya in the *Bṛhādāraṇyaka Upaniṣad* brings home this truth by appealing to experience. That Reality is of the nature of bliss is declared in many a passage of the Upaniṣads. The episode of Bhṛgu in the *Taittirīya Upaniṣad* illustrates the way in which *Brahman* is ascertained to be of the nature of happiness. Bhṛgu approached his father, Varuṇa, with a burning desire to know *Brahman* and got from him the definition of the qualification *per accidens* of *Brahman*, viz. its causality of the origination, sustentation and destruction of the universe. With this definition as his postulate, he decided through inquiry that gross matter, vital air, mind and intellect cannot be the cause of the world and discovered that *ānanda* (bliss) is *Brahman*. "From bliss, indeed, all creatures come into being; in bliss they live; and unto bliss they return. Hence, bliss is *Brahman*". Bhṛgu solved in this manner the fundamental problem of metaphysics (*PD* XI.12-13; *TaiUp* III.6).

Were *Brahman* of the nature of bliss, it should be the only reality without a second, as also self-luminous. The *Chāndogya Upaniṣad* reports a conversation between Nārada and Sanatkumāra where the latter instructs the former about the nature of the Infinite (*bhūmā*) which is *Brahman*. Prior to the creation of the world there was the Infinite, since there were not the threefold distinctions of empirical usage, viz. the cognizer, the cognition and the object cognized. "That is the Infinite wherein nothing else is perceived, nothing else is heard and nothing else is known" (*ChāUp* VII.xxiv.1). The Infinite alone existed in the beginning with nothing else as opposed to itself. Wherever there is the non-existence of empirical distinctions, there the non-dual self alone remains. The Infinite which is the "full" (*pūrṇa*) is experienced in the states of sleep, *samādhi* and swoon to be self-luminous and of the nature of bliss. That which is of the nature of bliss is *eo ipso* non-dual and self-luminous. "That, verily, which is great (*bhūmā*) is bliss; there is no happiness in the finite (*alpa*)" (*ChāUp* VII.xxiii.1). The objects of sense yield no unmixed pleasure. Even the little amount of enjoyment that seems to result from them is enshrouded in misery and pain. And so Sanatkumāra declared that there is no happiness in the finite (*PD* XI.14-17).

"Now, let there be no happiness in duality; but how is there happiness in the non-dual? If there were happiness, it would be apprehended; and if it were apprehended, there would be the empirical distinctions again which would negate the non-dual." If thus it be objected, the reply is: let there be no bliss *in* the non-dual, since the non-dual itself *is* bliss. Nor does this fact require any evidence; for in respect of the self-luminous no evidence is needed. That the infinite, non-dual *Brahman* is self-luminous is evident from the experience of sleep. In sleep there is not the functioning of the senses. Nor can that experience be established through inference from the sleep of another person. Means of valid knowledge like perception and inference are not capable of establishing the experience of sleep. But still we cannot deny such an experience; and hence it is self-luminous (*PD* XI.23, 32).

The experience of sleep which reveals the self to be non-dual and self-luminous indicates also that it is of the nature of bliss. From the non-existence of misery and pain in sleep we can well conclude that there remains in that state happiness or bliss. Scripture declares:

> Crossing the bund of the experiences of waking and dream, the *puruṣa,* though blind, becomes one who is not blind, though wounded, becomes one who is not wounded, though suffering from disease, becomes one who is not suffering from disease.
> – *ChāUp* VIII.iv.2

Nor may it be said by quoting the example of an inert object like the stone that mere absence of pain does not guarantee the presence of happiness. In the case of stone, etc. there cannot be even a suspicion of misery or pain, and hence also of happiness. But in the case of beings which are subject to happiness and misery we can say that when one of them is non-existent the other is present. Further the non-existence or existence of misery in the self is directly experienced, not inferred. Since in sleep the non-existence of misery is experienced, we say that there is in that state the manifestation of happiness. If there were no happiness in sleep, why should men prepare their beds smooth and soft? Comfortable beds are not intended merely for the removal of pain; for, if that were so, only those who are suffering from such pains as are caused by disease, etc. should be in need of them (*PD* XI.33-39).

The happiness that is afforded by soft beds, etc. is, no doubt, external and extrinsic. Tired of its avocations, the empirical soul seeks happiness in such objects of enjoyment as bed, etc. It experiences the reflection of its own bliss in the psychoses of the intellect. This is what is known as *viṣayānanda,* and it is not completely free from misery. It is only the semblance of bliss;

and the shadow cannot be a substitute for the substance. In sleep there is experienced happiness which is not the product of anything else. Scripture declares that the *jīva* in sleep experiences its identity with *Brahman* which is of the nature of bliss. By means of illustrations it indicates what the *Brahman*-bliss experienced in sleep is like. Just as a bird which is tied by means of a thread flies in vain to various places in search of rest and returns at last to the abode to which it is bound, even so, the mind which is the adjunct of the *jīva*, roams about in waking and dream in order to reap the fruits of its merit and demerit, and when its *karma* perishes, it gets resolved in its material cause, viz. nescience; and when the mind ceases to function, the *jīva* becomes one with the supreme. Just as a falcon wings its way in the sky gets exhausted and returns to its nest, even so the *jīva* runs to the experience of sleep longing for *Brahman*-bliss. Like a suckling babe which is free from attachment and aversion, or like an emperor who has reached the summit of human happiness, or like a knower of *Brahman*, learned in the sacred lore, who is at the helm of the happiness of knowledge, the *jīva* experiences unalloyed bliss in the state of sleep. Scripture compares the *Brahman*-bliss that is manifest in sleep to the happiness which a person experiences in company with his consort. In both the varieties of experience there is not the cognition of the objects which belong to the external and the internal worlds. Such passages of scripture which declare that in sleep a father becomes non-father, etc. (*BṛUp* IV.iii.22) show that the *jīva* loses its *jīva*-hood and hence also its transmigratory nature; and when *jīvatva* is removed in sleep, *Brahman* alone remains. The conceit in the body is the root-cause of all the sorrows of life; since that conceit is non-existent in sleep, the *jīva* is said to have transcended misery and pain. *Kaivalya Upaniṣad* 13 says:

> During the time of sleep when everything is resolved, the *jīva* which is obscured by *tamas* attains the nature of happiness.
>
> – *PD* XI.40-58

Scripture is not the only testimony for the existence of happiness in sleep. There is also the evidence of the experience of all who say after waking up from sleep: "Happily did we sleep; we knew nothing in our sleep". Thus there is the reflective cognition of happiness and nescience which were experienced in sleep. Reflective cognition is grounded in experience, for without the latter the former is not possible. Nor may it be said that since in sleep there are no recognized means of knowledge there can be no experience of happiness and nescience. The experience of happiness in sleep which is no other than *Brahman*-bliss requires no instrument of knowledge, because it is self-luminous; and nescience is revealed by *Brahman* which in so doing is not in need of any external channel of cognition. That the self-luminous bliss experienced in sleep is *Brahman* is declared by the *Bṛhadāraṇyaka Upaniṣad* in the text, "*Brahman* is intelligence-bliss" (*PD* XI.59-61; *BṛUp* III.ix.28).

Granting that the bliss experienced in sleep is *Brahman*, it may be said:

> The *jīva* which has the intellect for adjunct remembers that it slept happily without knowing anything. Since experience and the cognition thereof must have the same locus, the *jīva* conditioned by the intellect must have experienced happiness and nescience in sleep.

But this statement is not sound, for in sleep the intellect and mind which are the products of nescience get resolved in their cause; and since the adjunct, the intellect, is non-existent, there cannot be the *jīva* as conditioned by the intellect. What experiences happiness and nescience in sleep is the *ānandamaya* self; and the remembrance of that by the *vijñānamaya* self is intelligible because the self is the same in both the states of experience, although the adjuncts may vary (*PD* XI.63).

In the moment immediately antecedent to sleep there is the psychosis of the intellect which is turned inward and wherein there is the reflection of bliss; and later, the same psychosis along with the reflection of bliss gets resolved in the form of sleep and comes to be called *ānandamaya*. The *ānandamaya* self has for its adjunct nescience which is associated with the residual impression generated by the inward-turned psychosis of the intellect; and it experiences in sleep *Brahman*-bliss which is its true nature by means of the psychoses generated by nescience. In sleep there is not the conceit "I am enjoying happiness", etc. because the psychoses of nescience, unlike the psychoses of the intellect, are subtle and not clearly manifest (*PD* XI.63-66).

The Upaniṣads like the *Māṇḍūkya* and the *Tāpanīya* set forth that the *ānandamaya* enjoys *Brahman*-bliss by means of the subtle psychoses of nescience.

> The mass of intelligence, which has become one in the state of sleep is the *ānandamaya*, which enjoys bliss through the channel of the psychoses possessing the reflection of intelligence. – *MāUp* 5

The self which assumes many forms in the states of waking and dream becomes of a single consistency in sleep; and the intelligence which is reflected in nescience serves as the channel for the enjoyment of bliss (*PD* XI.67-68). Again, due to the force of *karma*, the *jīva* awakes from sleep and gets involved in the troubles and turmoils of the transmigratory life. *Kaivalya Upaniṣad* 13 says that awaking from sleep is caused by *karma*:

> Again, due to conjunction with the *karma* of the previous life, the same *jīva* dreams and awakes.

An examination of the moment immediately succeeding the termination of sleep gives us intimation of the *Brahman*-bliss experienced during sleep; for there is then the persistence of the residual impression of *Brahman*-bliss which is borne out by the fact that a person who has just got up from sleep remains calm and collected without any thought of external objects. But being prompted by *karma*, the *jīva* loses sight of its blissful nature and gets entangled once again in the vicious circle of *saṁsāra* (*PD* XI.74-75).

So far, we have seen how there is the experience of *Brahman*-bliss in the state of sleep, how it is self-luminous and non-dual, as also how there is the indication of the bliss immediately prior to sleep and an intimation thereof in the form of residual impression immediately subsequent to sleep. The happiness which is the result of the residual impression of bliss is experienced whenever there is happiness which is not due to the objects of the external world. This is what is called *vāsanānanda*. What is known as *viṣayānanda* is the reflection of bliss in the mental psychosis which has turned inward after the desire for external objects is destroyed through attaining them. *Vāsanānanda* and *viṣayānanda* are products of *Brahman*-bliss, the former being its residual impression and the latter being its reflection in the psychoses which cognize objects of sense. But both of them point towards their generator, viz. *Brahman*-bliss (*PD* XI.85-88).

Through an analysis of the state of sleep we found that there is every kind of evidence for the experience of *Brahman*-bliss. We shall now point out how the residual impression of bliss experienced during the state of waking serve as a ground for asserting the existence of *Brahman*-bliss. The *vijñānamaya* self, which is the agent in waking, experiences both pleasure and pain as also the balanced state where there is neither pleasure nor pain. The enjoyment of pleasure and pain is the product of *karma*, while the state of indifference expresses the innate nature of the self. In the enjoyment of the external objects and in day-dreams there is the experience of pleasure and pain; and in the intervals between pleasures and pains there is the experience of the state of silence which is the expression of the real nature of the supreme bliss. In those moments of carefree indifference men are observed to say, "We are free from woes and worries; we are happy". It must be noted, however, that even these moments of calm and peace do not directly manifest *Brahman*-bliss, for what we have is only the residual impression of that bliss. Cool-ness is felt on the outer surface of a vessel containing cold water; but that coolness is itself not water. Similarly, during moments of equipoise there is the experience of the residual impression of bliss which is not the bliss itself. But just as coolness on the surface of the vessel is the basis for inferring water inside the vessel, even so, the residual impression is the indicator of the existence of *Brahman*-bliss (*PD* XI.93-98).

Summary of Results

Through the objective approach we found that the objects of sense are lovable only insofar as they contribute to the happiness of the self and through the subjective analysis of sleep and the states that are antecedent and subsequent thereto we discovered that there is the manifestation either of supreme bliss or of its residual impression when unobscured by the virile and dull psychoses of the mind. Reality, we said, is bliss because of its infinitude. The word *Brahman* which comes from the root *bṛha*, *bṛhi* (to increase) signifies greatness. *Brahman* is great because it is unexcellable, free from limitation due to space, time or other things (*VPS*, pp. 179-80). And it is of the nature of bliss, because it is great.

6

The Witness-Self

VEDĀNTA has been defined as the science of the self (*ātma-vidyā*). Now, what is the self? Is it the physical body, a colony of cells? Or is it the cognitive and conative organs? Or is it the *manas*? Or is it cognition (*vijñāna*)? Or is it the void? Or is it the agent of actions and the enjoyer of fruits? Or is it the mere enjoyer, characterized by being the witness? Or is it the taintless *Brahman*, whose essential nature, we said, is existence, knowledge, bliss?

Different Views about the Self

AMONG the Lokāyatas (Materialists), who adopt perception as the only means of valid knowledge and who recognize the reality of the four elements alone, some think that the physical body is the self. They base their theory on the fact that the body is cognized as the substrate of the cognition "I" in such usages as "I am a man, I know", etc. (*VPS*, p. 181; *PD* VI.60-61). And they quote as evidence the scriptural texts, "That, verily, is this person, who is constituted of the essence of food (matter)" (*TaitUp* II.i.1), "That *Brahman* is this self, constituted of the earth, constituted of water, constituted of air, constituted of ether, constituted of fire", etc.

Even when the body exists there is no cognition without the activity of the senses (*VPS*, p. 181). And when the *jīva* departs, the physical body is observed to perish (*PD* VI.62). That which is inert and perishable cannot be the self. The senses alone are intelligences and they constitute the self. So say another section of the Lokāyatas. The co-presence and co-absence of the senses with cognition may be explained on the assumption that the senses are instruments of cognition. But the adherents of the view that the senses are the self maintain that to assume the senses to be the material cause of cognition is more suitable than the assumption of their instrumentality. The senses, they say, which are the substrates of the cognition "I" in "I am one-eyed, I am dumb", etc. and which are intelligences, are to be recognized as each the self. And they cite as evidence the scriptural passage, "They said unto speech, 'Do thou sing unto us'; saying 'So be it' speech sang unto them" (*BṛUp* I.ii.2), etc. The body, however, is said to be the substrate of the cognition "I" and is figuratively spoken of as being intelligence only because it is the locus of the senses which are the self. It may be said that, if there be many selves inhabiting a single body, there would be no personal identity such as is experienced in the recognition "The same 'I' that formerly saw the colour now hears the sound". And, further, it may be objected that, if the senses be the selves, colour, taste, etc. would be simultaneously enjoyed and not in sequence. But both the contentions are wrong. In order that there may be recognition and enjoyment in sequence oneness of intelligence is not necessary. What is needed is location in one body. In a house which is inhabited by many men, at the marriage of each one of them the others are accessories. Similarly, in the case of the senses that are located in a single body, at the time of the enjoyment of any one of them the others are accessories (*VPS*, p. 181).

In the experience of dream there is cognition even without the activity of the senses. Hence, the senses cannot be the loci of cognition, nor can they be the substrates of the cognition "I". The senses of sight, etc. are instruments, and not the material cause, of cognition. It was said that recognition is possible in respect of many selves even because of their being located in a single body. But that does not stand to reason because of the contingence of recognition even among persons living on a single floor. Hence, the followers of the Pāñcarātra system are dissatisfied with the doctrine that the senses are the selves; and they advocate the view that *manas* is the self. Cognition is caused in dream by the bare *manas*. Recollection and personal identity are made possible by it. The senses are its instruments and the body is its support (*VPS*, pp. 181-82; *PD* VI.67). Such texts of the scripture as "*manas* sang", etc. are said to favour this view.

The Vijñānavādins hold momentary cognition to be the self. Recognition is intelligible because of the similarity of cognitions. Flames, though different, appear to be identical because they are similar. In order to establish *karma*, knowledge, bondage, release, etc. it is not necessary to assume a persisting cognition, since that is achieved even because of the cognitions belonging to a single succession of cause and effect (*VPS*, p. 182). The scriptural text, "Which is the self? That which is a mass of cognition" (*BṛUp* IV.iii.7) supports the doctrine that cognition is the self.

In the state of deep sleep, there is not seen even cognition. Hence, the void alone is the self, says the Mādhyamika. If there were cognition in sleep, then, there would be the presentation of content too, since cognition without a content is impossible. It may be said that only those cognitions which are in the states of waking and dream require a basis, not the cognitions of sleep. But this is irrational. Why should cognition have content in other states and not in sleep? Nor may the non-existence of content in sleep be inferred on the ground that a person who has awakened has no recollection of a content in sleep. If the non-existence of a thing be inferable from the non-recollection thereof, then, even because there is invariable non-recollection of cognition in sleep for one who has awakened, let there be no cognition in sleep. There can be no dispute, says the Mādhyamika, about the void. The generation of the cognition of the real by the void which is opposed in content to that cognition is intelligible even as there is the generation of the determinate cognition by the indeterminate cognition. One who gets up from sleep has the cognition of reality "I exist". But that cognition is not true, since it is devoid of the cause consisting in an immediately antecedent cognition. Hence, the void alone is the true (*VPS*, p. 182). "Non-existence, verily, this was in the beginning" (*TaitUp* II.vii.1), says scripture in support of this doctrine. Thus, the Nihilists maintain that the void is the self.

The void cannot be the substrate of the cognition "I". If the cognition "I" be possible in the case of the void, then, there would be that cognition even in cases like the son of a barren woman. Even the doctrine of the Vijñānavādins is not intelligible. A series of momentary cognitions cannot account for personal identity. Empirical usage as having a single agent cannot be brought about by several selves existing in a single succession. A person knows a thing to be advantageous, then desires to possess it, strives and attains it, and then derives happiness therefrom. If the self that derives happiness be not the same self that desired to possess that advantageous thing, how can such unsublated recognition as "The same 'I' that knew this thing, now desires it" be accounted for? There must be admitted a permanent self. And this self is not of the form of cognition, since no apposition is experienced between the two in the form "I am cognition". It is only the relation of possessor and property that is experienced in the form "Mine is this cognition". And this experience is not figurative, like "my self", since it is never sublated. When it is proved that cognition is not the self but only a property thereof, it is needless to say that the body, senses and *manas*, which are related to the self as its properties, cannot be the self. The designation as "I" in respect of the body, etc. however, is due to superimposition. Thus argue those who advocate the doctrine that the self is the agent of actions and the enjoyer of fruits. The self they hold to be beginningless, indestructible and the subject of migration, of the nature of entering and departing from an infinite number of bodies. There is observed for the self-experience of happiness and misery even immediately after the origination of the body. This is impossible if the self had not existed even earlier as the agent of merit and demerit. Nor can destruction be demonstrated in the case of the self. Destruction cannot be of itself, since destruction without a cause is not admitted by others than the Saugatas. Nor is destruction possible from another, since for the partless self, there cannot be conjunction with a cause of cognition. Even if it were somehow possible, in order to effect cognition with another there must be *karma*. And *karma* would establish only the permanence of the self, not its destruction; for if the self were destroyed, there would be none to enjoy the fruit of that *karma*. If the self be unchanging, enjoyment is impossible for it. Hence, change, in the nature of the fruit of activity, must be admitted in the case of the self. Agency, which is of the nature of entering into activity, belongs to it (*VPS*, pp. 182-83).

The body, which is an aggregate of the five elements, cannot be the agent of actions and the enjoyer of fruits. The Lokāyatas declare enjoyership in the case of the body. But does enjoyership belong to each of the elements constituting the body distributively or in the aggregate? Even on the first, the elements cannot be the enjoyers all at the same time. If enjoyership belonged to them simultaneously, then, since they would be active in respect of their respective objects without mutual dependence, there would be no reciprocal relation of subsidiary and principal among them, and consequently no aggregation. And if there be enjoyership for the elements even without the aggregate, then, they would be enjoyers even outside the body. Nor is there enjoyership for them in sequence, since the said unintelligibility of aggregation remains unremedied. It may be said that is intelligible through the relation of subsidiary and principal on the analogy of the marriage of several bridegrooms in sequence. But there is no parity of the instance with what is illustrated. Just as for each bridegroom there is a distinct bride as the object of enjoyment, there is not for each of the four elements a specific object of enjoyments. Even assuming that there is a distinct object for each of the elements, when there is simultaneous proximity of all objects, sequence in enjoyment is not intelligible. Thus, enjoyership cannot belong to each object distributively either simultaneously or in sequence. Nor is enjoyership possible for them in the aggregate.

Intelligence, which is not existent in each of the elements, cannot be present in their aggregate. And enjoyership cannot belong to that which is not intelligent. It may be said that a particular capacity present in the aggregate need not necessarily be existent in each of the individuals constituting that aggregate and the case of the sesamum grains thrown into the fire may be cited as an instance. It is thus. Though in each of the sesamum grains thrown into the fire there is not the capacity to generate the flame, there is seen that capacity in their aggregate. Similarly, it may be thought, intelligence is an attribute of the elements, only when they are in aggregation. But, even then, what is the cause of the aggregation? Why should elements combine? It cannot be for the sake of future enjoyment. If future enjoyment be the cause of the aggregation, then the enjoyment would be in the relation of a subsidiary to the elements. And since, then, the elements would all of them be principals, there would not be the reciprocal relation of subsidiary and principal among them; and aggregation is not possible for what are not in the relation of subsidiary and principal. Nor can the enjoyment be the principal, since it is subsidiary to the enjoyer. Even the example of the sesamum grain is irrelevant, because what is called the aggregate cannot be demonstrated by the Lokāyata. Mere location of the enjoyment and the enjoyer in one place cannot be called an aggregate; for, if that were so, there is the contingence of intelligence and enjoyment existing everywhere in the case of the elements which are pervasive. If the aggregate be the whole produced by the elements, is that different from them, or not?

If different, there is the contingence of the acceptance of a fifth real over and above the four elements. If non-different, then, there would be only the elements and not an aggregate. And no other relation is possible, since difference-cum-non-difference is not admitted. Since the aggregate itself is not established for the Lokāyata, he cannot maintain that enjoyership is possible for the elements in the aggregate. Nor is enjoyership invariable only in someone element; for in the proximity of all, whereby can it be determined that enjoyership belongs to one particular element alone and not to any other (*VPS*, pp. 184-85)?

Certain sections of the Lokāyatas hold that enjoyership belongs to the senses and certain others think that it belongs to the aggregate of body and senses. But these two views are to be refuted by the same line of reasoning as set forth above (*VPS*, p. 185).

Another section of the Lokāyatas regard *manas* as the self. Now, what is *manas*? It is eternal, partless and atomic in size, say the Logicians. But *manas* is not eternal, since it is finite like a pot. It has parts, since it is an instrument, like the sense of sight. And it is not atomic in size, since it has parts and has conjunction and disjunction like any other finite object. Hence, *manas* cannot be the self and agency and enjoyership cannot belong to it. What is the self is none of these. The *ātman* is not an epi-phenomenon, an appendage of the body. It is neither a bundle of bones, nor a neural process, neither a colony of cells nor a system of electrons. However much the scientist may try to modify his conception of matter and interpret it in terms of force and energy, electrons and protons, he will not be able to bridge the gulf that yawns between matter and spirit. The self is not molecular motion or radio-activity. It is not only metaphysical but also metapsychical. However subtle mind may be, it is also material. Mind, like gross matter, is subject to origination and destruction, and is sublated in the experience of sleep. Hence, it is the agent and enjoyer, say the Mīmāṁsakas. And they quote in their favour such scriptural texts as "The permitter, knower, agent" (*PraśnaUp* IV.9), "In dream the *jīva* is the enjoyer of happiness and misery", etc. (*KaivalyaUp* 13).

The Sāṁkhyas do not grant agency to the self. That which is omnipresent and partless cannot be an agent. The self is non-active, intelligent. Activity in the form of motion or transformation does not belong to it. Agency cannot be natural to the self; nor can it be adventitious. Even for the possibility of adventitious agency, association with a cause of agency is needed; and that is not possible in the case of the partless self. Though the self is the a non-agent, it is the enjoyer; and its enjoyership consists in being the witness of what is cognized. Hence, the self is the enjoyer alone; this is the view of the Sāṁkhyas (*VPS*, pp. 189-90). And they say that the scriptural text, "One of those two eats the tasty berry, that is the intellect; the other shines without eating" (*ŚvetUp* IV.6), etc. supports their doctrine.

The final position of the Advaitin, however, is that the self is non-different from the taintless *Brahman* which is of the nature of truth, knowledge, bliss. This inner self is not inert, since it is understood to be self-luminous through perception, inference and revelation. That the experience of sleep is evidence for the self-luminosity of Reality, we have seen already. The self is the witness-intelligence which, while being self-luminous, illumines all other objects. Though the Sāṁkhyas regard the self as the witness, they fail to reach the truth because they hold to the doctrine of plurality of *puruṣa*s. The self is but one in all bodies, since everywhere it is known by the cognition "I" with a single form, like "cow-ness" (*VPS*, p. 189). The difference of bodies cannot be the ground for assuming a difference in selves. The bodies are products of nescience; and because of being conditioned by them, there appear to be many *jīva*s. But in reality, there is only oneself which is not different from *Brahman*.

The Nature of Witness-Self

Now, which is this witness-self that is said to be non-different from *Brahman*?

The author of the *Kaumudī* says that the witness is some form of the Lord which permits the *jīva* to be active and to refrain from activity, but which is itself indifferent and non-active. Though it is some form of the Lord, the witness is not the abode of causality. Hence, its immediacy is intelligible. While manifesting the nescience, etc. present in the *jīva*, it is inner to the *jīva*. And in sleep, it is known as *prājña* (*SLS*, vol. II, pp. 44-45).

In the *Tattvaśuddhi* it is said that just as the this-ness, which really belongs to nacre, appears to belong to silver, even so the witness, which is really of the constitution of *Brahman*, appears to be of the constitution of the *jīva* (ibid., p. 45).

Some Advaitins hold that the *jīva*, conditioned by nescience, is itself the witness, because it is the direct seer. The nature of being the witness is directly possible in the *jīva* which is non-attached, indifferent and luminous. Agency, etc. are imposed on the *jīva* when there is brought about its identification with the internal organ. But in its own nature, the *jīva* is indifferent (*SLS*, vol. II, p. 45).

Some others maintain that the *jīva* is the witness, not as conditioned by the omnipresent nescience, but as conditioned by the internal organ. Nor may it be said that, since what is conditioned by the internal organ is the cognizer, it cannot be the witness. The *jīva* as *qualified* by the internal organ is the cognizer; but as *conditioned* the internal organ as an adjunct, it is the witness (ibid., p. 46).[1]

In the *Kūṭasthadīpa*, Bhāratītīrtha defines the witness as the *kūṭastha*, the immutable, unchanging, eternal, flawless intelligence. The immutable intelligence which is the substrate of the two bodies – subtle and gross – is called the witness, because

[1] See also note on pp. 177-78.

it directly superintends the two bodies and is unmodified (ibid., p. 43). The preceptors of old have defined the *kūṭastha* as the witness of the mind and its modifications. Scripture declares the immutable to be existence, knowledge, bliss. In states other than sleep, swoon and *samādhi*, knowledge of objects is acquired through the functions of psychoses. The psychoses of the internal organ manifest the two bodies at intervals. But from the absence of psychoses at other times we cannot infer the non-existence of intelligence. The immutable witness is the silent spectator of all the changing moods and the fleeting moments. It is the foundational intelligence which reveals the existence as well as the non-existence of psychoses.

The Vedas and the Purāṇas declare that the self is the witness which illumines both the presence and the prior non-existence of psychoses (*PD* VIII.56). It is real, because it is the abode of the unreal world. It is of the nature of intelligence, since it illumines all inert things. Being ever the object of infinite love, it is of the nature of bliss. Because it is the source of all auspicious things and because it is the basis of all entities, it is unalloyed bliss. In this manner the Śaiva Purāṇas and scripture distinguish the *kūṭastha* from the changing world, the finite *jīva* and the non-absolute *Īśvara* (*PD* VIII.47-49).[2] The Vedāntins proclaim with one voice that the self is absolutely real, self-evident and uncontradicted by any fact of experience (*PD* VIII.66). The *kūṭastha* is unattached, impartite and immutable. It produces nothing, nor is it produced by anything else. In reality, there is no dissolution, no creation; there is no one bound, no one longing for release and none liberated. This is the supreme truth. But this real nature of the self is beyond the reach of speech and mind. Hence, scripture teaches the truth, basing itself either on the world, the *jīva* or *Īśvara*. It adopts whatever mode of teaching would easily reveal the truth. The wise discern the real

---

2 For a detailed account of the natures of *jīva* and *Īśvara*, see Chapter 7.

through the aid of scriptural testimony; but the ignorant wallow in darkness unable to get at the truth (*PD* VIII.71-74).

In the *Nāṭakadīpa*, the witness-intelligence is compared to the lamp set on a dramatic stage. The lamp gives light to the manager of the drama, to the actors and to the audience without any distinction; and it shines even if the theatre be emptied of all persons. Similarly, the witness manifests egoity, the intellect and the objects, and continues to shine even when they are non-existent. It cannot be said that the intellect is enough to illumine the objects, for it shines only by borrowed light. It is the self-luminous immutable intelligence that is the giver of all light. The sense of egoity may be compared to the proprietor of the drama, the objects to the audience and the intellect to the danseuse; and the various sense organs are auxiliaries or accompaniments which aid the actress. All these are without any distinction illumined by the witness. Just as the lamp on the dramatic stage illumines without moving and without being affected by the movements of the actors and the audience, even so the witness which is permanent and unchanging manifests all things both within and without (*PD* X.11-15).

The distinction between "inner" and "outer" which is dependent on the body has no reference to the witness. Those objects which are external to the body are called the "outer", and those that are within, the "inner". The impermanence and the vacillation natural to the intellect are superimposed on the witness-intelligence. But the witness neither goes in nor goes out. It appears as if it acts on account of its association with the intellect. It knows no "inner" and "outer" which are distinctions created by the intellect. Even to say that the self is omnipresent and all-pervasive is to superimpose on it the category of space. In itself, the witness is beyond all computation. If, then, it be asked how it can be known, the Advaitin replies, the self is not an object of apprehension. Because it is self-luminous, it shines ever without the help of any means of knowledge (*PD* X.16-25).

It is the light that never was on sea or land. It lends its lustre even to the luminaries of the sky.

In the *Citradīpa*, the concepts of *Brahman*, *kūṭastha*, *Īśvara* and *jīva* are explained and illustrated. *Brahman* is unconditioned like the ether at large. *Kūṭastha* is also immutable, but appears as if conditioned; hence, it may be compared to the ether defined by a pot. *Īśvara* and the *jīva*, both of them, are reflections. In the water that is present in a pot, there is the reflection of the sky along with clouds and the stars that are strewn in the sky. Just as the sky in the water is a reflection of the ether at large in the water contained in a particular pot, even so the *jīva* is a reflection of *Brahman* in the intellect which belongs to a particular body. In the clouds which are constituted of subtle particles of water there is a huge reflection of ether. If the reflection of ether in the pot-water be small, the reflection of ether in the clouds is large. *Īśvara* may be compared to the latter kind of reflection. But both *Īśvara* and the *jīva* are, as we said, reflections of intelligence. The *kūṭastha*, which is non-different from *Brahman*, is defined by the two bodies, subtle and gross. It is called *kūṭastha* because, while being the substrate of those bodies, it is immutable like the anvil (*PD* VI.18-22).

The pro-nouns "I", "you", "he", "it", etc. are used to signify different things by different persons. What is "I" to me is not "I" to another. An identical object is "I", to itself, "you" to another and "he" or "it" to a third. What is common to and constant in them all is selfhood. Just as in the case of the illusory appearance of silver, silverness is superimposed on *this*, on the immutable self *I-ness* is superimposed. In empirical usages like "Devadatta *himself* goes", "You yourself see", "I *myself* am not well", etc. we find that while selfhood (*svatva*) is constant, I-ness (*ahantā*) is not so. The self is the *kūṭastha* and the "I" which signifies the *cidābhāsa* is an imposition thereon (*PD* VI.38-39).

In the *Tattva-Pradīpikā* (p. 373) Citsukha distinguishes the witness which is the seer (*draṣṭṛ*) from the cognizer (*pramātṛ*).

In sleep, though there is not the proximity of the instruments of valid knowledge, the witness manifests nescience. Hence, its non-inclusion in the cognizer is intelligible. The cognizer is that which knows through the means of valid knowledge. The witness is not thus. Then, it may be thought that, since in waking, etc. there is the function of the means of knowledge, the witness would not be what establishes knowledge. But this is not so. Since the witness is included in the *jīva*-self, the nature of being subsidiary to empirical usage is intelligible for the witness-perception. Nor is there no evidence in respect of the witness, since there is evidence of the inference.

> Caitra's desire, etc. are apprehended by this perception which is different from the non-eternal knowledge which apprehends this, since it is the perception of this, like the perception of this pot, etc.

Desire, etc. cannot be cognized by the senses, because they are supersensuous. Nor can mind cognize them, since desire, etc. constitute the mind. If desire, etc. be known by mental perception, there is the conflict of objectness and agency in one and the same thing. Hence, a perception which is brought about by what is other than these must be admitted; and that is the witness-perception. The witness is not what is qualified by nescience; nor is it that of which nescience is a qualification *per accidens*. But it is that which has nescience as its adjunct.[3]

---

[3] That which persists in the effect so long as it lasts and brings about a distinction is a qualification (*viśeṣaṇa*) as the blue colour is of the lily. But that which does not so persist and yet effects a distinction is either an adjunct (*upādhi*) or a qualification *per accidens* (*upalakṣaṇa*). Of these, too, that which is coterminous with the effect is an adjunct; and that which, while remaining only for sometime, effects a distinction, is a qualification *per accidens.*

kāryā-'nvayitvena tu bhedakaṁ yat, tad vīśeṣaṇaṁ, nailyaṁ ivo 'tpalasya; ananvayitvena tu bhedakānām upādhito-'palakṣaṇatā prasiddhā । tayor api yāvati-kāryaṁ avasthāyi bheda-hetor upādhitā, kādācitkatayā bhedadhī-hetur upalakṣaṇam.

We have seen above some of the ways in which the witness has been conceived of by Advaitins. While some preceptors hold it to be identical with *Īśvara*, Bhāratītīrtha and Citsukha maintain that the witness is the true nature of the *jīva*. But, there is no conflict between the two views, since in the final position of the Advaitin, *Īśvara* who is non-different from *Brahman* is also non-different from the *jīva*.

7

Īśvara and Jīva

CAUSALITY of the universe is the qualification *per accidens* of *Brahman*; and it constitutes the essential nature of *Īśvara*. *Īśvara* is *Brahman* seen under the limitation of *māyā*.[1] The second aphorism of the *Vedāntasūtras* states the definition *per accidens* of *Brahman* as the cause whence result the origination, sustentation and destruction of the world. This definition is of the essential nature of *Īśvara*, who is *Brahman* qualified by *māyā* (*VPS*, pp. 194-95).

The Cause of the World

All the Advaitins do not subscribe to the view that *Īśvara* is the cause of the world. Some hold that pure *Brahman* is the cause and some others maintain that the *jīva* is the cause of the universe. The followers of the *Saṁkṣepa-Śārīraka* say that pure *Brahman* is the material cause (*SLS*, vol. II, p. 13). Those who uphold the theory that perception is creation (Dṛṣṭi-sṛṣṭivāda) regard the entire world as the fabrication of the *jīva*'s intellect. Just as dream-cognition, *Īśvaratva*, etc. are all mental constructions made by the *jīva* (ibid., p. 16). Bhāratītīrtha does not seem to support either of these views regarding the cause of the world. In the *Vivaraṇa-Prameya-Saṁgraha* he expounds the *Vivaraṇa*

---

1 For a discourse on *māyā*, see Chapter 8.

view according to which *Īśvara*, or *Brahman* qualified by *māyā*, is the material cause (*SLS*, vol. II, pp. 13-14). The world cannot be suspected to be a product of the *jīva*, he says, for all *jīva*s who are qualified by agency and enjoyership and are of the nature of name and form fall within the product (*VPS*, p. 201). In the *Pañcadaśī*, though the *Vivaraṇa* view that *Īśvara* is the primal cause is maintained, subsidiary causality is attributed to the *jīva*. Some Advaitins who make a difference between *māyā* and *avidyā* say that the universe beginning with ether, etc. is the product of the *māyā* located in the Lord and that the internal organ, etc. are the products of the subtle elements which are created by the nescience of the *jīva*. According to Bhāratītīrtha, *Īśvara* and the *jīva* are the joint creators of the world. But there is this difference: while the Lord is the principal author, the *jīva* is only a subsidiary parent. In respect of the existence of the world *Īśvara* is the ground, whereas in respect of its enjoyment the *jīva* is the locus. The nature of the creation by the *jīva* is psychical rather than physical. The universe is a product of *Īśvara* and an object of enjoyment for the *jīva*.[2]

Creation, Transformation and Illusory Appearance

Now, what kind of causality is recognized in respect of the Lord? Is it efficient causality alone, or material causality alone, or both? The first and second alternatives are not possible, since if *Īśvara* were either the efficient or the material cause alone, he would be finite, infinitude being impossible for him. Hence, it must be admitted that he is the material cause as well as the efficient cause (*abhinna-nimitto-'pādāna-kāraṇa*). There is no unintelligibility whatever in the material cause being itself the efficient cause. The world has a material cause which is non-different from the efficient, since it is generated as preceded by knowledge, like the happiness, misery, attachment, aversion, etc. present in the self. That the dual causality belongs to *Brahman* qualified by

---

2 *PD* IV18: *Īśa-kāryam jīva-bhogyam* ।

māyā is established by the creational text which declares efficient causality in "That desired" and material causality in "May I become many" (*ChāUp* VI.ii.3; *VPS*, pp. 196-97).

The dual causality is declared of *Brahman* as its qualification *per accidens*, only in the view of the doctrine of illusory manifestation. The material causality of *Brahman* consists neither in origination, as by the primal atoms, nor in transformation, as of Primal Nature. The Vaiśeṣikas and others who hold the view of absolute creation say that something originates from something else, as cloth from threads; and they attribute the creation of the world to the conjunction of primal atoms. The Sāṁkhyas and those who are in sympathy with their view of transformation characterize the world as a transformation of Primal Nature, as curd is of milk. When a thing attains a state which is different from its present one, it is called transformation; when a thing, while not abandoning its prior state, appears to be of a different state, it is known as illusory manifestation (see *PD* XIII.6-9).

> That change, which is of the same grade of reality as the thing, is transformation; what is not of the same grade of reality is illusory manifestation; or, change, which is of the same nature as the cause, is transformation; the effect, which even without being non-different from that (cause) is yet difficult to state apart from that, is an illusory manifestation; such is the distinction between transformation and illusory manifestation. – *SLS*, vol. I, p. 153; vol. II, p. 13

Brahman can be neither the originating cause nor the transformed cause. What is partless by nature cannot originate something *de novo*;[3] nor can it get itself transformed into something else. If

3 Pringle-Pattison 1917: 302-03: "The idea of creation as a special act or event that took place once upon a time represents the universe as in no way organic to divine life. ... Such a conception of creation belong to the same circle of ideas as the waving of a magician's wand."

Brahman were to abandon the earlier form and get transformed into another form, then, subsequent to creation, there would be destruction of *Brahman* of the form of knowledge and bliss. If, again, at the stage of dissolution, that *Brahman*, which is devoid of the form of knowledge and bliss, be transformed into *Brahman* that is knowledge and bliss, even thus, since at any moment that *Brahman* might transform its nature, there is the contingence of non-release. Nor is there any evidence in respect of transformation. Scripture in the text "The unborn self, the great, the firm" (*BṛUp* IV.iv.20) predicates immutability of the self as opposed to transformation. And *Brahman* is immutable because it is partless (*VPS*, p. 204).

It may be objected that the transformation is possible even in the case of the partless. This is how it is argued: conjunction which is inherent in a part of the whole is indirectly preceded by the conjunction of the partless primal atom. The parts conjoin and produce the whole, but the parts by themselves are constituted of atoms; and if there were no conjunction of atoms, how would the production of the parts be possible? Necklet, etc. are said to be transformations of gold. But gold is but a colony of primal atoms; and without a transformation of the primal atoms which are partless, how is transformation possible for gold? Hence even of the partless, transformation must be admitted (*VPS*, p. 204).

Now, what is this transformation? Is it the increase of parts through one's own parts coming to have a conjunction other than the earlier conjunction, like the lump of clay coming to have the form of a pot? Or is it the increase of parts through the conjunction with other parts, like milk becoming curd through the conjunction with the parts of the buttermilk poured into the milk? Neither of these is possible in the case of *Brahman* which is partless. Nor is it possible for *Brahman* to attain a different state either like the ageing of the young or like the twig becoming a post; for if *Brahman* were to transform itself in the form of the world in that manner, it would not become *Brahman* again and there is the consequent contingence of non-release. Verily, the aged man does not become a youth again; nor does the post grow into the form of a tree. Nor does transformation consist either in the conjunction of one thing with another like the atom becoming a dyad through conjunction with another atom, or in motion like water becoming a river, or in the rise of another quality like the assumption of a different colour by a ripe fruit; for to define transformation in any of these ways would be over-extensive. In the ether that is conjoined to another thing, in the bee that moves about and in the cloth wherein redness has appeared, there is not observed any transformation of substance. Nor is transformation the origination of another substance associated with the material cause; for though such transformation be possible in the case of the whole, the transformation of the parts is difficult to state. The necklet, for example, is the product of the whole and not of the parts of gold. Though the necklet be not the product of the parts, the parts may intelligibly persist in the necklet through the channel of the whole. Without a change in the loci, the parts, there can well be a change in the located, the whole. Origination and destruction are non-existent in the primal atom; but they are seen in the dyad. It may be said that attributes other than origination and destruction must change in the loci in order that they may change in the located; but, no. The generality "potness" is not present in the potsherds, but it is inherent in the pot. Nor is a change of state for the pervaded, the whole, unintelligible in the absence of a change of state for the pervaders, the parts; for without a change of state for the pervaders, generality and quality, there is seen a change of state in the substance pervaded. Even if transformation of the parts be admitted, that transformation must be prompted by the transformation of the whole. And this kind of transformation is not possible in the case of *Brahman* which is not a part of anything else (*VPS*, pp. 204-05).

It was urged that transformation of the partless *Brahman* is intelligible like the conjunction of primal atoms. Now, what is meant here? Is it stated that the perceptible conjunction of the whole is inherent in the primal atoms? Or is it assumed that the conjunction of the whole is preceded by the conjunction of the primal atoms? Not the first, since if conjunction of the whole were inherent in the primal atoms, it would be imperceptible even as the colour, etc. which are present in the primal atom are imperceptible. Nor is the second alternative, which assumes that the conjunction of the whole is preceded by the conjunction of primal atoms, intelligible; for conjunction in respect of the whole itself is intelligible without conjunction of primal atoms, like the inherence of "potness" in pot without its presence in the potsherds. The parts, however, may persist in the conjunction through the channel of the whole. This we observed already. Hence, the example of the conjunction of primal atoms is not valid; and it is not possible to infer on that ground the transformation of the partless. The creationist doctrine and the view of transformation having been thrown overboard, it must be admitted that *Brahman* illusorily appears as the world (*VPS*, p. 205).

Īśvara, the Material Cause of the World

The disputants do not agree as to what the material cause of the world is. The Sāṁkhyas regard the *pradhāna* as the material cause. All the modifications that constitute the world, they say, have for material cause the generality of happiness, misery and delusion whichever accompanies them. What is always persistent in a product must be the cause of that product. Basin, etc. are interpenetrated by clay; hence, clay is their material cause. The Sāṁkhyas next point out that there cannot be a plurality of causes for the world. What are limited and multiple, and are modifications must have a single undifferentiated material cause, like basin, etc. which have clay for their material cause.

Thus, the Sāṁkhyas infer that the *pradhāna* or *prakṛti*, which is constituted by the three *guṇa*s in an undifferentiated state, is the material cause of the world.[4] The Nyāya–Vaiśeṣikas postulate primal atoms as the material cause of the world. They argue that a produced substance must have as its material cause what is smaller in size than its own size. A piece of cloth, for instance, is produced by the threads which are smaller in size than its own size. Just as the threads join together and constitute a cloth, the primal atoms by a process of conjunction become the world. The Śūnyavādins consider the void to be the material cause. They maintain that every product is preceded by non-existence since it has a prior state which while being capable of being cognized is not cognized. The Yogas declare Hiraṇyagarbha to be the material cause; and the Śaivas assert that Paśupati is the material cause (*VPS*, p. 209).

All these views, in the opinion of the Advaitin, are wrong. The Sāṁkhya theory that the generality of happiness, misery and delusion is the material cause of all modifications cannot bear reasoning. Happiness, etc. which are external cannot be the cause of pot, etc. which are external. On the ground that all modifications are accompanied by the generality of happiness, etc. it is not possible to state that the latter is the cause of the former. Qualities like whiteness accompany cloth and generality like "potness" accompanies pot; but whiteness is not the material cause of cloth, nor is "potness" the cause of pot. The Logicians argue that a produced substance must be a product of a thing smaller in size than its own size. But this is not always the case. Two long and broad silk cloths twisted together become the

---

4 *VPS*, p. 208:
vimatāḥ sarve vikārāḥ sukha-duḥkha-moha-sāmānya-prakṛtikāḥ, tadanvita-svabhāvatvād, ye yad-anvita-svabhāvās te tatprakṛtikāḥ, yathā mṛdanvitā mṛt-prakṛtikāḥ śarāvādayaḥ, tathā vimatāḥ sarvavi- kārā avibhaktaikaprakṛtikāḥ parimitatvād anekatvād vikārātvācca śarāvādivad iti sāṁkhyāḥ pradhānam anumimate ।

rope-substance. Here, the rope-substance is produced by two things which are larger in size than its own size. Further, the Logician must admit that primal atoms have parts, since their product, the dyad, has parts. The reasoning of the Śūnyavādin also is inconclusive. A product is not preceded by a state which is not cognized, while being capable of being cognized. The prior state of the pot is clay; and clay is perceptually cognized. As for the views of the Yogas and the Śaivas, they are to be rejected because they conflict with the Veda (*VPS*, p. 209).

What are non-intelligent like the *pradhāna* and primal atoms cannot be the cause of distinctly regulated creation. The universe is a cosmos and not a chaos. The rhythmic movement of the suns and the stars, the music of the spheres, the enchanting song of the nightingale, the beautiful form of the black antelope – all these cannot be the handiwork of either a blind force or of a chance coincidence of atoms colliding together. Without the postulation of an intelligence possessing omniscience and omnipotence, the regulated creation of the universe is not intelligible. The world is of the form of an arrangement that cannot be conceived even by the mind. How can that which is not omniscient and omnipotent create such a world? That the cause of the world, *Īśvara*, is omniscient is declared by the scriptural text, "He who is omniscient" (*MuṇḍUp* I.i.9).

The Svabhāvavādin wants to do away with all extraneous causes. Thinking that the four elements alone are real, that perception is the sole means of valid knowledge and that the doctrine of nature is alone the absolute truth, he says that every product is originated by its very nature. But his view is extremely defective. A product cannot be its own cause, because of self-dependence. Nor is a product originated without a cause, since there would be simultaneous existence and non-existence of an object, if it be not produced by a cause. Hence, the doctrine of the Advaitin that the omniscient, omnipotent *Īśvara* is the cause remains unshaken (*VPS*, p. 210).

Ideas of God

Even non-Advaitins like the Vaiśeṣikas, Yogas and Naiyāyikas admit of God who is omniscient and omnipotent. But their idea of God differs vitally from that of the Advaitin; and while they reach their conclusion through bare reasoning, the Advaitin takes his stand on scripture and utilizes such argumentation as is favourable to the declarations of Śruti. The Vaiśeṣikas argue that the universe must have a creator who knows all, e.g. the material cause, etc. since it is a product, like a house. But, here, the reasoning is not sound. There is nothing to prevent the world from having many creators or a non-omniscient creator. A house, verily, may be the product of many men; and it does not require omniscience on the part of one who builds the house. The Yogas regard God as the terminus of the capacities for cognition and lordship. These capacities increasing in degree terminate somewhere, since they are properties that increase, like size. This argument of the Yogas is defective. Even some of those who maintain that there is no *Īśvara* say that there are deities which are the termini of the capacities for cognition and lordship (*VPS*, pp. 190, 211). According to the Yogas, the Lord is a *puruṣa-viśeṣa* (special soul) who is not conjoined with blemishes, *karma*s, fruits and their residual impressions. Like the *jīva*, he is intelligent and unattached. If like the finite self, God be without attachment, how can he be the "prime mover" of *prakṛti*? The follower of the Yoga has a ready answer to give. God is not an ordinary *puruṣa*, he is a *puruṣa-viśeṣa*, a distinguished soul (*primus inter pares*). It is because of his supremacy that he directs the universe, controls the course of creation. Otherwise, the universe would be like a kingdom without a king, an army without a captain. Of the Lord, scripture declares the directorship of the universe in the text, "For fear of him wind blows; for fear of him move the sun and the stars" (*TaitUp* II.viii.1). Since God is without the blemishes which pertain to the *jīva*s, he can well be the controller of the world. It is no doubt true that even the *puruṣa*s are by nature undefiled; but since they do not discriminate themselves from the products of *prakṛti*, say the Yogas, blemishes, *karmas*, etc. belong to them (*PD* VI.105-08). This view is, as we saw, not sound. If God be only the foremost among the finites, he ceases to be God with an infinity of perfections. Such a view of God would satisfy neither the philosophical intellect nor the religious heart. The Naiyāyikas believe that the Lord is the dispenser of the fruit of *karma* such as merit and demerit, and argue that in order that he may do his work he must possess knowledge of that fruit, even as an earthly master should know the fruit of service before granting it to his servants. Now, this inference does not distinguish the Lord from the deities, etc. admitted by those who maintain that there is no *Īśvara* (*VPS*, pp. 190, 211). The Logicians predicate of the Lord such attributes like cognition, effort and desire, and they regard these qualities as eternal. *Īśvara* differs from the *jīvas* only in the nature of his attributes, not otherwise. His attributes are eternal, while those of the *jīvas* are not. "He has desires that come true, resolves that are real" (*PD* VI.109-10; *ChāUp* VIII.i.5). The Naiyāyika view is not valid for the reason that it does not regard God as the material cause of the world. If God be only an efficient cause, he cannot be infinite and eternal. The views of the Vaiśeṣikas, Yogas and Naiyāyikas are partial and not perfect. The Vaiśeṣikas think of God as the omniscient creator on the analogy of the potter that makes a pot or an engineer that builds a house. The Yogas consider God to be the apex of the pyramid of souls, the locus where terminate the capacities for cognition and lordship. And the Naiyāyikas regard him as the dispenser of justice. Even the Advaitin advances some such arguments to establish God. We have already seen how the argument from design is advocated by him. But he never errs like the others in regarding the arguments as inferences. Argumentation helps us to have a cognition of the possibility; while the task of inference is to give us certitude about the thing. Inference cannot yield us God, because he is supersensuous and suprarational. All inference about God is bound to be vitiated by defects such as we have seen above. There is no harm, however, if such argumentation as is auxiliary to scripture be brought into use. The same syllogisms of the Vaiśeṣikas and others, though defective as inference, are valid as possessing the character of argumentation (*tarka*) which is the cause of the cognition of possibility in respect of *Brahman* established by scripture. Another defect, as we have observed already, is that none of these views regards God as the material cause. And if God be not the material cause, he must be a conditioned, finite and imperfect being, limited by the material out of which he has to mould the universe (*VPS*, p. 212).

Having set aside some of the metaphysical attempts to define God, we shall now turn to a few of the theological ideas of God. Some there are who regard Hiraṇyagarbha as God; and they cite the *Udgītha-Brāhmaṇa* as supporting their doctrine. Some others consider Virāṭ to be the Lord; and they quote in their support the text: "He has a thousand heads, a thousand eyes and a thousand feet". Still others say that the four-faced Brahmā is the sole creator. Worshipping him for the sake of progeny, they assert that there is no God other than he. The Vaiṣṇavas hold that Viṣṇu is the supreme deity. The Śaivas maintain that Śiva is the overlord. There are other sectarian views championed by partisans in religion who torture the texts of Śruti in order to fit them in the procrustean bed of their pre-formed theories. The conceptions of God vary from the sublime to the sensuous, from the most lofty to the most ludicrous (*PD* VI.111-21).

All these views the Advaitin regards as imperfect attempts at gauging the nature of God. To him God is both the material cause and the efficient cause. He takes his stand on the declaration of Śruti, "Know *māyā* as the primal cause, and the Lord as the wielder of *māyā*".

Is Īśvara a Reflection?

In the *Citradīpa*, Bhāratītīrtha defines *Īśvara* as the reflection of intelligence in the impressions of the intellects of all beings and compares him to the reflection of ether in the water-particles that constitute the cloud. *Māyā* is like the cloud, the impressions of the intellect are like the particles of water present in the cloud, and the reflection of intelligence is like the reflection of the sky in the water-particles. The reflection of intelligence in *māyā* is the *māyin*, the Supreme Lord. Scripture declares that he is the omniscient inner ruler, the source of the entire universe.[5]

The *Citradīpa* view that the reflection of intelligence in the nescience qualified by the impressions of the intellects is *Īśvara* comes in for criticism.[6] It is thus: what is the adjunct of *Īśvara*? Is it bare nescience, or nescience as associated with the impressions, or bare impression? If bare nescience be the adjunct of *Īśvara*, there would be conflict with the view that *Īśvara* is the reflection in the nescience qualified by the impressions of the intellect. Nor is the second alternative that the adjunct is nescience as associated with the impressions sound, for it is in keeping with the law of parsimony to regard nescience alone as the adjunct. It may be said that if bare nescience be regarded as the adjunct there would not be established omniscience for the Lord, and that the impressions of the intellects are said to be the qualification of nescience so that omniscience may be possible for the Lord. But this is wrong. When it is possible to establish omniscience through the *sattva*-psychoses of nescience, it is futile to accept the impression of intellect as the qualification of nescience. Further, omniscience cannot be established through the impressions of the intellects. There is not for each impression the capacity to apprehend all things. Hence, we must regard all impressions as the qualification of nescience, if omniscience is to

---

5 *PD* VI.156-57; *ŚvetUp* IV.10:
māyāṁ tu prakṛtiṁ vidyānmāyinaṁ taṁ maheśvram ।
tasyāvayava-bhūtaistu vyāptaṁ sarvamidaṁ jagat ॥

6 *SLS*, Commentary, p. 77; *Vṛtti-Prabhākara* (Hindi), pp. 337-38.

be established. But except at the time of *pralaya* (deluge), it is not possible for all impressions to exist together at the same time. And so omniscience is not established through impressions. The third alternative that the bare impressions are the adjuncts of *Īśvara* is also unintelligible. Is *Īśvara* the reflection in each of the impressions? Or is he the one reflection present in all the impressions? On the first alternative, there would be many *Īśvara*s, since the impressions of the intellects of the innumerable *jīva*s are many. And moreover, parviscience would have to be predicated of *Īśvara*, since the impression of each intellect is limited in its scope for knowledge. Nor is the second alternative intelligible. Except in *prulaya*, all the impressions cannot exist at the same time; and there cannot be a single reflection in many impressions. Hence, concludes the critic, bare nescience is to be regarded as the adjunct of *Īśvara* and the assumption of the impressions of the intellects as the qualification of nescience serves no useful purpose.

Bhāratītīrtha identifies *Īśvara* who is the reflection of intelligence in the impressions of the intellects of all beings with the blissful self of the sleep state described in *Māṇḍūkya Upaniṣad* 5 (*PD* VI.138). But how can the blissful self of the sleep state which is the *jīva* be the omniscient Lord? The same *vijñānamaya* self which functions in waking and dream is called *ānandamaya* in sleep. If the *ānandamaya* be *Īśvara*, then, in waking and dream there would be no *Īśvara*, since from these two states the sheath of bliss is absent. And further, there must be admitted a separate *Īśvara* for every *jīva* in sleep. In all the relevant scriptural texts the *jīva* is vested with five sheaths. Bhāratītīrtha himself declares so in the *Pañcakośa-Viveka*. Hence, it is not intelligible to accept the view that the Lord is the blissful self of the state of sleep.

In the *Brahmānanda*, Bhāratītīrtha says that the blissful self of sleep is but the *jīva*. The intention of the great preceptor is not to declare that the blissful self of sleep is *Īśvara*. For the

Supreme Self there are three qualified cosmic forms and three qualified individual forms. In the *Citradīpa*, with the example of the artistically worked cloth, pure intelligence and its three qualified cosmic (*adhidaivata*) forms are described. A piece of canvas is first bleached, then stiffened with starch, sketched with lines and finally filled in with paint. Similarly, the self which is by nature pure intelligence is called Antaryāmin (*Īśvara*) when it is associated with *māyā*, Sūtrātman (Hiraṇyagarbha) when it creates the subtle universe, and Virāṭ when it is the cause of the gross world. The individual forms of the self are three. When in sleep the internal organ is resolved, the witness of the bare nescience is *prājña*; and it is called *ānandamaya*. In dream, that which has a conceit in the individual subtle body is *taijasa*. In waking, what has a conceit in the individual gross body is *viśva*. The Māṇḍūkya Śruti includes the *adhyātma* forms in the *adhidaiva* forms to facilitate the passage from the conditioned to the unconditioned. Hence, the identification of *Īśvara* with the blissful self of sleep or with the reflection of intelligence in the impressions of the intellects of all beings has for purport the declaration of the truth that the *adhidaiva* and *adhyātma* forms are but the forms of the same Supreme Self.

Īśvara, Hiraṇyagarbha and Virāṭ

Under the three cosmic forms the Self comes to be called, as we saw, *Īśvara*, Hiraṇyagarbha and Virāṭ. *Īśvara* is *Brahman* qualified by *māyā*. He is the material and the efficient cause of the world. He is like the bleached canvas which is stiffened with starch, pure but serving as the substrate of world-creation. Hiraṇyagarbha or Sūtrātman is the cosmic subtle form of the Self. He is of the nature of all *jīva*s put together; for he has conceit in the subtle bodies of them all. He possesses the powers of action, knowledge, etc. Just as early in the morning or late in the evening the world appears to be immersed in twilight, in the form of Hiraṇyagarbha the universe is presented in an indistinct manner. Just as the canvas stiffened with starch is sketched with lines, the form of the Lord is invested with the subtle bodies, the non-quintuplicated elements. Like the grains which shoot their sprouts, *Īśvara* who is the womb of the universe attains in the form of Hiraṇyagarbha the tender stage of the sprout. He is the seed of the worlds, he is the sprout of the spheres (*PD* VI.200-203). The form of Virāṭ is the full-blown stage of the universe, comparable to the world in the noonday glare, the canvas filled in with paint, or the grains which have borne their fruit. In the Viśvarūpādhyāya of the *Yajurveda* and in the Puruṣasūkta, Virāṭ is described as of the cosmic form comprising all beings from the highest Brahmā down to a blade of grass (*PD* VI.204-05). All things are his visible forms. Each being is a fragment of his cosmic vesture. He is the mighty Lord whose crown is the heaven and footstool the earth:

Whose dwelling is the fight of setting suns,
And the round ocean, and the living air,
And the blue sky, and in the mind of man;
A motion and a spirit that impels
All thinking things, all objects of all thoughts,
And rolls through all things.
– *Tintern Abbey* – Wordsworth

The Jīva and Its Vestures

The *jīva* is a reflection of intelligence (*cidābhāsa*) in the impure-*sattva*-predominant *avidyā*.[7] More correctly, the *jīva* is the substrate intelligence plus the subtle body plus the reflection of intelligence therein (*PD* IV.11). It is the self endowed with a psycho-physical organism. Just as the ether defined by the pot, the pot with water, and the reflection of the sky in the water

7 In order to make a difference between the Immutable and the *jīva*, Bhāratītīrtha defines the *jīva* simply as a reflection. But this distinction is rather strained; and he himself relinquishes it in many places. See *PD* I.17.

constitute the pot and its content, similarly the intelligence which is the substrate as defined by an individual mind–body system is the *jīva*. The individual self gets itself involved in misery and metempsychosis. It is caught up in a vortex of ceaseless change. Deluded by *avidyā*, the *jīva* identifies itself with the mind–body composite and deems itself to be the enjoyer of the sweets and bitters of life. It acts in order to enjoy and enjoys in order to act. Like the worms that are carried away in a wild stream from one whirlpool to another, the *jīva* is driven from birth to death and from death to birth in a continuous cycle of empirical existence (*PD* I.30).

The cosmos which has its origination in the Lord's contemplation (*īkṣaṇa*) finds its completion in the production of *jīvatva*. Of the entire external world of the living and the non-living the Lord is the artificer. Of the internal world of transmigratory existence which begins in the state of waking and ends in release, the *jīva* is the author. The *jīva* is the progenitor of its own microcosmic world. That *jīva*, being deluded by *māyā* and established in the body, creates everything. In waking it alone finds satisfaction in the manifold objects of enjoyment like woman, food, drink, etc. It is the agent of actions and the enjoyer of the fruits thereof.

> Even in dream, the *jīva* is the enjoyer of pleasure and pain in a world created by its own *māyā*. If in waking the *jīva* sports with the external world, in dream the sphere of its ravings is the internal world of fiction and fancy. At the time of sleep when all is resolved, it attains the form of bliss, being overpowered by *tamas*. And again due to conjunction with the *karma* of its previous life, the same *jīva* dreams and wakes. – *PD* VII.4

The *jīva* is tossed from one birth to another, from one state of existence to another, like the weaver's shuttle, without cessation. It lives in the cocoon of its own making. From death to death it travels by the force of its delusion.

The impure-*sattva*-predominant *prakṛti* is *avidyā* (nescience). The self having *avidyā* as the adjunct is the *jīva*. It is endowed with a psycho-physical organism for the sake of enjoyment. It is said to possess three bodies: causal, subtle and gross. The causal body of the *jīva* is nescience; and as qualified by that body, it is known as *prājña*. The causal body (*kāraṇa-śarīra*) is so called because, as a particular aspect of *prakṛti* which is the parent of the subtle and gross bodies, etc. it is the cause (*kāraṇa*) and because it is destroyed (*śīryate*) by true knowledge (*PD* I.17).

The subtle body (*sūkṣma-śarīra*) consists of the five organs of sense, the five of action, the five vital airs, mind and intellect. From the *tamas*-predominant *prakṛti* the five great elements, viz. ether, air, fire, water and earth spring forth. From the *sattva*-parts of these five elements are born respectively the five organs of sense; and those parts together produce the internal organ, which owing to a difference in function is divided into mind (*manas*) that deliberates and intellect (*buddhi*) that decides. From the *rajas*-parts of the five elements are created respectively the five organs of action; and from them as a collective whole the five vital airs are derived. These seventeen factors go to make up the subtle body of the *jīva* which, as having conceit therein, comes to be called *taijasa* (*PD* I.18-24). The gross body (*sthūla-śarīra*) of the *jīva* is its particular physical frame which is a composite of the quintuplicated elements. When the *jīva* has conceit in its physical body, it is called *viśva* (*PD* I.29). Thus, the three forms of the *jīva* are conditioned by the three vestures it wears. There is also another way of characterizing the three forms of the *jīva*. The *pāramārthika* (absolute) self is the substrate of the subtle and gross bodies. The *prātibhāsika* (apparent) self is the subject of the dream world. And the *vyāvahārika* (empirical) self is the agent and enjoyer of the waking experience.

Is the Jīva One or Many?

Among Advaitins there are some who hold that there is only

one *jīva* and others who maintain that there are many *jīvas*. A section of the Eka-jīva-vādins argues thus: There is only a single *jīva* animating only one body. The other bodies are non-animated like the ones seen in dream. The entire universe is illusorily posited by the nescience which belongs to that *jīva*. All empirical usage is apparent like dream-cognitions. There is not even the distinction between the bound and the released, since the *jīva* is single. The release of Śuka, etc. is assumptive like the release of persons seen in dreams (*SLS*, vol. II, p. 27). In the view of the Eka-jīva-vādin, other selves "are such stuff as dreams are made on, and our (their) little life is rounded with a sleep".[8]

The world of the living and the non-living is a fiction created by a single *jīva* animating a single body (Eka-śarīraika-jīva-vāda).

Another section of the Eka-jīva-vādins is not satisfied with the view that there is only one animated body. It holds that Hiraṇyagarbha which is a reflection of *Brahman* is the one principal *jīva*. The other *jīvas* are reflections of this principal *jīva* and are similar to the apparent clothings put on the bodies of human beings sketched on an artistically worked cloth. Thus, this section of Advaitins adopts the view of a single *jīva* with many distinctive bodies (Saviśeṣāneka-śarīraika-jīva-vāda) (*SLS*, vol. II, p. 28).

A third group of Eka-jīva-vādins contends that, since Hiraṇyagarbhas vary with each aeon, it is not possible to determine which Hiraṇyagarbha is the principal *jīva*. Hence it prefers the view of a single *jīva* animating many bodies without distinction (Aviśeṣānekaśarīraika-jīva-vāda). The non-recollection of one's happiness, etc. by another is explained as due to the difference of bodies. In all these three varieties of Eka-jīva-vāda there is no distinction between the bound and the released, since there is only a single *jīva* (*SLS*, vol. II, p. 28).

Such of those Advaitins who do not agree with the views set forth above resort to the view of many *jīvas*, through the

[8] Shakespeare, *Tempest*, Act IV, Scene 1.

admission of the internal organ, etc. as adjuncts of the *jīva*. The *jīvas* are many because of the plurality of adjuncts. And since the *jīvas* are many, the distinction between bondage and release is recognized (*SLS*, vol. II, p. 28).

It is difficult to determine which of these theories Bhāratītīrtha favours. By his assumption of the distinction between the bound and the released, and by his drawing a difference between the apparent world of dreams and the empirical world of everyday existence, it would appear that he supports the view of many *jīvas*. In the *Tattvaviveka*, he declares that the *jīvas* are many because of the difference in the grades of impurity present in *avidyā* (*PD* I.17). The *jīvas* are of many kinds, the *devas*, humans, sub-humans, etc.

At one place in the *Vivaraṇa-Prameya-Saṁgraha*, however, Bhāratītīrtha writes as one who maintains the view of a single self.[9] If he be asked how, then, could there be the distinction between the bound and the released, he replies: You who ask of me about the distinction between bondage and release, *you alone* are the self, the one consistency of intelligence; all *jīvas*, other than you whether already released, being released or to be released, are posited by your nescience, as in dreams. Scripture, no doubt, declares about the release of Vāmadeva, etc.; but it has the purport of praising *Brahman*-knowledge. And this being the case, there is no room for doubt as for whom there are bondage and release whether in the state of transmigration or in the state of release. Thus, in the sight of each person, he alone is the self, all others being illusorily posited by his nescience. As for the non-recollection of the happiness, misery, etc. of one individual by another, that is due to the difference of bodies; for in the case of even a single self non-recollection is seen in respect of past bodies (*VPS*, p. 265).

---

9 *VPS*, p. 243. The *vivaraṇakāra* is believed to have advocated the view of one *jīva*. Hence, Bhāratītīrtha's leanings to this view in the *Vivaraṇa-Prameya-Saṁgraha*.

This view of Bhāratītīrtha borders on solipsism. We have already seen how in interpreting the *Bṛhadāraṇyaka Upaniṣad* "For the love of the self everything is dear", etc. he dangerously comes near subjectivism. But one feels on reading Bhāratītīrtha's works that he is not a subjectivist. The difficulty of expounding Advaita arises when one has to speak from two levels of reality. From the standpoint of the Absolute, there is no world and no *jīva*. Hence, the question about the number of *jīva*s does not arise there. But from the empirical point of view, difference of *jīva*s has to be acknowledged. The subjectivistic and solipsistic tendencies in Bhāratītīrtha are adventitious and not essential. Even in the passage we quoted above, he does not style himself as Eka-jīva-vādin. He purports to say that the self which is of one consistency of intelligence is single and that all *jīva*s are posited by nescience; and this self he identifies with the real self of his interlocutor.

In explaining the view of a single *jīva* with many distinctive bodies (Saviśeṣāneka-śarīraika-jīva-vāda), Appayya Dīkṣita takes the illustration of the artistically worked cloth from the *Citradīpa*. From this it may be surmised that Bhāratītīrtha is an upholder of the doctrine of one *jīva*. But there is no evidence for this in the *Citradīpa*. Hiraṇyagarbha is not described there as the principal *jīva*. He is defined as the inner self conjoined to the subtle bodies of all beings. The *jīva*s are called reflections of intelligence (*cidābhāsāḥ*) and not apparent *jīva*s (*jīvābhāsāḥ*). They are compared to the human figures with apparent clothes on sketched on the canvas in order to distinguish them from non-intelligent things.

Relation between Jīva and Īśvara

How are the Lord or *Brahman*[10] and the *jīva* related? Are they different from each other? Or is there a relation of difference-cum-non-difference between them? Or are they non-different?

---

10 *Īśvara*, as we said, is but *Brahman* qualified by *māyā*.

There cannot be real difference between the Lord and the *jīva*, since perception, etc. are not evidence therefor (*VPS*, p. 242). Perception is not the evidence, since the *jīva* and the Lord are super-sensuous (*VPS*, p. 265). Perception is dependent on sense-contact and sense-contact is not possible either with the *jīva* or with *Īśvara*. Nor can the mind without the help of sense-contact apprehend the difference between the Lord and the *jīva*, since it is an auxiliary to *pramāṇa* and not an independent means of valid knowledge. Similarly, inference is not an evidence for the difference of the *jīva* from the Lord. The Advaitin admits empirical difference caused by nescience; and hence no purpose would be served by an inference which establishes adventitious difference. As for real difference, that is not possible to be inferred, since there is inertness as an extraneous adjunct conditioning all inferences formulated for establishing the difference of the self. Nor is presumption an evidence in respect of difference, since there is nothing unintelligible in the absence of real difference. If the Lord were really different from the *jīva*, there would result non-selfhood for him. Nor does non-cognition establish the difference of the *jīva* from the Lord. For *anupalabdhi* (non-cognition) to be possible, the mind must have the non-cognition of what is capable of being cognized; but the Lord is not capable of being cognized by the mind.[11] The evidence of scripture is definitely against difference. Śruti condemns difference in such texts like:

> Then, he who worships a different God, saying "He is different, I am different", he does not know.
>
> – *VPS*, p. 241; *BṛUp* I.vi.10

> From death to death he goes who sees difference here as it were.

and

> There are no differents whatever here. – *BṛUp* IV.iv.19

[11] For a fuller criticism of difference, see *Bheda Dhikkāra*.

The Bhedābhedavādins say that there is difference-cum-non-difference between the *jīva* and *Brahman* because of such sacred teaching as "He who stands within the self", "This that is within all is thyself" (*BṛUp* III.iv.1), etc. But they have to state whether the difference between the *jīva* and *Brahman* is removed by knowledge or not. If the difference be not removed, there would be no release. If it be removed, then, what is that knowledge which removes it? It cannot be such knowledge as has difference-cum-non-difference for content; for that knowledge cannot remove difference which is a part of its own content. If it be said that some other knowledge having non-difference alone for content removes difference, then, what is the means of valid knowledge which originates the knowledge of non-difference? The sacred teaching cannot be the originator thereof, since, in the view of the Bhedābhedavādin, it has for content difference-cum-non-difference. Even admitting that there is somehow the generation of the knowledge of non-difference, there would be illusoriness for difference, if removable by knowledge. Nor may it be said that while ignorance is removed by knowledge, difference perishes through ritual acts alone; for scripture declares that the removal of difference is caused by knowledge in "He who knows *Brahman* becomes *Brahman* itself" (*MuṇḍUp* III.ii.9). Then it may be thought that there is no illusoriness for difference, though removable by knowledge, as for the antecedent non-existence of knowledge which also vanishes with the dawn of knowledge. Even thus, how are there both difference and non-difference of the *jīva* from *Brahman*? Is the *jīva* non-different from *Brahman* through that aspect in respect of which there is difference, or through some other aspect? On the first alternative, non-difference too would be removed on the removal of difference, because the aspect which determines difference is identical with that which conditions non-difference. On the second, ritualistic acts cannot remove the difference which is an attribute of the *jīva* that is of the nature of the partless *Brahman*. It may be said that the difference is discarded through knowledge. But even then, if the *jīva* be qualified *per accidens* by that difference, then the *jīva* would be no other than *Brahman*; and thus there would be no place for the relation of difference-cum-non-difference. If, on the other hand, difference be an essential attribute of the *jīva*, then, when difference is destroyed, the *jīva* too would perish. It may be said that, even though the qualified form as the *jīva* may perish, the *jīva* in the aspect of the substrate of the qualification remains to enjoy release consisting in identity with *Brahman*. But then it must be logically admitted that even in the stage of transmigration the *jīva* is that same substrate-aspect, which has attained identity with *Brahman*; for that which is the locus of release cannot be different from that which is the locus of transmigration. It is not that one self transmigrates while another is released. Hence, difference is not essential to the *jīva*. Scripture does not support the view of difference-cum-non-difference. It condemns, instead, difference and declares non-difference in such texts as "It is to be seen as one alone" (*BṛUp* IV.iv.20), "Other than this there is no seer" (*VPS*, p. 231; *BṛUp* III.vii.23), etc. The Bhedābhedavādins wrongly cite such scriptural texts as "He who stands within the self", etc. in support of their view. These passages do not declare difference-cum-non-difference. On the contrary, they teach non-difference after restating the difference established through delusion (*VPS*, p. 232).

In order that the eternal release of *Brahman* may be distinguished from the eternal bondage of the *jīva*, the *jīva* is declared to be different and non-different from *Brahman*. If there be absolute non-difference, it is asked, how could *Brahman* itself create the world for its own transmigration? How could the pure become impure (*VPS*, pp. 241-42)?

Before an answer can be given to this question, it is necessary to consider critically the concept of difference-cum-non-difference. Difference-cum-non-difference is possible only where there is either the relation of the general and the particular, or the relation of quality and the possessor of the quality, or the relation of effect and cause, or the relation of the qualified and the pure, or the relation of part and whole. But none of these relations is intelligible as between the *jīva* and *Brahman*. It may be said that there is the relation of part and whole, because of the traditional code "In the world of *jīva*s, a part of me alone" (*BhG* XV. 7) and the scriptural text "All beings are a quarter of him" (*ChāUp* II.vii.6). But, no. The scriptural passage "Without *kala*s" (*ŚvetUp* VI.19) declares that the self is partless; and the traditional code and Śruti text quoted above assert the littleness of the *jīva* in order to declare the infinitude of *Brahman*. Indeed, if *Brahman* have parts, it would be mutable like a pot which is created by the parts. This defect may be overcome by regarding "having parts" as due to adjuncts like the intellect. But even then, real difference would not be established. Verily, the edge of a razor cannot really cut the partless ether. The internal organ, etc. are not capable of really differentiating *Brahman* from the *jīva*; for it is inconceivable how *Brahman* could create adjuncts for its own evil. It cannot be said that the creation of adjuncts is for the sake of the *jīva*, for prior to that creation there is not established the difference of *jīva* from *Brahman*. *Karma*, nescience and residual impression cannot be the cause of differentiation, because they are not adjuncts of the *jīva*. It is only the internal organ which is a substance that is an adjunct of the *jīva* (*VPS*, p. 242).

It may be thought that difference and non-difference between the *jīva* and *Brahman* are similar to the difference and non-difference that exist between, say, a blue lily and an yellow fruit. Though difference is natural between the lily and the fruit, they are non-different in their generic nature as substances. But this way of thinking is not valid. Between the *jīva* and *Brahman* there is declared apposition in "This self is *Brahman*". Such an apposition is not possible between the lily and the fruit. It would be absurd to say "The blue lily is the yellow fruit". However much he may try, the Bhedābhedavādin will not be able to make his position intelligible. Difference conditioned by adjuncts is superimposed on *Brahman*, and hence it is only a delusion. It cannot be maintained by him who holds the view of difference-cum-non-difference that the assumption of difference is for making the distinction between being a transmigrator and not being a transmigrator intelligible; for non-difference too being accepted by him the non-distinction continues as before. If he declares that the distinction is stated in dependence on the aspect of difference, then, even the Advaitin could easily explain the distinction as due to the conjunction and non-conjunction of nescience, etc. with *Brahman*. Nor may it be said that the existence and non-existence of conjunction in respect of one and the same thing are unintelligible; for the Bhedābhedavādin admits the existence and non-existence of difference in one and the same place. Even if non-difference be but oneness, difference and non-difference in one and the same place are certainly contradictory. It is said that though the *jīva* that is a part is a transmigrator, there is not that character for *Brahman*, the whole. But such a view is quite irrational. How can the transmigratoriness of the part remain without affecting the character of the whole? Hence, the very ground for postulating the view of difference-cum-non-difference is slippery.

It was said by the Bhedābhedavādin that if there were absolute non-difference, impurity consisting in transmigration would have to be predicated of *Brahman*. But he is himself unwittingly involved in the defect he wishes to avoid. On his view, there can be no non-transmigratoriness for *Brahman*. On the contrary, being non-different from all *jīva*s and all worlds, *Brahman* would itself be the repository of the entire host of defects. On the view of the Advaitin, however, in *Brahman* there is not any defect; the pure does never become impure. The darkness, etc. of the reflection, verily, do not belong to the prototype. Difference between *Brahman* and the *jīva* is not envisaged by scripture. Besides condemning difference, it declares non-difference in such texts like "This is thy self, the internal ruler, immortal" (*BṛUp* III.vii.3; *VPS*, pp. 242-43).

Pratibimbavāda and Avacchedavāda

Although all Advaitins subscribe to the doctrine of non-difference – otherwise they would cease to be Advaitins – they differ in the mode of expounding the doctrine. Some of them consider both the Lord and the *jīva* to be reflections of *Brahman*. Some others regard the Lord as the prototype and the *jīva* as his reflection. Still others hold the *jīva* to be intelligence defined by nescience. Yet others maintain that the *jīva* is neither a reflection nor nescience-defined-intelligence but that it is *Brahman* which has forgotten its infinitude. Bhāratītīrtha records some of these views at the end of the seventh *varṇaka* (section) in the *Vivaraṇa-Prameya-Saṁgraha*, following the *vivaraṇakāra* and says that all of them are final positions. Some Advaitins, he declares, draw a distinction between *māyā* and *avidyā*, regard *Brahman*, which is in the position of the prototype and endowed with the energy of *māyā*, as the cause and the *jīva*s as reflections, each separately conditioned by *avidyā*. Some others, without making a difference between *māyā* and *avidyā*, hold that the pure *Brahman* reflected in *māyā* is the cause and that the *jīva*s are bound by *avidyā*. The author of the *Brahmasiddhi* advocates a subjectivistic view. According to him, the *jīva*s themselves create the world due to delusion. They are separately deluded in respect of *Brahman* envisaging it as of the form of the world, because of their own nescience. Their worlds correspond and are not identical. Each *jīva* is circumscribed by its own creation. Each one is involved in a circular panorama. *Brahman*, however, is spoken of as the cause figuratively, because it is the substrate of the world. There is also another way in which the subjectivistic view is set forth. *Brahman* alone through its own *avidyā* is said to manifest itself illusorily in the form of the world, as in dreams, etc. (*VPS*, pp. 224-25).

Among post-Śaṅkara Advaitins, there has arisen a controversy over the way in which the *jīva* is to be regarded. The Pratibimbavāda, favoured by the *vivaraṇakāra* and endorsed by Bhāratītīrtha in the *Vivaraṇa-Prameya-Saṁgraha*, declares the *jīva* to be the reflection of *Brahman* which as the prototype is *Īśvara*. The Avacchedavāda which is ascribed to Vācaspati and those of his way of thinking regards the *jīva* as intelligence defined by nescience. Śaṅkara uses the analogy of reflection and that of pot-defined ether in order to make clear the adventitious nature of *jīvatva*. To his mind there seems to have been no discrepancy between regarding the *jīva* as a reflection and considering it to be nescience defined intelligence. Those who came after him, however, strained the analogies and ranked themselves either as Pratibimbavādins or as Avacchedavādins.

This is how the *Vivaraṇa* view is explained: the *jīva* is a reflection of intelligence present in egoity; and since there is no difference between the prototype and the reflection, the *jīva* is non-different from *Brahman*. The reflected face in a mirror, for example, is not other than the prototype. It is identical with the original face, with certain traits such as facing oneself, being located in the mirror, etc. superimposed thereon. The experienced difference between what is present on one's shoulders and what is present in the mirror is sublated by the recollection of oneness in the form "This face is mine". Further, if there were difference, reflection would be impossible. What is called reflection is neither a seal imposed on the mirror by the face, nor is it a transformation of the very parts of the mirror, due to the proximity of the prototype. The reflection is not a seal, because it is not always seen that the prototype and the reflection are of the same size and because there is no conjunction between the face and the mirror. And it is not a transformation of the parts of the mirror, because of the contingence of the continuance of that reflection, even on the removal of the prototype which is the efficient cause. Moreover, merely because of the proximity of the face, the parts of the mirror cannot get transformed into the form of the face; otherwise, a sculptor, when he wants to fashion an image out of mirror-material, would only bring the prototype into the proximity of a mirror, instead of engaging in such activities as chiselling, etc. Further, the transformation in the form of a facial reflection is not sound, because when the mirror is felt through touch by the hand, it is an even surface that is cognized and not the condition of having depressions and prominences like the eyes, the nose, etc. Hence, there is not another face in the mirror. It is the prototype that appears as if in the mirror. And it is the location of the reflection in the mirror, etc. that are illusory and not the reflection itself (*VPS*, pp. 65-67).

The Advaita-vidyācārya, who does not brook the identification of the reflection with the prototype, maintains that the reflection is but a creation. He says that children and savages look for a face behind the mirror. They do not cognize the reflection to be identical with the prototype. The sublating cognition denies not merely the location of the original face in the mirror; it makes known the unreality of the reflection. The *ācārya* goes on to attribute a theory to the advocates of the *Vivaraṇa* view, which theory, however, finds no support in the *Vivaraṇa-Prameya-Saṁgraha.* In the *Siddhāntaleśa*, the followers of the *Vivaraṇa* are made to say that "in reflection, rays of light proceeding from the eyes of the observer are turned back by the reflecting medium, go back to the prototype face and apprehend it" (*SLS*, vol. I, p. 33). This is certainly an implausible theory; and it comes in for rightful criticism. But Bhāratītīrtha himself, who was an adherent of the *Vivaraṇa* view or at least an exponent thereof in the *Vivaraṇa-Prameya-Saṁgraha*, seems to reject this theory. He says (*VPS*, p. 67) that those, who think that there is no reflection at all and that the rays from the eyes reflected by the mirror turn back and apprehend the prototype itself as non-discriminated from the mirror, are in the wrong. They are to be refuted, he adds, even by the patent experience of the reflection facing oneself, etc. Though the simultaneous existence of the face in two different places is impossible, it can be intelligibly explained by regarding the existence in the mirror as a product of *māyā*.

A more formidable objection against the Pratibimbavāda is the impossibility of a reflection of intelligence. How can the colourless, non-material *Brahman* be reflected in a colourless medium, i.e. nescience? Bhāratītīrtha replies that the reflection of even the non-material is possible just as the non-material ether as qualified by the clouds, stars, etc. located in itself, is reflected in water. Of pure *Brahman*, however, there is no reflection; reflection is predicated of *Brahman* only as qualified by *māyā*. There is also evidence for the *jīva* being a reflection. Scripture declares, "It became the reflection of each form" (*BṛUp* II.V.19; *KaṭhaUp* V.ix.10); the traditional code proclaims, "It is seen as one and as many, like the moon in water" (*Brahmabindu* 12); and in the *Vedāntasūtra* we read, "For the same reason there is the comparison to the reflection of the sun, etc." (*VedSū* III.ii. 19; *VPS*, p. 68).

Incidentally, there is a criticism in the *Vivaraṇa-Prameya-Saṁgraha* of the *avaccheda* view. If the *jīva*, like pot-ether, be defined by an adjunct, it is asked, does *Brahman* too exist in the midst of the adjunct of the *jīva*, or does it not? If it existed, there would be a duplication of intelligence in the adjunct of the *jīva*. But no such duplication is seen in the case of the ether in the pot. And if *Brahman* be non-existent in the adjunct, it would cease to be the omnipresent controller of all. Therefore, the *jīva* is not defined by an adjunct like pot-ether. The example of pot-ether is given in the sacred teaching in order that the non-attachedness of the self may be understood. Scripture has no purport in establishing the *jīva*-hood of the defined. The duplicated existence of intelligence, however, is not a defect on the view of the *jīva* as a reflection. Just as in the midst of knee-deep water there exists both the natural ether that is of the volume of the water and the reflected expansive ether, in the adjunct of the *jīva*, viz. egoity, there may intelligibly be present both the original and the reflected intelligence. Thus, the *Vivaraṇa* view is that the reflection is of the nature of the real prototype and that illusoriness belongs to the character of being a reflection and of the difference, error, etc. which bring about that character (*VPS*, pp. 68-69).

There is a criticism of the Avacchedavāda in the *Pañcadaśī*. The Avacchedavādin believes that there is no need for assuming a reflection of intelligence. The immutable defined by the intellect is the *jīva*. Just as movement, etc. which really belong to the pot are superimposed on the ether defined by the pot, the departure from and the advent into the world, which are in truth conditioned by the movement of the mind, are illusorily attributed to the intelligence defined by the intellect. When, thus, it is possible to account for the migrations and misery of the *jīva* through the mere limitation brought about by the adjunct, viz. intellect, it is prolix, says the Avacchedavādin, to assume a reflection of intelligence. But Bhāratītīrtha would not agree to this view. If bare definition be the cause of *jīvatva*, then, even the intelligence defined by pot, etc. would be *jīva*. The unattached self does not become the *jīva* through bare definition or limitation; otherwise, even hills and dales would be *jīva*s and there would be no distinction between the living and the non-living. Nor may it be said that the intellect differs from pot, etc. in being clear and pure; for as defining adjuncts they are not really different from the latter. Rice-grains may be measured out either by a vessel made of wood or by one made of metal. In either case it makes no difference to the measuring out of the rice-grains. We do not get more rice in the one and less in the other. Similarly, the self is conditioned equally by the intellect and by other adjuncts like pot, etc. There is no distinction whatever in the matter of defining or limiting the self. Thus, if the definition of the self by the intellect be what constitutes *jīva*-hood, then, it may be said with equal validity that even such extraneous adjuncts like pot, etc. convert the self into the *jīva*.

The Avacchedavādin may maintain that in the example of measuring out the rice-grains, though the two vessels equally and without any difference whatever measure out the grains, there is this distinction between them, that while the wooden vessel has no capacity for reflection, the one made of metal has. But this is a contingence of the acceptable. While the non-intelligent objects like pot, etc. do not have the capacity to reflect, the intellect, the adjunct of the *jīva*, has; and it is this reflection of intelligence that is distinctive of *jīvatva*. Hence, mere definition of the self does not invest it with *jīva*-hood. Where the adjunct is the intellect, there the self is reflected; and this reflection of intelligence is what is known as the *jīva* (*PD* VIII.27-31).

Much of what has been said against the *avaccheda* view is unconvincing. Arguments can be advanced even against the *pratibimba* view.[12] Some of them we have already seen and the replies given by the upholder of that view are hardly convincing. As we said, the controversy in question is artificial, since it makes too much of analogies, whose purport is only to illustrate the illusory nature of *jīvatva*.

In the *Pañcadaśī*, Bhāratītīrtha holds what is known as Ābhāsavāda which is a variety of the Pratibibavāda. While the *Vivaraṇa* view regards the reflection as real and identical with the prototype, according to the theory propounded in the *Pañcadaśī*, the *ābhāsa* is wholly illusory. It may be asked how there can be non-difference of the *jīva* from *Brahman*, if the former be totally unreal. To this it is replied that the apposition between the *jīva* and *Brahman* is through sublation. Bhāratītīrtha reduces even *Īśvara* to a reflection. The intelligence reflected in *māyā* is the Lord; and the intelligence reflected in *avidyā* is the *jīva*. The

12 See *SLS*, pp. 93f. for a detailed criticism of the Pratibimbavāda.

distinction between *māyā* and *avidyā* is this, that while in the former there is a predominance of pure *sattva*, in the latter there is a dominance of impure *sattva*.

The reflection theory may be advantageous insofar as it defines the relation of the *jīva* to *Brahman* clearly by employing a common analogy. But there is nothing to be said in favour of that variety of Pratibimbavāda which holds *Īśvara* too to be a reflection. If the Lord too were a reflection, there would be nothing to distinguish him from the *jīva*. He would be as helpless as the finite self. And since *Īśvara* also is a reflection, there would not be the relation of the controller and the controlled between him and the *jīva* (*SLS*, vol. I, pp. 39-40).

We had an occasion to point out that the view that the *jīva* is a mere reflection is adventitious in the *Pañcadaśī*. Bhāratītīrtha, in that work, struggles between two divergent views, the reflection theory which he adhered to in the *Vivaraṇa-Prameya-Saṁgraha* and the *avaccheda* view that he supports in the *Dṛg-Dṛśya-Viveka*. The example of the fourfold distinction in ether is an attempt to combine the theories of reflection and definition. Bhāratītīrtha compares the *kūṭastha* (immutable witness) to ether defined by pot and the *jīva* to the reflection of the sky in the pot-water. That this is a fruitless distinction, he soon recognizes and in the *Dṛg-Dṛśya-Viveka* he includes the immutable in the *jīva*-aspect and teaches only a threefold division of intelligence. There are three ways in which the *jīva* can be conceived: as intelligence defined by the internal organ, as the reflection of intelligence and as one posited by dreams. The first is the absolutely real *jīva* (*pāramārthika*) and for it alone there is apposition in the principal sense with *Brahman*. The other two are illusory and they are to be sublated. That the theory of *avaccheda* is considered by Bhāratītīrtha to be superior to the other two views is evident when he says that the scriptural texts like "That thou art" declare the identity of the defined *jīva* with the partless *Brahman* and not either of the apparent *jīva* or of the *jīva* posited by dream.[13]

Thus there would seem to be a gradual transition in the works of Bhāratītīrtha from the Pratibimbavāda to the Avacchedavāda. It does not really matter whether the example of the pot-defined ether be given or the analogy of reflection be cited. What the preceptors of Advaita aim at teaching is the non-difference of the *jīva* from *Brahman*.

---

13 *Dṛg-Dṛśya-Viveka*, *śl.* 32, 34.

8

Māyā

Brahman and Māyā

TRUTH, knowledge, infinitude is *Brahman*. Mutable, non-intelligent, finite and perishing is the world. *Brahman* is pure, attributeless, impartite and immutable. The world is a manifold of changing phenomena, fleeting events and finite things. *Brahman* is bliss. The universe is "a vale of tears". The problem for the Advaitin is to solve how from the pure *Brahman* the impure world of men and things came into existence. It is on this rock that most of the monistic systems break. The absolutist has to explain how the one became the many. In the previous chapter we found *Brahman* to be the material cause and the efficient cause of the universe. If *Brahman* be the cause of the world, will not the blemishes of the latter pertain to the former also? Will not the non-difference of *Brahman* be destroyed? Will not *Brahman* cease to be truth, intelligence, bliss? The answer to these questions was foreshadowed even in the seventh chapter. *Brahman* is neither the originating cause nor the transformed cause of the world. It illusorily appears as the world; and it suffers nothing by such appearance. The faults and foibles of the world cannot affect the purity of *Brahman*. The attributes of a serpent do not really belong to the rope. The rope remains in its own nature even at the time when it is mistaken for a snake. The impurities seen in the reflection do not spoil the prototype face. The world which is an illusory manifestation of *Brahman* has not the capacity to create discord and distress in the blissful self. But the Advaitin cannot make such an easy escape. It will not do if he stops with saying that *Brahman* appears as the world. He will have to account for the appearance. No inquirer into truth will be satisfied with the knowledge *that Brahman* illusorily appears as the world. In order that the system of Advaita may become intelligible, the upholder of that view has to state *how* the Real appears as the transitory world. Without the assumption of an extraneous principle which effects the illusory manifestation, it is not possible to account for the world-appearance. There must be admitted some principle or power which superimposes the manifold of sense on the supersensuous and supreme *Brahman*. This principle the Advaitin calls *prakṛti* (primal nature), *māyā* or *avidyā* (nescience).

Both *Brahman* and *māyā* cannot independently be the material causes of the world. Hence, we must combine the two and admit only one material cause. Three ways of combination are possible. Just as two strands conjoined together make a rope, *Brahman* and *māyā* are the material cause of the world, in a relation of equal primacy. The elements of reality and manifestation are caused by *Brahman*; and the elements of inertness and change are produced by *māyā*. Or, the potency of *māyā* alone may be characterized as the material cause. But, since potency always depends on the potent, it would have to be said presumptively that even *Brahman* that possesses the potency is the material cause. Or, since *Brahman* is the substrate of *māyā*, though material causality may belong directly to *māyā* alone, for *Brahman* too material causality cannot be avoided. Of these three views, the first maintains that material causality in the principal sense belongs to *Brahman* qualified by *māyā*; and the other two hold that it belongs to *māyā* alone. But on all the three views, *Brahman* is only figuratively the material cause.

Bhāratītīrtha records these views without stating his preference for any one of them (*VPS*, pp. 207-08).

Māyā and Avidyā

Some Advaitins draw a distinction between *māyā* and *avidyā*. Bhāratītīrtha in the *Pañcadaśī* distinguishes *avidyā*, the impure-*sattva*-predominant *prakṛti* from *māyā*, the pure-*sattva*-predominant *prakṛti*. The former is the adjunct of the *jīva* and the latter the adjunct of the Lord (*PD* I.16).

In the *Vivaraṇa-Prameya-Saṁgraha*, however, Bhāratītīrtha follows the *Vivaraṇa* tradition of not making any difference between *māyā* and nescience (*avidyā*). Those who want to maintain a difference argue thus: *māyā* is that which does not delude its abode and conforms to the desires of the agent; nescience is that which deludes its abode and does not conform to the desire of the agent. But, this distinction is not valid. It cannot be conclusively proved that in the case of *māyā* there is non-delusion of the abode. Viṣṇu, in his incarnation as Rāma, was deluded by his own *māyā*. Nor is it an invariable rule that nescience deludes its own abode; for he who sees the reflection of a tree in water is not deluded and does not doubt the uprightness of the tree. It may be said that, because the tree on the bank is seen, there is no delusion. But, in that case, even for him who performs a magical feat, there is non-delusion only because of his knowledge how to get out of the effects of his magic. The nature of *māyā*, however, is to delude. The spectators are deluded by the feat. If, indeed, they had the knowledge of the remedy, they too would certainly not be deluded. It was said that *māyā* does, while nescience does not, conform to the desire of the agent. But even this mode of distinction is not sound. In the case of *māyā*, the agent is independent only in respect of efficient causes such as spells and drugs. And that kind of conformity to desire is observed even in nescience. When the eye is pressed with the finger-tip, there is the delusive perception of two moons. He who sees two moons has perfect control over the efficient cause which originates the delusion. Hence, to distinguish between *māyā* and *avidyā* on the ground that they are to be defined differently is not rational. A common definition can be stated and it is this: while being indeterminable, *māyā* or *avidyā* is the cause of obstruction to the presentation of the true and of the presentation of the erroneous.[1]

Nor may it be said that the word *māyā* is applied only to real things like spells, drugs, etc. since spells, etc. are not called *māyā*. It is only the seen magical feat that is termed *māyā*, not the unseen spell, etc. which are the efficient cause. The spell, etc. which are real cannot be the material cause of the indeterminable magical feat. There must be assumed some beginningless, indeterminable material cause which is denoted by the word *māyā*; and the application of the same word to the effect, the magical feat, is intelligible because of the non-difference between the material cause and its effect. Hence, there is no point in distinguishing *māyā* from nescience on the ground that the former relates only to real things (*VPS*, p. 37).

Scripture in the text "Know *māyā* to be the primal cause" (*ŚvetUp* IV.10) declares that *māyā* is the material cause of all. In "Again, at the end there is the removal of the all *māyā*" (*ŚvetUp* I.10) nescience which is removable by right knowledge is denoted by the word *māyā*. And there is the express mention of the oneness of *māyā* and nescience in the traditional code:

> That, on whose entry into the heart, the *yogin* crosses over the extensive nescience, *māyā*, obeisance to that immeasurable one, who is of the nature of knowledge. – *VPS*, pp. 37-38

In empirical usage, however, there is a distinction made between *māyā* and nescience. But that is intelligible even in respect of one and the same thing as conditioned by different adjuncts.

---

[1] *VPS*, p. 37: *anirvacanīyatve sati tattvā-'vabhāsa-pratibandha-viparyayā-'vabhāsayor hetutvaṁ lakṣaṇam taccobhayor avśiṭam* ।

When *prakṛti* generates projection or when it conforms to the desire of the agent, it is called *māyā* in empirical usage. When it obscures or when it is independent of the agent's will, it is known as nescience. Apart from this adjunct-conditioned distinction, there is no difference between *māyā* and nescience (*VPS*, p. 38).

The Indeterminability of Māyā

We had occasion, in the second chapter, to study *māyā* from the epistemological standpoint. We found that error has for its material cause ignorance which is of the nature of an existent, beginningless and indeterminable. In the present chapter we shall take account of the metaphysical bearings of *māyā*.

Māyā can be studied from three different standpoints.[2] The man in the street considers the world of *māyā* to be real (*vāstavī*); he who is learned in scripture regards it as unreal (*tuccha*); and the metaphysician who mainly trusts the powers of his intellect maintains that it is neither real nor unreal (*anirvacanīyā*).

The ordinary run of mankind does not doubt the reality of the world. Common sense tells the man in the street that he is living in a world of realities. He does not question the veracity of what he sees. Being caught up in the meshes of *māyā*, from death to death he travels. The theorist of the First Look gives the man of the world a philosophical sanction for his unsophisticated view. He regards the finite particulars as absolutely real. Since a criticism of Realism is immanent in the sequel, we refrain from stating the arguments against that view here.

To the man who is endowed with scriptural learning, *māyā* is that which is not. As an illustration of the unreal nature of the world, a parable is related in the *Yoga-Vāsiṣṭha*. An old nurse once told her ward a fantastic fable for his amusement:

---

[2] *PD* VI.130:
tucchā 'nirvacanīyā ca vāstavī ce 'ty asau tridhā ।
jñeyā māyā tribhir bodhaiḥ śrauta-yauktika-laukikaiḥ ॥

> There were three handsome princes, two of them were not born and the other was not even in the womb of his mother. Virtuous by nature, they lived in a town which was absolutely non-existent. Leaving the city of void, they, who were endowed with clarity of mind, beheld on their way fruit-bearing trees flourishing in the sky. Then, after sporting in the forest, they lived happily in the land of the future. – *PD* XIII.22-26

The boy, who evinced a keen interest in the story related by the nurse, believed all that she had told him to be true. As the princes, their adventure and the future city appear to us to be mere creations of the nurse's imagination, so the existence of the visible world seems to the enlightened to be unreal and imaginary.

To the metaphysician, *māyā* is a riddle, a sphinx which is impervious to all attempts at probing into its nature. To logic, *māyā* is a puzzle. Wonder is its garment; inscrutable is its nature (*PD* VI.139). What is not possible to be defined or determined while being the object of clear perception is called *māyā* in empirical usage. People call that fact *māyā* which defies their rational powers. This world appears most clearly to our intellect; but its nature is beyond the possibility of comprehension. Inquiry into the nature of the world is a thankless task. Even the learned flounder and fail. They are at a loss to answer such questions as these: how from the vital fluid are the body, senses, etc. created? How do they become conscious? It cannot be said that it is natural for vitality to create body, senses, etc. since co-presence and co-absence do not exist between vitality and body, etc. Where there is impotence, no procreation is seen. In respect of problems like these, "I know not what" is the only last resort. Inquiry into the causal relations and connections of the facts of the world leads us into and not out of, ignorance. It may give us worldly knowledge; but it cannot lift us out of nescience. It is on account of the puzzling nature of the world that the wise compare it to the *fata morgana*. What greater magic is there than this world? The semen in the womb springs to consciousness; it is invested with various limbs; it passes through the stages of infancy, youth, old age, etc.; it eats, drinks, speaks, smells, hears and moves. Can there be a greater miracle than this? Like human organisms, even trees, etc. puzzle our wits. How tiny is the seed and how big the tree that comes out of it? Hence, the whole universe is *māyā*, indeterminable (*PD* VI.42-48).

Māyā is the power of *Brahman*. It cannot be really different from *Brahman*-intelligence, since, if it were really different, the scriptural texts declaring non-difference would be contradicted. Nor can it be non-different from the Absolute, since identity is not possible as between the intelligent and the inert. Nor can it be both different and non-different since contradictories like difference and non-difference cannot reside in one and the same thing. Similarly, *māyā* is not real, because of conflict with the scriptural declaration of non-difference. Nor is it unreal, because there would be no other primal cause of the world. It cannot be both real and unreal because of contradiction. *Māyā* is not possessed of parts. If it had parts, it would have a beginning and consequently, the Lord and the *jīva* who are reflections therein would come to have a beginning. Further, the *māyā* with a beginning would require another *māyā* as its cause, and thus there is the contingence of infinite regress. Nor is *māyā* partless, because of the contingence of its not being the primal cause. It is the cause, indeed, only of things which are constituted of parts. It cannot be both with parts and without parts, because of conflict. Hence, since it is not possible to determine the nature of *māyā* in terms of any of the human categories, it is called indeterminable (*anirvācyā*).[3]

As heat is to fire, *māyā* is to *Brahman*, neither different nor non-different from it. Heat which is the power of fire is not

---

3 Commentary on *SLS*, p. 67. See Bradley 1908: 511: "The fact of appearance and of the diversity of its particular spheres we found was inexplicable".

different from fire; nor is it identical therewith. If it were non-different from fire, then it must be found always therein. But we observe that fire does not burn, when it is influenced by spells (*PD* XIII.12). In the *Yoga-Vāsiṣṭha* we have a description of the power that is located in *Brahman*. The Supreme *Brahman* is eternal, full, non-dual and omnipotent. As waves are to the sea, so are the powers to *Brahman* which are neither identical with nor different from it.

> By whatever power the self is pleased, that power gets manifested. ... Observe, Rāma, how the power of intelligence which belongs to *Brahman* is found in the various bodies. There is in the winds the capacity to move; in the rocks there is manifested the power of immobility; there is fluidity in water and in fire the power to consume. In ether there is void, in perishable objects the power to get destroyed.[4] ... Just as within the shell of an egg there is a great serpent, even so in the self the world exists. Everything is located in *Brahman* as the tree with its roots and sprouts, leaves and branches, flowers and fruits exists potentially in the seed. ... As the earth produces its harvests according to the particular soil and season, so the powers that belong to *Brahman* manifest themselves differently in accordance with the difference in place and time.
>
> – *Yoga-Vāsiṣṭha* III. C.7-9, 11, 22; *PD* XIII.14-19

An objection that suggests itself to the critic is: how can there be an entity which is neither real nor unreal? A thing must be either real or unreal. The contradictory of the *sat* is *asat* and that of the latter is the former. The Advaitin's reply to this contention is: by stating that *māyā* is other than *sat* we do not predicate its unreality in the sense of empty nothingness. It is not real in the sense that it does not bide for ever. That alone is real which is not sublated at any time. *Māyā* is sublated by the light of wisdom. And so it cannot be real. Nor is it unreal in the

[4] Cf. Carlyle, Thomas, 1837, *The French Revolution*: "There is power in the rotting leaf; how else could it rot?"

sense of void. *Māyā* is existent but not real. Unreal the world is, non-existent it is not.

On the ground that it is inexplicable *māyā* cannot be denied. It is inferred from its product, viz. superimposition. Because of the unintelligibility otherwise of superimposition which is indeterminable, there is indeterminability of its material cause, *māyā*. And because of the unintelligibility otherwise of its being the primal cause, there is beginninglessness; and if it had a beginning, there would be the need for succession of material causes and a primal cause would not be established (*VSP*, p. 18). Thus, therefore, it is settled that the material cause of superimposition is nescience (*māyā*) which is beginningless, indeterminable and of the nature of an existent.

The Locus and Content of Māyā

What is the locus of *māyā* and what is its content? The *Vivaraṇa* view is that the Self is the locus and content of ignorance. Ignorance does not require the difference of locus from content, since it is not of the nature of an act. Its residence in and obscuration of one and the same self is intelligible, since it is an obscuring agent, like the darkness present in a room (*VSP*, p. 46). Nor may it be said that ignorance appears as located in the self as qualified by egoity and not as located in intelligence in general; for this appearance is an illusion. In empirical usage, we say "Iron burns"; but it is not really iron that burns. There is the appearance of reciprocal relation because of the relation of combustion and iron to the single fire. Similarly, both ignorance and the internal organ are related to the self; and hence, the appearance of apposition. In reality, however, ignorance is located in the self and not in the internal organ. Further, since the relation of the self to nescience is seen in sleep, even in the absence of the internal organ, the internal organ is not the locus of nescience. If it be said that the unattached intelligence being the locus of nescience is unintelligible, then, let the qualified intelligence be the locus. Even thus, location of ignorance in intelligence is difficult to avoid. The real unattachedness of intelligence is in no way affected, since its property of being the locus of ignorance is assumptive. Therefore, the locus of ignorance is intelligence in general. But ignorance is said to be located in the *jīva*, because of its leaning to the side of the *jīva* (*VPS*, p. 48).

Bhāskara holds that the internal organ alone is the locus of ignorance. But if the internal organ be the locus, then, there would be constant omniscience for the self. This, indeed, is not in the scope of what is experienced. And if the self is non-omniscient, then since at some time it does not know something, ignorance is certainly admitted therein. Bhāskara may think that though non-apprehension and illusory cognition be located in the self, ignorance which is of the nature of an existent is located in the internal organ. Even then, what is meant by ignorance? Is it merely what is other than knowledge? Or is it what is opposed to knowledge? On the first, it would be a defect like the film in the eye, jaundice, etc. On the second, it would be removable by knowledge. But how is the removal of ignorance located in the internal organ by the knowledge located in the self possible? Verily, Yajñadatta's ignorance of a certain thing is not removed by the knowledge thereof present in Devadatta. Therefore, the self, and not the internal organ, is the locus of ignorance (*VPS*, p. 48).

It may be urged that the location of nescience in the self which is of the nature of luminosity is self-contradictory. But is the conflict in what is of the nature of luminosity being the locus of ignorance experienced or inferred? Experience presents no conflict. Ignorance is established by the witness-intelligence. And in the form "I am ignorant" the self being the locus is experienced. Nor is the conflict inferred. The self's manifestation is not the ground of its not being the locus of ignorance. The opponents of Advaita, who maintain that the self is manifested by originated cognition, have to admit that it is the locus of ignorance. Otherwise there is the contingence of omniscience at the instant the self is manifested. The self, it may be said, is of a nature opposed to ignorance, because of luminosity, like a psychosis of the internal organ. But this inference is not valid, since there is inconstancy in respect of the manifestation that manifests ignorance. Nor may it be argued that the self is opposed to conjunction with ignorance, since it is self-luminous, like the consciousness acceptable to the Prābhākaras; for, there is no example, the consciousness being itself the self (*VPS*, p. 46).

If *Brahman* be the locus of nescience, how can there be for it omniscience, etc.? We have already said that the property of being the locus is only assumptive. There is oneness between the prototype and the reflection (according to the *Vivaraṇa* view); but though the darkness, etc. present in an impure mirror be superimposed on the reflection, they do not destroy the fairness of the prototype. Similarly, though the *jīva* be the locus of nescience, *Brahman*'s omniscience would remain unhindered. Reason, we said, cannot account for the presence of *māyā* in the self. But still, as Viśvarūpācārya says, since nescience is well established, it cannot be denied (*VPS*, pp. 46, 49).

Is *māyā* located in the whole of *Brahman*? Or only in a part? It cannot cover the whole of *Brahman*, since the *jñānin*'s realization is of the *māyā*-less *Brahman*. If it be held that *māyā* occupies a part of *Brahman*, then, does the space occupied by nescience belong to *Brahman* as its part? Is that spatial attribute real? Or is it an unreal superimposition? If it be real, scripture which declares that *Brahman* is partless would be invalidated and *Brahman* itself would be finitized. If it be a superimposition, is it of the nature of the gross and subtle universe, or of the nature of the *jīva* and *Īśvara*? Is it to be characterized as time, as void or as *māyā*? Or is it something other than these six categories? The spatial attribute of *māyā* cannot be identified with the universe which is but a product of nescience. Nor can it be of the nature of the *jīva* and the Lord who are conditioned by *māyā*. Nor is it time which is a manifestation of nescience, nor *śūnya* which is mere void. It is not of the nature of *māyā*, since, then, there would result logical fallacies culminating in infinite regress. And as there is no other alternative, with nothing else can the spatial attribute be identified. Hence, space cannot even be superimposed on the spaceless *Brahman*. But from the point of view of empirical existence, *māyā* must be regarded as residing only in a part of *Brahman*. The Veda declares that all beings, sentient and non-sentient, constitute but a quarter of *Brahman*, three quarters remaining unobscured and self-effulgent. In the *Gītā*, Śrī Kṛṣṇa observes that he supports the entire universe by a portion of himself (*BLG* X.52). "Pervading the whole world, He is ten inches in excess" (*ŚvetUp* III.14). And the *Vedāntasūtra* IV.iv.19 tells us, "*Brahman* transcends the cosmos which is but a product, a modification". Though *Brahman* is partless and indivisible, it seems as if divided and possessed of parts. This is due to the superimposition effected by *māyā*. Scripture answers him, who asks whether *māyā* is located in the whole or a part of *Brahman*, in his own language, imposing particularities on the impartite Reality (*PD* II.54-58).

Now, though the self-luminous intelligence be the locus of nescience, how is it the content of nescience? How can that which is constantly manifest be the content of ignorance? In respect of a pot which is manifest to us we do not plead ignorance. The self which is ever luminous, how can it be enshrouded in *māyā*? Can darkness cover the effulgent sun? To this objection, the Advaitin replies: a thing that is revealed by a means of valid knowledge is not a content of ignorance, since a means of valid knowledge is that which removes ignorance. A pot that is perceived through the senses is not the content of ignorance, because it is revealed by a *pramāṇa*. But that which is known by the witness-perception, whether it be pot, etc. or intelligence itself, can intelligibly be the content of ignorance. The witness-intelligence does not remove ignorance. On the other hand, it is what establishes that ignorance. In spite of opposition to all evidences and reasonings, we accept the existence of ignorance, because it is revealed by the witness. *Māyā* does not brook inquiry, as darkness the sun. And not brooking inquiry is an ornament to, and not a defect in, nescience. Thus, it is settled that *māyā*, while residing in the self, obscures it also (*VPS*, pp. 49-50).

Māyā Obscures the Self and not the Not-self

Māyā has two aspects: obscuring (*āvaraṇa*) and projective (*vikṣepa*). It obscures the self and projects the world. But does it obscure the not-self too? Or does it not obscure? For the obscuration of the not-self there is neither evidence nor fruit. The evidence for the obscuration should be stated in the form "This object, say, pot, is obscured by ignorance"; and this form should be apprehended by a *pramāṇa*. But that is not possible, when there is cognition of pot as well as its non-cognition. Even in such empirical usage as "I know not the thing stated by you" there is not experienced ignorance as relating to an object. Objects of ignorance and their relations are superimposed on the witness-intelligence and are experienced by it. There is between ignorance and the object the relation of cause and effect, and not the relation of obscurer and that which is obscured; for obscuration is not possible in the case of what has been superimposed. There is no obscuration at the time when the object is cognized; and no time there is when it is not-cognized, since what is superimposed, like the two moons, etc. is constituted of the cognition alone. If obscuration be admitted in the case of what is superimposed, then nowhere would there be its presentation; for, the superimposed, not being within the sphere of *pramāṇas*, its obscuration would not be removed. That which is knowable by a *pramāṇa* may, because of being real, somehow be obscured. But that which is removable by a *pramāṇa*, how can there be obscuration for it? The not-self, which is the superimposed, is removable by a *pramāṇa*. Hence, there is no evidence for the obscuration of the not-self (*VPS*, pp. 18-19).

The fruit too is difficult to demonstrate. Obscuration has the fruit of obstructing a contingent luminosity. But, there is no contingence of luminosity of itself in the not-self, because it is inert. Nor is there the contingence of luminosity on the strength of a *pramāṇa*, since obscuration, which is removable by a *pramāṇa*, cannot serve as an obstacle either to the *pramāṇa* or to the luminosity caused thereby. Nor may it be said that there is a contingent luminosity in the not-self on the strength of intelligence; for when obstruction results even from the obscuration of intelligence, it is futile to assume a distinct obscuration in respect of the not-self. If it be admitted that one and the same ignorance which is located in the self obscures the not-self, then, when there are the manifestation of even a single object and consequent removal of ignorance, there is the contingence of immediate release for all. As for assuming a different ignorance for every object, that is without any ground. If in the desire to remedy the contingence of immediate release differences of ignorance for every object be admitted, there would result prolixity of assumptions. Therefore, the view that the not-self too is obscured cannot bear reasoning (*VPS*, p. 19).

Now, what is meant by obscuration of the self? Is it destruction of luminosity? Or is it an obstruction to luminosity in its function of producing the manifestedness of the object? Or is it the expectancy of some other auxiliary without which that production is not possible? Not the first, since luminosity which is the essential nature of the eternal self cannot be destroyed. Nor are the second and the third alternatives possible. What the object requires is only the luminosity of intelligence manifested by the psychosis of the internal organ. Apart from this, there is no need to admit a separate manifestedness. Thus, it may be argued that obscuration even in respect of the self is difficult to demonstrate. The Advaitin recognizes the futility of the task of determining the nature of obscuration. It is because of this that he characterizes nescience as being indeterminable. But merely because of the difficulty of demonstration, nescience cannot be denied. It is inferred even from the empirical usage of ignorant folk who say, "A true self, which is above appetite, etc. and known to the discriminating, does not exist; it is not manifest." Such an empirical usage is not possible without the self being obscured. Thus, while obscuring the self, *māyā* projects the not-self without obscuring it.

The Possibility of Superimposition

The projective power of *māyā* superimposes the unreal on the real, the not-self on the self. In order that superimposition may be possible, there must be

1. the residual impression brought about by the cognition of a real object,
2. defect in the object of knowledge,
3. defect in the cognizer,
4. defect in the instrument of valid knowledge, and
5. a knowledge of the general nature alone of the substrate without a knowledge of its particularities.

Silver is superimposed on nacre not by him who has never seen silver before, but only by him who has seen real silver elsewhere. In order that silver may be superimposed on nacre, one must possess the residual impression caused by the prior knowledge of real silver. A serpent is not superimposed on nacre; nor is silver imposed on a rope. There must be similarity between the substrate of superimposition and what is superimposed thereon, i.e. there must be some defect in the object of erroneous cognition. Further, there must also be in the subject who superimposes such defects like desire to possess silver and in the instruments of knowledge like the sense of sight such defects like jaundice, etc. And finally, the substrate must be cognized in its general nature and its particularities must remain obscured. What is seen in front must be cognized as "this", and not as "nacre". If nacre be not apprehended even as "this", there would be no superimposition. Nor would there be superimposition if what is in front be cognized as nacre.

Now, in the case of the self, asks the opponent of Advaita, how can there be superimposition, since none of the causes thereof exists? The first condition of superimposition requires that he who superimposes must possess the residual impression of his prior cognition of a real object which is now by him superimposed. What is imposed on the self, according to the Advaitin, is the host of bondage consisting of egoity, etc. But egoity, etc. are not real. Hence, how can there be the residual impression caused by a cognition thereof? To this objection the Advaitin's reply is: what is required for superimposition is the residual impression of the prior cognition of the thing which is superimposed. But that thing which was cognized earlier need not be real. Even the residual impression of an illusory object may serve as a cause of superimposition. It is not necessary that one should have seen a real snake before mistaking a rope for a snake. It is enough even if one has seen an illusory snake produced by magic. Hence, there is no rule that the residual impression generated by a *pramāṇa* is an adjunct but not one generated by delusion (*VPS*, p. 70). And the residual impression of egoity, etc. is easily established because the stream of transmigration is beginningless (*VPS*, p. 52). The body, etc. which are presented in each earlier superimposition and persist in the form of residual impressions, are the cause of each subsequent superimposition.

Nor may it be said that, because of the unreality of egoity, body, etc. there can be no imposition of them; for, they are imposed even because of the bare cognition of them, and so, their reality is not a cause of the superimposition. Indeed, in the case of the illusory cognition of nacre-silver, what is superimposed is the identity of the real and the non-real, the nacre and the silver (*VPS*, p. 14).

Defect, we saw, is of three kinds: similarity, etc. present in the object, obscuring film, etc. present in the instrument and desire, etc. present in the seer. Without defect, superimposition is not possible. But in the case of the superimposition of egoity, etc. the self itself is in the position of all the three called object, instrument and the seer, since everything else falls under the category of the superimposed. And in respect of the non-dual self of undefiled nature, predication of defects is not possible. Hence, how can there be the imposition of egoity, etc. thereon (*VPS*, p. 43)?

To this the reply is: even in the flawless, non-dual self, there is the defect which is called nescience. It is of the nature of the non-real, and the evidence therefor is the scriptural text:

> Just as those who do not know the land, though repeatedly passing over the hidden treasure of gold, do not attain it, even so all these people go to *brahmaloka* day after day, but do not attain it, being obstructed by the non-real (nescience).
>
> – *ChāUp* VIII.iii.2

From this passage we understand that at the time of sleep there is non-manifestation of *Brahman*-intelligence, because there is the veil of nescience which is of the nature of the non-real (*VPS*, p. 45).

Now, the causal aggregate of superimposition is the similarity created by the qualities or parts of the substrate and of the superimposed. Silver is imposed on nacre because of its similarity thereto. But there is no similarity whatever between the self and the not-self which are opposed to each other like light and darkness. Hence, it is asked, how is superimposition of egoity, etc. on the self possible? The Advaitin's reply to this contention is that the superimposition of agency, etc. on the self is due to the external adjunct, egoity. And in the case of a delusion due to an extraneous adjunct there is no need of similarity. The redness of the hibiscus flower is imposed on crystal without there being the least similarity between the flower and the crystal. It may be said that, even though the superimposition of agency, etc. be somehow possible, the imposition on the self of substrates like egoity, etc. which is without extraneous adjuncts, is unintelligible. But this is not so. Similarity is possible for the self with egoity, etc. through the attribute of being "the import of a word". If it be said that the self can have no attribute, then, let not similarity be the causal aggregate in respect even of the delusion not due to adjuncts. The delusion "The conch is yellow", which is not due to adjuncts, is brought about without any similarity between the conch and yellow. There is, of course, in this case the defect due to excess of bile in the cognizer. But similarly, in the self, we found, there exists the defect, viz. nescience, which is the cause of all superimposition (*VPS*, p. 13).

The substrate of superimposition, it was pointed out, is that which is apprehended in its generality, but not apprehended in its particularity. But how can the self which has neither generality nor particularity be the substrate? In respect of the self, though partless and self-luminous, an unapprehended particularity is possible. This is how: just as on letters like "A", which are partless and manifested in their entirety, the shortness, length, etc. present in the audible sound, are superimposed, even so in the self there is the delusion of identity with the body, etc. (*VPS*, p. 52). In the self there does not certainly exist a distinction of general and particular. But still, just as the rope-substance is cognized through a form common to a staff, a snake, and a streak, similarly, the self too is cognized by the disputants as of a form common to the body, senses, *manas*, intellect, void, agent, enjoyer, the omniscient and *Brahman*. Just as the common form of the rope-substance is itself the generality, the common form through which the self is cognized may be the generality. Hence, there is no unintelligibility whatever in the self being the substrate of superimposition (*VPS*, p. 180). And substrateness is possible even for the indeterminate, since determinateness is not a determinant of substrateness. What is needed for a thing to be a substrate is the mere manifestation of immediacy; and this is established in the case of the self-luminous intelligence (*VPS*, p. 84).

Now, how is it possible to superimpose egoity, etc. on the inner self? In every case of superimposition the substrate is the content of cognition by the same sense organ as what is superimposed. But in respect of the self that is not possible, since it is not the content of the cognition "thou". The Advaitin's reply to this contention is that it is not a requirement of superimposition that the substrate should be a content. What is needed is only the presentation of the substrate and the superimposed as in union in a single cognition. And in the cognition "I" the self and the not-self are presented as in union. The self, however, is not the content of this cognition. It is the internal organ, which is superimposed on the self and pregnant with the reflection of the self, that appears in the form of the cognition "I" (*VPS*, p. 53).

The contention that the self cannot cognize what is superimposed on itself, since it is the substrate, like the crystal, the Advaitin easily disposes of. The crystal is not capable of cognizing what is imposed on itself, because it is inert. But the self is of the nature of self-luminous intelligence. Hence, it is able to apprehend what is superimposed on itself. It can be the substrate as well as the subject who sees the delusion (*VPS*, p. 65).

Of all the charges levelled against the doctrine of superimposition, the most serious is this: the not-self and the self are opposed to each other as darkness and light. Nowhere can the one be of the nature of the other. They are destitute of identity, because they have contradictory natures. The not-self is the sphere of the notion "thou";[5] and the self is the sphere of the notion "I". How, then, can such contradictory things, like the self and the not-self, be superimposed each on the other?

What the Advaitin's rejoinder to such a question is we have indicated already. Superimposition in the case of the self is certainly in conflict with reason. It does not brook inquiry. But it is because of this character of superimposition that it is called indeterminable. Logic has its limits. It cannot annul the perceptually experienced fact of superimposition. How reason aids experience in testifying to the *fact* of nescience, although it is incapable of accounting therefor, we have seen above.

We started our discussion on *māyā* with the statement that the Advaitin is not satisfied with the knowledge *that Brahman* illusorily appears as the world and that he seeks to know *how* it so appears. But we are now forced to conclude that the intellect cannot thoroughly explain. The postulation of *māyā* makes out that the world by its very nature is inscrutable. To the intellect it seems to be a welter of contradictions. But, it may be asked, is not this position a veiled confession of the inability to explain *how*? It is a legitimate demand of the intellect not to be satisfied with mere observation of facts but to attempt to explain them. "Curiosity", which is inherent in man, is "the craving of reason that the facts discriminated in experience be understood. It means the refusal to be satisfied with the bare welter of fact" (Whitehead 1933: 180). But the human mind cannot achieve any finality in its adventure of ideas. In his Seventh Epistle, Plato declares that a final system can never be verbally expressed. The popular mind is satisfied with explanations which appear ridiculous to the man of culture. But even science and philosophy are not able to fulfil the task of thorough explanation. What is explanation today becomes mere observation tomorrow.

---

5 More accurately the not-self is the sphere of the notion "this"; but in order to exhibit the opposition in a telling manner it is said to be the sphere of the notion "thou".

> The certainties of science are a delusion. They are hedged around with unexplored limitations ... whenever some new mode of observational experience is obtained, the old doctrines crumble into a fog of inaccuracies. ... It [human thought] only dimly discerns, it misdescribes, and it wrongly associates. But always there remain the same beacons that lure. Systems, scientific and philosophic, come and go. Each method of limited understanding is at length exhausted. In its prime each system is a triumphant success; in its decay it is an obstructive nuisance. The transitions to new fruitfulness of understanding are achieved by recurrence to the utmost depths of intuition for the refreshment of imagination.
>
> – Whitehead 1933: 198, 203-04

The Advaitin recognizes the inherent *want* in the intellect. What the scientific causal concepts do over and above the popular notions which are crude is to state in more precise terms the relation between the antecedent and the consequent. But the real nexus which connects the cause and effect science is unable to define. Hence, it is that the philosophical sciences turn to teleology. The *how* which science seeks to know is nothing more than a precise definition of the *that*. In order that knowledge may be more systematic and complete we must discern the *why* of a fact. Teleology tries to explain phenomena in terms of the final cause. But even here nothing satisfactory is achieved. The problem is shifted from the antecedent to the consequent. All systems which depend mainly on reason reach a point whence they cannot proceed. Materialism is not able to explain how matter passes into life. Absolute idealism, dogmatically states that *somehow* the appearances are transmuted and transformed in the Absolute so as not to create a discord in the perfect orb of Truth. Realizing that discursive thinking cannot transcend its own limitation, the Advaitin does not attempt the impossible, and he turns to "the utmost depths of intuition for the refreshment of imagination". His reasoning is always based on the intuitions of the Upaniṣadic seers. The mind which is a product of *māyā* cannot in full measure apprehend the nature of its parent. The realization of the limits of reason marks a high level in philosophic knowledge. Even to know the limitations of the intellect is to approach very near the truth.

Perception, inference, presumption and revelation are the evidence for superimposition. There is in the world empirical usage of the form of cognizer, cognized, etc. This is accomplished only after superimposing on the self the assemblage of body, organs, etc. qualified by class, etc. The empirical usage in the form "I am a man", "I am a god", "I am a beast", etc. is brought about by the illusory transference of the attributes of the not-self to the self. Thus, perception is an evidence of superimposition. Similarly, there is the testimony of inference. In sleep there is no superimposition and hence in that period there is not the empirical usage of cognizership, etc. The periods of waking and dream possess the empirical usage of cognizership as preceded by superimpositions, because they are periods other than the period of sleep. Presumption too is evidentiary in respect of superimposition. The empirical usage of cognizership, etc. is not intelligible in the absence of the superimposition of identity with the body, etc. Superimposition and empirical usage are causally connected. In sleep, when there is no superimposition, the empirical usage is not cognized. In waking and dream there is the said empirical usage which cannot be except as caused by superimposition. The evidence for superimposition in scripture is such a text like "A brāhmaṇa is to sacrifice" (*VPS*, p. 96).

The witness-intelligence is the substrate of superimposition. On it are imposed in sequence the internal organ, the organs of sense and action, the body, the objects external to that and the attributes of all these. There are two forms of superimposition as "I" and "mine". In respect of riches, etc. which are relatively remote to the self, there is invariably the superimposition of relation alone in the form "mine". In respect of the son, wife, etc. there is sometimes, due to extreme affection, the superimposition of oneness too. The superimposition of oneness is still greater in respect of the body; and in respect of the internal organ it is invariable. When the son is adorned with ornaments, etc. the father exclaims "I myself am adorned". Everyone points to his body and says "I am this". Superimposing the attributes of the body, such as leanness, etc. on the self, we say "I am lean, I am dark". The attributes of the organs are imposed on the self in the empirical usage "I am dumb, I am an orator, I am blind, I am a seer". In "I am desirous, or angry" the attributes of the internal organ are transferred to the self. And the internal organ is superimposed on the witness-intelligence as one with it (*VPS*, pp. 91-93).

Analysis of the World

The disputants differ in their analysis of the world which, according to the Advaitin, is a product of *māyā*. The Bhāṭṭas analyse the world into substance, quality, activity and generality. The Śaivas hold that there are five categories: the world which is a product, the Lord who is the cause, Yogic trance, the performance of ceremonial baths like the Triṣavana, and release which marks the end of misery. The Vaiśeṣikas enumerate six categories. To the four given by the Bhāṭṭas they add particularity and inherence. The classification given by the Kṣapaṇakas (i.e. Jainas) consists of seven factors: *jīva* which may be either bound, released or eternally perfect, *ajīva* which is fourfold, viz. *pudgalāstikāya*, *dharmāstikāya*, *adharmāstikāya* and *ākāśāstikāya*, *āsrava* (sense-activity), *saṁvara* (activity in the form of calmness and equanimity), *nirjara* which consists of acts that exhaust merit and demerit without residue, bondage and release which is upward motion. The older Prābhākaras classify the phenomena of the world into eight categories, viz. substance, quality, activity, generality, particularity, dependence, potentiality and the unseen result. The modern Prābhākaras substitute inherence, number and similarity for particularity, dependence and the unseen result. According to the Naiyāyikas, the categories are sixteen, viz. *pramāṇa*s like perception and inference, *prameya*s (objects of knowledge), doubt, fruit of activity, example, final position, members of the syllogism, *tarka* (*reductio ad absurdum*), *nirṇaya* (ascertainment), *vāda* (debate), *jalpa* (disputation), *vitaṇḍā* (destructive criticism), *hetvābhāsa*s (logical fallacies), *chala* (quibble), *jāti* (wrong objection) and *nigrahasthāna* (occasion for reproof). The Sāṁkhya categories are twenty-five and they are: the eleven organs of sense and action, the five *tanmātra*s (subtle essences of elements), the five gross elements, individuation, *mahat* (or *buddhi*, intellect), the unmanifest and spirit (*VPS*, pp. 200-201).

It requires no argument to understand how the classificatory schemes given above are unsatisfactory and some of them even fantastic. The Vedāntins reduce the phenomena of the world to three or two categories. Name, form and activity constitute the stuff of the universe; or leaving out even activity, we can say that the world is a medley of name and form. In an earlier chapter we had occasion to see how a thing is constituted by five factors, reality, intelligence and bliss which form the essential nature of *Brahman* and name and form which go to make up the illusory world.

Illusoriness of Creation

The world-creation is an illusory product of *māyā*. Evidences like scripture, traditional code, perception, inference and presumption go to prove the illusoriness of creation. Scripture in the passage "Know *māyā* to be the material cause" (*ŚvetUp* IV.10) shows that the world is a product of *māyā*. The traditional code "My *māyā* which is difficult to transcend" (*BhG* VII.14) declares of creation that it is of the nature of indeterminable *māyā*. The perception of the non-existence of objects like pot proves the illusoriness of creation. Inference too makes known the illusory nature of the world. From the fact that all things, though different, are interpenetrated by one nature it can be inferred that they are posited in a single thing that is constant in them all. This is just like the reflections of the moon in water, etc. being interpenetrated by the nature of the moon. Presumption too is an evidence of the illusoriness of the world. The origination and destruction of the world are unintelligible in the absence of illusoriness. What is neither originated nor destroyed is either the absolutely real *Brahman* or the void. The world is originated and destroyed; hence it is illusory (*VPS*, pp. 198-99).

Brahman Unaffected by Names and Forms

Names and forms are superimposed on *Brahman* as pictures are painted on the canvas. When names and forms are realized to be mere superimpositions, the real nature of *Brahman* becomes known. Names and forms are recognized to be unreal, just as a man standing on the edge of a tank knows his reflection in the water to be unreal. There may be innumerable day-dreams flitting across the mental arena; but no man in his senses pays any heed to them. They are evanescent, ever-fleeting. So also are names and forms and their empirical usage. Boyhood is not found in youth and youth is not recovered in senility. The deceased father never comes; nor does the dead past ever return. Thus, there is no real difference between day-dreams and the facts connected with this world. Hence, though the world may continue to appear, the cognition that it is real must be given up. When the objects of the world are seen in their true colour, the intellect is set free to indulge in the contemplation of *Brahman*. Like the historian who does not lose his individual identity in the roles that he happens to play, the intellect, though attending to the affairs of the world, does not lose sight of the real. Just as the rocks that lie buried in the riverbed are not affected by the flow of the stream, even so the immutable *Brahman* remains unchanged in spite of the fleeting things of the world. The appearance of the world in *Brahman* is like the reflection of the heavens in the mirror. Without looking at the mirror it is not possible to behold the reflection of the sky. Similarly, without the thought of *Brahman*, there is not even the thought about names and forms. Superficial cognition of *Brahman* is vouchsafed even by the cognition of objects. But if that cognition is to be constant, we must cease from cognizing the world as real. When *Brahman* which is of the nature of truth, intelligence, bliss, is seen, the cognition of names and forms vanishes of its own accord (*PD* XIII.93-102).

9

The Path to Perfection

THE path to perfection lies in and through knowledge. Ignorance which is the root of all the imperfections and ills of the world can be destroyed only by knowledge. By knowledge what the Advaitin means is the final, immediate intuition of the non-difference of the *jīva* from *Brahman*.

Karma and Knowledge

The Mīmāṁsaka, however, does not accept the Advaitin's view regarding the means to release. He holds that release is attained through *karma*. The popular opinion about the Mīmāṁsā is that it is an inquiry into the religious rites ordained by scripture the performance of which leads to prosperity here and happiness hereafter. But earthly pleasure and heavenly enjoyment are not the goal of the system, though they might have formed an incidental ideal at a certain stage in its development. The Mīmāṁsaka admits that *karma* is the cause of bondage, but he does not agree to the view that all *karma*s are to be voluntarily relinquished. A seeker after release should abstain from *kāmya* (optional) and *pratiṣiddha* (prohibited) *karma*s; but he should never give up the performance of *nitya* (obligatory) and *naimittika* (occasioned) rites (*Naiṣkarmyasiddhi* I.10). Just as there results sin from indulging in prohibited acts, there is also sin as a consequence of not performing the obligatory rites. A *mumukṣu* (one who desires release) must not only be free from the error of commission; he must also be free from the error of omission. Scripture is the authority in matters of religious duty. What it prescribes one should do and what it prohibits one should not do.

That the entire Veda has injunction alone for purport is the doctrine of the Mīmāṁsaka. To the Prābhākara no proposition would be significant if it did not refer to an act. Though Kumārila admits that a word may connote an object unrelated to action, he does not grant an independent logical status to assertive propositions.[1] Hence, on the Mīmāṁsā view, texts about *Brahman* or the self are Arthavādas (eulogies) without any purport. Since all scripture is for the sake of ritual, there is validity for injunctive texts alone. Scripture has *codanā* (command for purport). It is incumbent on man to carry out the commands of the Veda and to abstain from acts which are prohibited.

As against the Mīmāṁsā view, the Vedāntin maintains that a proposition may have even existent things for purport. Such a statement as "A son is born to you" is not without significance. The ritualistic section of the Veda teaches religious duty (*dharma*). But the Upaniṣads have *Brahman* for purport. Religious duty which is what is to be done depends on human volition. But, for *Brahman* which is an existent there is no dependence on a human being. That which is dependent on a human being can be done, not done or done otherwise. In ordinary experience, Devadatta goes on horseback or does not go or goes on foot. His going, which is what is to be done, entirely depends on his will. Similarly, in the Veda too, religious rites are observed to depend on the will of man. Doing and not doing of an act are declared in the texts "In the *atirātra*, one uses the sixteenth cup", "In the *atirātra*, one does not use the sixteenth cup". Doing and doing otherwise are to be found in the passages "He offers oblation after sunrise" and "He offers oblation before sunrise". There are

[1] M. Hiriyanna's Introduction to the *Naiṣkarmyasiddhi*, p. xx.

in the ritualistic section of the Veda prescriptions like "He is to sacrifice with the Jyotiṣṭoma" and prohibitions like "Do not eat the flesh of any animal struck with a poisoned weapon". There is option at will in "He is to sacrifice with rice-grains or with barley". There is combination of the six sacrifices constituting the *darśapūrṇamāsa*. There are general rules like "Injure not any living being" and exceptions like "He is to kill the *agnīṣomīya* animal". In respect of certain modelled rites, there is the sublation of the basic material transferred from the model rite, e.g. there is the sublation of the *barhis* (sacrificial grass) consisting of *kuśa*, transferred from the model rite, by the *barhis* consisting of *śara*, taught in the modelled rite. When the *nāriṣṭa-homas* belonging to the model rite are performed in combination with the *upa-homas* of the modelled rite, it is called supplementation. There is differentiated option consequent on the differences of the section of the Veda to which one belongs. In one section it is taught "He offers oblation after sunrise", and in another it is declared "He offers oblation before sunrise". Thus, in the case of ritual acts, there is the possibility of dependence on a human being, prescription, prohibition, option at will, combination, general rule, exception, sublation, supplementation, differentiated option, etc. But these are not possible in the case of the existent *Brahman* (*VPS*, p. 213).

Brahman is not the fruit of an act. The fruit generated by an act in the object-causal-correlate is one of four kinds – origination (*utpatti*), attainment (*prāpti*), modification (*vikāra*) and purification (*saṁskāra*). Of these, origination, attainment and modification are not possible in respect of the eternally attained unchanging *Brahman* (*VSP*, p. 112). Nor may we suspect the possibility of purification consisting in the removal of impurities like ignorance, unrighteousness, etc.; for *Brahman* is ever pure. It is flawless and undefiled. In reaching a place, say, a village not attained before and in removing a disease, etc. not already remedied, there is required action in the form of movement, taking in medicine, etc. But, in the case of *Brahman* which is eternally attained as it were, what need is there for activity? What should be removed is ignorance; and for the removal of ignorance what is potent is knowledge. A person not knowing what is already attained like the gold ornament round his neck, desires to attain it again, and not knowing that there is no snake in the rope desires to avoid it. But what he desires is accomplished not by any act, but by mere knowledge (*VPS*, p. 234). Similarly, in the attainment of the eternally attained *Brahman* and in the remedying of the eternally remedied transmigration, what is the cause is the knowledge of the truth.

That the attainment of *Brahman* is figurative is evident from scriptural texts like "And being (already) released, he is released" (*KaṭhaUp* V.i), "Being (already) *Brahman*, he attains *Brahman*" (*BṛUp* IV.iv.6). Release has neither beginning nor end. If release had a beginning, there would be an end also to it. And if it has an end, it is a misnomer to call it release. Further, if release be accomplishable by an act, then, its relation to body, senses, etc. would have to be predicated, and there would be for it the capacity to increase and decrease (*VPS*, p. 239). And that which is subject to growth and decay is not imperishable. There is no embodiedness for the self in release. Release is the natural and eternal state of the self. It comes to be clouded by nescience and as a consequence the non-embodied appears as if embodied, the pure appears as if impure, the eternally attained appears as if unattained. When ignorance is removed by knowledge, *Brahman* is attained as it were.

Karma which is a product of ignorance cannot destroy its parent. The delusive cognition of the rope-snake is not removed by darkness which is its cause (*Naiṣkarmyasiddhi* I.24). Pain is the result of being embodied; the body has its root in the previously acquired merit and demerit; merit and demerit are the fruit of prescribed and prohibited acts; these acts are dependent on appetition and aversion; appetition and aversion are conditioned by attractiveness and unattractiveness which are superimposed on sense-objects, superimposition is caused by the world of duality which appears to be real on account of non-inquiry; the world of duality, however, is illusory, like nacre-silver and it is the result of the ignorance which obscures the non-dual self. Hence, ignorance of the self is the sole cause of all evil (ibid. I.1); and it is only knowledge that can remove ignorance. Delusion which is brought about by nescience is dispelled by the cognition of the true. Darkness is destroyed by light alone. The removal of nescience could be by knowledge alone, not by any act.

Nor is cognition itself an act of the mind, since, because of the fruit as well as the cause, there is difference between cognition and activity. The fruit of cognition is the manifestation of the object; and what is called the manifestation is of the nature of the self and hence it is unoriginated. The appearance of its origination, however, is due to the origination of the psychosis of the internal organ which manifests it. The fruit of an act, on the other hand, is originated. The cause of activity is effort preceded by human desire. Cognition, however, does not conform to human desire. Even what is undesirable like evil smell is cognized (*VPS*, p. 249). Not even by the most skilled can the fire existing in front be cognized in the form of a pillar, etc. Cognition is not generated by human effort. Desire controls such activity like turning the eyes, etc. and it has no power over cognition.

The view is advocated in some quarters that the means to release is *karma*-cum-knowledge. Those who sponsor this view quote as evidence such texts as "Knowledge and non-knowledge, he who knows both together" (*ĪśaUp* 11; *MaitrīUp* VII.9), etc. But this text does not enjoin the combination of *karma* with knowledge; for, in the rest of the text "Crossing over death by non-knowledge, by knowledge he enjoys immortality" (ibid.) the fruit of rites which are called non-knowledge is declared to be different from the fruit of knowledge. Nor is it possible to establish an injunction of the combination of knowledge and rites in "Perform those invariably, Oh lovers of the true" (*MuṇḍUp* I.ii.1), for mere rites alone are mentioned here and the word "true" does not refer to *Brahman*. Even the text "This self is to be attained by truth, by austerity, by right knowledge" (ibid. III.i.5) does not prescribe the combination, for the word "austerity" occurring in the text means contemplation and not rites like Agnihotra, etc. It may be said that the traditional code "Through *karma* alone did Janaka, etc. attain *saṁsiddhi*" (*BLG* III.20) enjoins *karma* as the means to release. But the word *saṁsiddhi* here connotes the purification of mind which is auxiliary to *Brahman*-knowledge and not the final release. Far from enjoining the combination of knowledge and rites, scripture directly denies the instrumentality of rites to release in "There is nothing to be done by him who has achieved (knowledge)" (*MuṇḍUp* I.ii.12), "Not by rites, not by children" (*MahānārUp* X.5), etc. *Taittirīya Upaniṣad* II.i.1 declares, "The knower of *Brahman* attains the highest". In the *Chāndogya Upaniṣad*, Nārada asks Sanatkumāra, "I have heard from men like you that the knower of the self crosses sorrow; and I, who am well versed in scripture, because of the lack of that knowledge, am in distress. Therefore, Oh Lord! enable me to cross the bounds of sorrow." And in the traditional code we read "The fire of knowledge reduces all *karma*s to ashes".[2]

Although there is not the instrumentality of rituals to release, *karma* is not without its use. Rites are to be performed until the rise of knowledge. They contribute, though indirectly, to self-realization. The followers of the *Bhāmatī* school consider *karma* to be useful in generating the desire to know, for it is declared by scripture:

> That (self) the brāhmaṇas desire to know through study of the Veda, through sacrifice, through gifts and through austerities like fasting. – *BṛUp* IV.iv.22

---

2 *VPS*, pp. 165-66; *PD* XI.8 and commentary; *BhG* IV.37.

According to the *Vivaraṇa* view, *karma* is useful in generating knowledge itself. Through the performance of obligatory rites there is acquired virtue which removes the impurity called sin. A person thus qualified becomes eligible for *Brahman*-inquiry. Mere rites may have prosperity as fruit; but, when conjoined with hearing, reflection, etc. they are useful in the generation of *Brahman*-knowledge. That rites through the channel of purification originate *Brahman*-knowledge is evident from such traditional codes like "Knowledge arises for human beings through the exhaustion of sinful deeds". But, since rites subserve knowledge only through the channel of purification, they are not proximate (*sannipātya*), but remote auxiliaries (*ārādupakāraka*).

The afore-mentioned utility of rites to knowledge is not inconsistent with the need for renunciation. Rites are to be performed up to the purification of the mind; and when the mind has been purified they are to be abandoned. Rites, we said, are remote auxiliaries in respect of knowledge; but renunciation is a proximate auxiliary, since it originates hearing of the Vedānta, etc. As Sureśvara says, rites, after directing the intellect to the inner self through purification, disappear like clouds at the end of the rainy season (*VPS*, p. 164).

Some people think that renunciation is enjoined for the disabled like the blind and the lame who are not eligible for rites. But they are thoroughly in the wrong. Renunciation is not for the weak. It is not the result of impotence. It is a potent weapon which can be wielded only by the strong and the skilled. It is not that only those who are ineligible for rites are to renounce, for scripture prescribes renunciation even for the student in "Renounce even from the students' order of life". When one realizes that attachment to the things of the world is the source of misery and turns away from them, one becomes eligible for renunciation. Scripture declares, "The day on which he is non-attached, that very day he is to renounce" (*VPS*, p. 163; *JābālaUp* 4).

Knowledge and Yoga

Although all Advaitins agree that knowledge is indispensable, some of them do not support the view that it is the *sole* means to release. Bhāratītīrtha, who in the *Vivaraṇa-Prameya-Saṁgraha* teaches the view of the *vivaraṇakāra* that knowledge gained from the study, etc. of the Vedānta is the only means to release, maintains in the *Pañcadaśī* that this is but one of the two paths shown by the Lord, viz. Sāṁkhya and Yoga. The path of Sāṁkhya is that of inquiry into the purport of the Vedānta texts. It is prescribed for those who are intellectually virile and are capable of understanding the meaning of scripture aright. But there are many, who, on account of either extreme dullness of intellect or the impossibility of the causal aggregate of inquiry in their case, are unable to undertake inquiry. For them, scripture recommends the path of Yoga which is that of constant contemplation of the attributeless *Brahman*. Both the paths lead to the same goal; but while the path of Saṁkhya is the right royal road to release, the path of Yoga is comparable to hit or miss guesswork, which nevertheless happens to succeed. In the *Dhyānadīpa*, Bhāratītīrtha compares contemplation to *saṁvādī-bhrama* (a delusion which culminates in a fruitful result). Both the light of a lamp and the light of a gem may be mistaken for a gem. Both are delusions. But the man, who mistakes the lamplight for the gem and approaches the place whence the light comes, gains nothing, whereas the person, who mistakes the light of the gem for the gem itself, obtains the precious stone. Both of them have delusive cognition, but unlike the former, the latter finds his cognition come true. One mistakes steam for smoke and infers the existence of fire. He hastens to the place where he thinks there is fire and as chance would have it, he finds fire there. The existence of fire does not make his inference valid; but still it serves the purpose of him who was in search of fire. A person, thinking that the Godāvarī is the Gaṅgā, bathes in that river or sprinkles its water on his head. Mistaking the Godāvarī for the Gaṅgā is no doubt a delusion; but still the sprinkling of the sacred water purifies the man and makes him holy. It is declared in the sacred texts that if a person utters the name of the Lord at the moment of his death, he attains heaven. A dying man may take the Lord's name even without intention. Yet, it is proclaimed that he reaches heaven. All these are cases of *saṁvādī-bhrama* (delusions that come true). The path of Yoga may be likened unto these. The *yogin* has not the knowledge of *Brahman* to start with. He begins his journey in ignorance, but he ends it in knowledge.

Contemplation is not needed for one who knows *Brahman*; and it is not possible in the case of one who does not know *Brahman*. Hence, it may be asked, where is the place for contemplation? Those who believe in Yoga as a path to perfection reply that even he who treads this way is not ignorant of *Brahman*. From the Vedānta learnt by *adhyayana* (study) he has a superficial knowledge of the oneness of *Brahman* and the self. The knowledge which he possesses is no doubt mediate; but that meditation on what is mediately known is possible is well proved by the worship of deities like Viṣṇu. A worshipper of images sees before him only idols made of stone or stock; but this does not in any way hinder his mediate cognition of the Lord. He does not debate or discuss whether there can or cannot be the presence of God in idols. Through instruction from a trustworthy person or through study of scripture he gets a mediate knowledge of the nature and form of the object of his adoration; and even without inquiry or discussion he meditates on the deity of his heart. Similarly, he who contemplates the attributeless *Brahman* starts his career of Yoga even without a direct apprehension of the real.

Nor may it be said that contemplation of *Brahman* without attributes is impossible; for just as in the case of meditation on *Brahman* with attributes, even in *nirguṇopāsanā* (meditation on the attributeless) there is the possibility of the repetition of cognition. If it be contended that meditation on what is beyond the reach of speech and mind is impossible, then, even the knowledge of such an object would not be obtained. If *Brahman*-knowledge be within the province of possibility, then even contemplation of *Brahman* must be possible. It may be said that *Brahman* is *known* to be beyond the sphere of speech and mind. Then, it can be maintained with equal legitimacy that the contemplation of *Brahman* is of the form that *Brahman* is not the sphere of speech, mind, etc. If contemplation invest *Brahman* with attributes, then, even knowledge of *Brahman* would convert it into an object possessed of attributes. If it be said that knowledge, having recourse to secondary implication, has for its sphere the attributeless *Brahman*, then, let meditation be on the secondary implication which is the cause of presenting *Brahman* devoid of attributes. It may be urged that there is the prohibition of contemplation in the scriptural text:

> That which is not thought by the mind, that by which, they say, the mind is thought, that alone is *Brahman*; know that, not this (other) which this (world) contemplates. – *KenaUp* 5

But there are also passages in scripture like "It is other than the known, and more than the unknown" which declare that *Brahman* is not what is known. The solution that *Brahman* is to be known in accordance with the meaning of scripture, i.e. that it is other than the known and more than the unknown – is common to the view of meditation also; for it is easy to hold that *Brahman* is to be contemplated as what is other than that which is contemplated by this world. Nor may it be asserted that the known-ness of *Brahman* is unreal, since that assertion holds good even in the case of contemplation. If it be said that the pervasion by the psychosis of the internal organ is what is known, that consideration is common also to what is contemplated. The possibility of contemplation is mentioned in the Upaniṣads like the *Praśna*, *Kaṭha* and *Māṇḍūkya*; and the denial of contemplation elsewhere is only apparent.

The fruit of the meditation on the attributeless is thus declared in the *Tāpaṇīya Upaniṣad*:

> That man who desires (viz. *upāsaka*, the one who meditates) becomes desireless. He desires the self and gets his desires fulfilled. His vital airs do not depart; they get resolved here in his own body. Being *Brahman*, he attains *Brahman*. He becomes of the nature of the self-luminous reality, intelligence, bliss, without body, sense organs, vital airs and mind.

The *Tāpaṇīya Upaniṣad* clearly sets forth that release is the final fruit of meditation on the attributeless *Brahman*. The *Praśna Upaniṣad* declares that he who contemplates the Absolute through the help of the three *matras* (i.e. *AUṀ*) is led to *brahmaloka* where it becomes possible for him to behold the supreme *puruṣa*. In the *Vedāntasūtra* (IV.iii.15), Bādarāyaṇa maintains that all those who contemplate the effected *Brahman* except those who take their stand on symbols are led to the world of Brahmā on the principle of *tatkratu* that "in whatever form they meditate on him, that they become themselves". "Those who do not take their stand on symbols he leads, thus Bādarāyaṇa (opines); there being no fault in the twofold relation (resulting from this opinion); and the meditation on that (i.e. *Brahman*) is the reason of this twofold relation." Those *upāsakas* who contemplate the attributeless and yet are not rid of desires reach the world of Brahmā and there they acquire the knowledge of the true and are released at the end of the world-aeon. The texts above cited which declare release as the ultimate fruit of contemplation are not in conflict with scriptural passages like "No other path is known" (*ŚvetUp* III.8; IV.15), since the capacity of contemplation to accomplish release is admitted to be only through the channel of knowledge.

That those who are not capable of achieving true knowledge through inquiry are eligible for the contemplation of the attributeless is declared in the *Ātma-gītā*. "He who is incapable of intuiting (*Brahman*), let him meditate on me free from doubts, in good time he will be firmly established in experience and will attain without fail the fruit of release." Just as there is no other means to obtain a treasure hidden in the bowels of the earth except digging, there is no other method except meditation on one's own self to gain the final goal. The *Ātma-gītā* explains the analogy thus: uprooting the body which is comparable to a huge rock and digging the field of the mind by means of the intellect as the spade, the inner treasure, the self, is to be attained. There are other passages which declare that even though there be no experience of *Brahman*, a man may think that he is *Brahman* and constantly ruminate on this thought, until this very thought matures into a fact. The seen fruit of meditation is that day by day the *upāsaka* discards the cognition of things which are other than the self; and this should be a sufficient reason why the path of contemplation is of supreme value to those who are incapable of inquiry. Destroying the conceit in the body through contemplation and beholding the non-dual self, the mortal *upāsaka* becomes immortal and attains *Brahman* even here, in this world.

In the eleventh chapter of the *Pañcadaśī* entitled *Yogānandam* the method by which the intellect is to be refined so that the supreme bliss may be attained is described. Bhāratītīrtha accepts the *Gītā* definition of *yoga* as separation from contact with pain and points out that it is to be achieved by constant and steady practice with a determined and untiring mind. Whatever drags the mind to the objects of sense and makes it waver and wander away should be regarded as an obstacle to the progress of a *yogin*. Renouncing all desires and restraining with his mind all his senses, the *yogin* should gain tranquillity and with a steady and steadfast purpose concentrate his mind on the supreme self. When thus the mind is restrained and withheld from sense-objects and the intellect is refined and tranquillity reached, the *yogin* experiences unexcellable bliss which is supersensible and grasped only by the intellect.

The same method of quieting the mind is taught in the Maitrāyaṇī *śākhā* by Sage Sākāyanya to King Bṛhadratha. Whatever the mind thinks that he becomes. When it is attached to the senses and their objects, it gets muddled and mutilated; but when it is centred in *Brahman*, it becomes of that form. That mind is impure which is in contact with desires; and that mind is pure which is completely free from the pestilence of desires, etc. Mind alone is the cause of the bondage and release of men; attachment to objects brings about bondage, while detachment from them effects release. Mind is to be purified and tranquillized by constant and vigilant practice. Just as the fire which is unfed by fuel cools down, even so when all the psychoses are destroyed, the mind gets dissolved in its source. When the channel of the mental flow is turned away from sense-objects and directed towards *Brahman* and when the mind gets attached thereto, then the bonds of *saṁsāra* break. Rid of its impurities through *samādhi*, the mind experiences unexcellable bliss which defies all description and which is apprehended by the tranquil mind alone.

The mental equanimity cannot be maintained for long; *samādhi* does not stay for ever. But still it gives the *yogin* a lasting taste of the supreme bliss. Even when he is out of the balanced state of mind, he thinks longingly of that bliss with the same ardour and intense fervour with which a woman contemplates the lord of her life. In moments of indifference when there is manifest the residual impression of bliss, he discerns the unexcellable bliss and concentrates his mind thereon. That the *yogin* is able to fix his mind on *Brahman* and at the same time carry on the activities of the world can be illustrated by examples. The crow which is said to see with only one eye directs its vision alternately through the two cavities. A man who is a master of two languages discerns meaning in both of them. He who stands in a river half-immersed with the scorching sun above experiences both the pleasure afforded by the cool waters and the pain inflicted by the piercing shafts of the sun. Similarly, the *yogin* is able to bear the miseries of the world and yet at the same time centre his mind in *Brahman*. Thus, unlike the ordinary run of mankind which unwittingly experiences *Brahman*-bliss only in sleep, the *yogin* perceives it even in the hours of waking and dream. To the Yogic perception, *Brahman* is revealed.

Bhāratītīrtha gives to *yoga* a place next to knowledge as a means of release. Though in the *Dvaitaviveka* he is inclined to say that the Yogic control of mind cannot yield lasting release, that the attempt to achieve liberation through that path is analogous to the effort to strengthen the curly tail of a dog and that release is not attained except through. *Brahman*-knowledge (*PD* IV.38-39), he recognizes in the latter chapters, as shown above, that *yoga* can also be a legitimate method of approach. The path of Yoga may be circumlocutory, it may involve delay; but nonetheless it is a path to the final beatitude. That the Sāṁkhya and Yoga have the same fruit. Bhāratītīrtha shows by quoting *Gītā* V.5 (*PD* XII.82):

> The place which is reached by the Sāṁkhyas is attained by the Yogas also. He who sees that the way of Sāṁkhya and the way of Yoga are one – he sees indeed.

The fruit of both the methods is the same, viz. the knowledge of the self. What is called discriminatory knowledge is the intuitive experience of the inner self gained through an inquiry into the purport of scripture. *Yoga* is the method of contemplation which culminates in self-knowledge. There is need for two paths because of the difference in the capacity of those who are eligible (*adhikārins*).

What is important in the position taken by Bhāratītīrtha in the *Pañcadaśī* is its liberal attitude to the question of method. The tendency to liberalize Advaita reached another stage in Madhusūdana who was the first to claim that the path of devotion (*bhakti*) leads to non-dual realization.[3] To

---

3 See P.M. Modi's translation of *Siddhāntabindu*, Appendix II.

Madhusūdana Sarasvatī, devotion is as good a means to release as knowledge. He draws his inspiration from the *Bhāgavata Purāṇa* which he ranks with the three *prasthāna*s (triple canon consisting of the Upaniṣads, *Bhagavadgītā* and *Vedāntasūtra*). His ardent love for Kṛṣṇa makes him regard the Lord of the *Gopī*s as the incarnation of the attributeless *Brahman*. He accepts the Bhāgavata view that of the two paths, *jñāna* and *bhakti*, the latter is superior, since it leads to the goal more quickly than the other. Though all his works bear testimony to his faith in the efficacy of *bhakti*, he develops the doctrine of devotion in full measure in the *Bhaktirasāyana* and the *Gūḍhārthadīpikā*. The manner of his exposition of the theme of *bhakti* reminds us of artistic experience. Rhetoricians do not include *bhakti* among the *rasa*s (sentiments) which they recognize. But Madhūsudana maintains that devotional love is the queen of *rasa*s. An excitant, an ensuant and an accessory constitute the causal aggregate which generates a *rasa*. The chief excitant for *bhakti* is the Supreme Lord and minor excitants are sandal paste, etc.; the ensuants are facial expressions, etc. and the accessories are distaste for the things of the world, etc. Twofold *bhakti* is advocated by Madhusūdana. *Bhakti* as the means is the actual process of being in love with God; and *bhakti* as the goal is the *summum bonum* or the beatitude where there is the everlasting experience of *Brahman*-bliss. Though Madhusūdana was liberal in the matter of the method, he was uncompromising with regard to the metaphysical basis of Advaita. To him must be given the credit of reconciling the philosophy of Advaita with the experience of a *bhakta*. Whether we agree with him or not in bestowing on *bhakti* the importance which he gives it, we cannot but admire the catholicity of spirit which animates his exposition of Advaita.

Eligibility and the Means to Release

Śaṅkara lays down a fourfold constitution for eligibility, viz. the discrimination of things eternal from non-eternal, non-attachment to the enjoyment of fruit here or hereafter, the possession in abundance of means like calmness and equanimity and the desire for release (*VPS*, p. 169). Of these four qualifications each earlier one is the cause of the gaining of each subsequent one. When there is the discrimination of things eternal from the non-eternal, there is non-attachment to the enjoyment of fruit here or hereafter; when there is the said non-attachment, there arises the desire for release as associated with calmness, etc. He who is fully qualified by possessing the fourfold requisite is to study the Vedānta texts under the guidance of a *guru* who is not only learned in the sacred lore (*śrotriya*) but is also well established in *Brahman* (*brahma-niṣṭha*). Scripture enjoins for him who is eligible, hearing (*śravaṇa*), as the principal, with reflection (*manana*) and contemplation (*nididhyāsana*) as subsidiaries. When by reasoning of the nature of reflection, the impossibility of the content of the Vedānta texts, consisting in the oneness of the *jīva* and *Brahman*, is refuted and by contemplation is obtained that concentration of the mental psychosis, which, while refuting the notions of the contrary, is capable of ascertaining the subtle object, there is generated by verbal testimony the unshakable immediate cognition of *Brahman*. That the principal texts of the Vedānta are directly the instrument (*kāraṇa*) of intuition is the *Vivaraṇa* view. Verbal testimony is capable of generating the immediate knowledge of the self-luminous *Brahman*. But when there is obstruction through the notions of impossibility and the illusory cognition of the contrary, there does not arise unshakable, immediate experience. Hence, the need for reflection and contemplation. That the testimony of the Vedānta is the cause of immediate knowledge of *Brahman* is evident from the use of the *taddhita* suffix in the text, "I ask you about the *aupaniṣada-puruṣa* (person propounded in the Upaniṣads)" (*BṛUp* III.ix.26). Therefore, verbal testimony yields even in the first instance immediate cognition and that cognition becomes unshakable later on the departure of the obstacle. Or, we may even say that verbal testimony at first gives rise to mediate cognition of *Brahman* and again generates immediate cognition on the removal of the obstacle. In any case, verbal testimony is directly the *karaṇa* (instrument), of *Brahman*-intuition (*VPS*, pp. 103-04).

Vācaspati, who regards verbal testimony as giving only mediate knowledge and who characterizes the mind as a sense organ, holds that deep meditation (*prasaṁkhyāna*) is the *karaṇa* of intuition. He inherits this view from Maṇḍana who considers knowledge generated by *śabda* (verbal testimony) to be mediate.[4] *Avidyā* can be removed only by immediate knowledge. Verbal testimony is unable to do this, since it signifies what is related (*saṁsṛṣṭa*) and mediate (*parokṣa*). Hence, the need for *bhāvanā* (meditation) which can transmute the mediate knowledge gained from verbal testimony into immediate intuition.

Sureśvara condemns this view in the *Naiṣkarmyasiddhi*. Mediacy or immediacy of the knowledge derived from verbal testimony depends on the character of the object of knowledge. Words can give only mediate knowledge of a mediate object. But of an immediate object, they can give also immediate cognition. *Brahman* is immediate and self-luminous. Hence, the principal texts of the Vedānta like "That thou art" are capable of giving rise to the immediate knowledge of *Brahman*. The final intuition in order to be true knowledge must be the result of a valid means of knowledge. Verbal testimony is, while *prasaṁkhyāna* is not, a *pramāṇa*.

While admitting the need for meditation as an auxiliary to knowledge, the followers of the *Vivaraṇa* school do not regard it as the instrument of intuition. Contemplation cannot be the distinctive cause (*karaṇa*) in the origination of *Brahman*-experience. Hearing, however, which is of the nature of the determination of purport, is the distinctive cause; hence to it

---

4 M. Hiriyanna's Introduction to *Naiṣkcarmyasiddhi*, p. xxv.

belongs the character of being the principal. Reflection and contemplation, which remove such mighty obstacles like the notions of impossibility and of the contrary, are helpful subsidiaries in the production of the fruit. To calmness, etc. and sacrifice, etc. which are remote auxiliaries, belongs the character of modus operandi. Therefore, as aided by moral discipline and disinterested action that constitute the modus operandi, and by such subsidiaries like reflection and contemplation that are helpful to the fruit, hearing alone, which is the principal, is the generator of unshakable, immediate experience (*VPS*, p. 103). This is the *Vivaraṇa* view. But both Vācaspati and the *vivaraṇakāra* agree in this that the path to perfection lies *in* and *through* knowledge; no other path there is: *nā 'nyaḥ panthā 'yanāya vidyate.*

10

Release

BRAHMAN-INTUITION is release. Defined negatively, the destruction of bondage is release. Bondage consists in the conceit bestowed by the *jīva* on the host of things, pleasurable and painful, that constitute the illusory world; and release is attained through knowledge that discriminates things eternal from the non-eternal, through the intuitive experience of the oneness of the *jīva* and *Brahman*.

Brahman-knowledge Is Bliss

Brahman-knowledge is of the nature of happiness or bliss. It marks the cessation of all sorrow; it signifies the culmination of all desires, the accomplishment of the unaccomplished as it were and the attainment of the unattained as it were. A man of illumination has no wants and is impelled by no desire. He has nothing to accomplish in this world or in the next. Nor is there anything left for him to be attained either here or hereafter. When he has achieved the supreme human goal, what need has he for the trinkets of this world? The entire choir of heaven and furniture of the earth seem naught before his divine vision. He revels in the bliss of *Brahman*; and the realization that he is non-different from the Absolute gives him felicity and peace (*PD* XIV.2-3).

Cessation of Sorrow

The happiness that is consequent on knowledge is characterized, first, by the cessation of sorrow. This is the negative aspect of release. Misery or sorrow is of two kinds – that which belongs to this world and that which is associated with the other world. That there is no misery in this world for him who has realized the self is proclaimed by *Bṛhadāraṇyaka Upaniṣad* IV.iv.12:

> If a man knows the self as "I am this", then, desiring what and for whose sake will he suffer in the wake of the body?

The afflictions of the body are

> possible for the man who does not see the self and consequently desires things other than it. He struggles desiring something for himself, something else for his son, a third thing for his wife, and so on, goes the round of births and deaths and is diseased when his body is diseased. But all this is impossible for the man who sees everything as the self.[1]

It is only when the *jīva* gets itself attached to the psycho-physical organism that there is for it misery and pain. But its true nature is existence–intelligence–bliss. When it discriminates its true nature from the illusory name- and form-world, then there is no more misery that is born of the superimposition on the self of agency and enjoyership. It is only when the *jīva* thinks itself to be the agent of actions and the enjoyer of fruit that it runs after the external objects of sense and comes to grief. The ailments of the body, the passions of the mind and the seeds of both which lie dormant in sleep – all these are inseparable attributes of *avidyā* and its products. When through the cognition of non-difference the supreme self is known, the *jīva* wakes from its slumber and shakes off the superimpositions of agency, enjoyership, etc. When it is realized that there is in reality neither an enjoyer nor objects of enjoyment, the root of all evil is removed (*PD* XIV.4-11).

The thought about merit and demerit is the cause of misery hereafter. For a person who has transcended the notions of merit

---

[1] Śaṅkara's Commentary. See Mādhavānanda's translation, p. 739.

and demerit, there can be no misery hereafter. Future *karma* does not bind him, because he lives in the world unattached like water on the lotus-leaf. He has no accumulated *karma*, since that has been burnt up in the flames of *Brahman*-knowledge. All his evils are burnt "just as the soft fibres of the *iṣīkā* reed would burn, when thrown into the fire" (*ChāUp* V.xxiv.3).

> As the fire which is kindled reduces all fuel to ashes, Oh Arjuna! so does the fire of knowledge reduce all *karmas* to ashes. – *BhG* IV.37, tr. Sarma

> He who is free from the notion of and whose understanding is unsullied – though he slays these men, he slays not, nor is he bound. – *BhG* XVIII.17

The actions of him who has attained release do not bind him. *Kauṣītaki Upaniṣad* III.1 goes to the extent of saying that even such heinous crimes as matricide, patricide, theft and infanticide do not affect him who is released. This does not mean, however, that the knower of *Brahman* can be a moral rake. His very nature cannot lead him to sinful ways. What scripture intends to declare is that he is a-moral and not immoral. His actions do not spring from him. Hence, he is not responsible for the actions which others attribute to him. When, thus, he is not bound by *karma*, merit and demerit which are the causes of misery in the other world do not affect him (*PD* XIV.12-17).

Attainment of Happiness

The positive aspect of release is that the man who is released attains the culmination of happiness. *Aitareyopaniṣad* IV.6 cites the example of Vāmadeva, who attaining the fulfilment of all desires, is said to have become immortal. *Chāndogya Upaniṣad* VII.xii.3 declares:

> There he moves about, laughing, sporting and rejoicing, be it with women, or conveyances, or relatives – not minding the body in which he was born.

Commenting on this passage in the words "That serene being resting in its own nature as the universal self, 'moves about' – sometimes as Indra, 'laughing' or eating all desired foods, high and low, sometimes sporting and rejoicing with women, etc. only in the mind by the mere force of will, these women, etc. – being those of the regions of Brahmā, or of this world; not thinking of the body that is born of the connection of man and woman, or that which was bom for himself – i.e. into which he was born; as any thought of the body would only cause pain, as the body abounds in pain",[2] Śrī Śaṅkara pertinently points out that this scriptural passage is an eulogy of the knowledge of the self. Hence, this text must not be literally understood as allowing moral lapses in the case of the *jñānin*. As was remarked already, the knower of *Brahman* by his very nature cannot be immoral. To say that he transcends ethical considerations is one thing and to say that he is immoral is another. While the former is true, the latter is a gross misrepresentation and distortion of the purport of scripture.

After defining the self as existence, intelligence, infinitude, *Taittirīya Upaniṣad* II.i.1 declares that he who knows it (the self) placed in the innermost recess, the transcendent *ākāśa*, realizes all his desires along with the omniscient Brahmā. In the calculus of happiness which the *Upaniṣad* gives there is found a description of the grades of happiness; and it is declared that the happiness which the knower of *Brahman* attains defies all calculation. Pleasures that are empirical lie within the frontiers of *māyā*; the bliss that the *mukta* (released one) enjoys belongs to the realm of *vidyā*. His happiness is not extrinsic. It is born of discrimination and not delusion. He is unafflicted by desires; and he is happy, because he is desireless.

In the supreme bliss which is *Brahman*, there are no such distinctions as happiness and the experiencer thereof. There

---

[2] See Ganganath Jha's translation, vol. IV, p. 296.

is scriptural evidence for the non-existence of even the least difference in *Brahman*. No channel is needed for experiencing that bliss, since it is eternally established, ever attained. What is required is the destruction of nescience; and when that is accomplished, the self-luminous *Brahman* shines of its own accord.[3] Thus, the bliss that is experienced by the knower of *Brahman* is different from the happiness that is enjoyed by others not merely in degree but also in kind. *Brahman*-bliss is the real of which all the other pleasures may be called appearances. The *jñānin* enjoys unalloyed bliss; and hence scripture declares that all his desires are fulfilled. Because he has realized that he is the self of all, he sings the *sāman* (chant), "I am the food! I am the food-eater, etc." (*TaitUp* III.x.5). For him, there is no distinction between enjoyment and the one who enjoys. His is the distinctionless happiness of non-difference.

The satisfaction that results from sense-objects is dependent and limited, whereas the satisfaction consequent on *Brahman*-knowledge is without any limit and determination (see *Tṛptidīpa* 52ff.). When that supreme solace is gained, all obligations are fulfilled and all desires are quenched. To the *mukta* who is a non-agent and non-enjoyer there may occur activities which are scripturally declared or empirically necessary; but by them he is in no way bound. Even though there is nothing for him to be accomplished in this world or in the next, he may act in accordance with scriptural injunctions in order to save the world. His physical organism may worship the deity, bathe in the holy waters and take to the life of the mendicant. His speech-sense may recite the Vedic texts or his mind may study the system of Vedānta. His intellect may contemplate the form of Viṣṇu or become merged in the bliss of *Brahman*. But he does nothing, nor does he make others do anything. He is the witness of all things and thoughts without any conceit in the way of the senses and in

---

[3] Sureśvara's *Vārttika*, p. 145.

the functions of his mind. His ignorance has taken to flight and he knows no misery born of *saṁsāra*. He has achieved his life's end, attained as it were the eternally attained greatest human goal. There is nothing in the world to equal his contentment. His bliss knows no bounds. This is the state of him who has transcended the travails and turmoils of transmigration.

Different Views about Release

The conception of the *summum bonum* as positive distinguishes Advaita from nihilistic Buddhism, the Vijñānavāda and the Nyāya–Vaiśeṣika. The Mādhyamika defines release as the cessation of the stream of cognitions eclipsed by the object-forms.[4] But, since that stream of cognitions is the nature of the self, the cessation thereof is not a human goal. Not indeed does any one have the desire to extirpate the self which is the object of supreme love. According to the Vijñānavādin, release is the origination of the stream of pure cognitions rid of the dirt of object-forms. But, is this origination the human goal of the cognitions that constitute the stream or of the stream itself? Not the first, since the cognitions that are momentary perish of their own accord. Nor the second, since the stream of impure cognitions ceases to exist by the time the stream of pure cognitions comes into being. How, then, can the latter be the human goal of the former? There is the contingence of different loci for bondage and release. The Logicians regard the destruction of misery without a residue as release. Now, to what kind of misery does this destruction refer? The destruction of past miseries is not to be accomplished, since they are already removed. The present miseries, however, are discarded by the generation of the opposite qualities that serve as antidotes. And the removal of the miseries that are to come is impossible. The non-existence of misery cannot independently be the human

---

4 *Tattva-Pradīpikā*, p. 349.

goal, since it is subsidiary to the manifestation of happiness.[5] Nor is there the contingence of the reverse being true, since it cannot bear reasoning. Is happiness the generator of the non-existence of misery, or is it its manifester? In neither of the ways is happiness the subsidiary. In the self, even while there is experienced the non-existence of all miseries, there arises happiness all of a sudden from the hearing of sweet melodies generated by the *vīṇā*. Nor may it be said that, because in the case of him who stands in a cool lake half-immersed on a hot day there is observed happiness even while there is misery, the non-existence of misery is not subsidiary to the cognition of happiness; for it is not admitted that happiness is invariably manifested by the non-existence of misery alone. What is invariable, however, is that the non-existence of misery certainly manifests happiness.

The cessation of misery, says Maṇḍana,[6] is not itself happiness, since happiness and misery may coexist at the same time, as in the cited case of a man half-plunged in a cool tank with the scorching sun above. Happiness admits of grades; and grades are possible only in the case of what is existent and not in the case of the non-existence of misery which is an *abhāva*. All seek happiness and not the mere cessation of misery. They are prepared even to go through hazards and hardships in order to gain happiness. It may be said that what is sought is the extinction of desire and the consequent extinction of misery through the enjoyment of the desired object. But as Maṇḍana points out, desire does not die through enjoyment. Bhāratītīrtha says that desire is quenched not by enjoyment, but by the cognition of defect in the object (*VPS*, p. 159). Hence, absence of desire does not amount to happiness. When, thus, it is settled that absence of misery is not happiness, it will not be difficult to see that the human goal which is sought by all is positive bliss. Though the highest bliss which constitutes the

5 *Tattva-Pradīpikā*, p. 357.

6 *Brahmasiddhi*, pp. 1-3.

nature of *Brahman* and with which we are identical is eternally attained, it seems through delusion as if it were not attained. And when by knowledge the True is cognized, *Brahman*-bliss is attained as it were.

The Jīvan-mukta

The attainment of *Brahman*-bliss need not synchronize with the decease of the body. The *jīvan-mukta* is he who is released even while being embodied. There is for him the persistence of the body until the fruition of the residue of *prārabdha-karma*. Though knowledge of Truth destroys *avidyā* that is the material cause of all *karma* without exception still it does not remove *prārabdha-karma*, since it is itself the fruit of that *karma* (*VPS*, p. 263). The continuance of the body even after the destruction of nescience is intelligible on the analogy of the potter's wheel rotating for some time till the momentum is spent even after the propelling rod is removed. According to the Logicians, the effect continues to remain for a while after the removal of the cause. In the case of momentary effects it may be admitted that they remain only for one moment after their causes are destroyed. But in respect of the body which is a product of beginningless nescience, says the Advaitin, we must allow a considerable lapse of time before it can be finally resolved (*PD* VI.54).

Prārabdha-karma perishes by enjoyment. Both the released and the bound have alike to reap the consequences of their *prārabdha*. Both have to walk in a path strewn with thorns; but while the enlightened walk with shoes on, the ignorant have no such protection to enable them to pass unhurt. The vulgar are led astray by their whimsical moods, whereas the wise regard themselves as witnesses and not victims of their moods. Two travellers wend their way on the same road; and both of them are equally fatigued. One of them knows that the destination is near and so he quickens his pace in the hope of reaching it soon.

But the other is heavy of heart and not knowing that his place of rest is nigh he plods on with staggering steps.[7]

The *mukta* who has transcended nescience is not affected by the ruffle of the empirical life. If he be discomfited at any time, it is due to his aversion to the objects of sense. That he is not in tune with the enjoyment of the world is patent from the fact that he gets disgusted with it very soon. Desires do not multiply in his case. Desire is like a burnt seed impotent to produce fresh sprout. In the case of the ignorant desires do not die with enjoyment. Fulfilled desires bring in fresh ones. Like fire fed by fuel, they grow from more to more. But enjoyment which is combined with discernment does not breed new desires. The sun of knowledge scorches the seed of desire making it ineffectual to sprout forth and yield fresh fruits.

The desire of the *mukta* is unproductive because he knows the worthlessness of the desired object. Just as fried grains are useful for eating and not for sprouting, similarly, the desires of the knower of truth give him slight enjoyment, but do not entail in their train any more of their kind. The *karma* which has begun to take effect perishes when it has borne its fruit. Since *prārabdha* is the cause only of enjoyment, it dies with the destruction of its product. There can be misery only when there is the delusion that the object of enjoyment is real. The person who possesses true knowledge is devoid of such delusion; and hence he is not bound by his *prārabdha*. Apprehending the world to be of an impermanent, indeterminable nature, comparable to the dream and the *fata morgana*, how can the released be attached to it? Who, except those who are perverse, will drink poison after knowing its fatal consequence? When the illusory nature of the world is well cognized, attachment to sense-objects ceases along with the cessation of the cognition of reality in them.

---

[7] These analogies found in the *Pañcadaśī*, however, suggest that the *jīvan-mukta* is not really released, but that he is an *āsanna-mukta*, one for whom release is imminent.

Knowledge is not the destroyer of *prārabdha*, since it does not bring about the resolution of the world. It reveals only the illusory nature of the universe and by that the latter is not resolved. Just as people, while not denying the fact of a magical show, know it to be fictitious, the knower of truth, while not discarding the enjoyment generated by *prārabdha* possesses the cognition of the illusoriness of the world. The obstinacy of *prārabdha* is in compelling the *jīva* to enjoy pleasure and suffer pain and not in postulating the reality of the objects of enjoyment. Knowledge and *prārabdha* are not contradictories, since they have different contents, like the colour and taste of a substance.

If the body were to fall off even at the time of release, then there would be no preceptor to teach Advaita. And if there be none to teach, how are the study and realization of Advaita principles possible? If it be asserted that true knowledge is incompatible with the cognition of duality, then Sage Yājñavalkya and others would not have been preceptors. If the non-cognition of duality were the criterion of release, then all beings should be released in sleep. If in sleep there be no release because of the non-existence of true knowledge, then knowledge of the true and not non-cognition of duality is the cause of release.

The *jīvan-mukta* lives *in* the world, but he is not *of* it. He awaits only the fruition of the residue of his *prārabdha*. Even in reaping the fruits of his *karma* he is unattached and does not lose his balanced deportment. He is compared to a child or a lunatic, since he has no conceit in his actions. To his synoptic vision there is neither action nor agent, neither enjoyment nor enjoyer. He has transcended the temporal process; and temporal categories have no meaning for him. He revels in the bliss of non-difference that has not come to be, but which was, is and will ever be.

Conclusion

We are coming to the close of a rapid survey of the magnificent mansion of Advaita built by many a mighty intellect on the sure foundations well and truly laid by Śaṅkara. We have taken note of some of the doctrinal differences in Advaita. These differences add to the strength of the system and they in no way detract from it. Though the main subject of our study was the philosophy of Advaita as expounded by Bhāratītīrtha-Vidyāraṇya, we have not omitted to draw freely from the works of other preceptors. In order to suit different tastes and temperaments, teachers of Advaita adopt different methods of setting forth their doctrine. They have taken liberties with regard to minor details. As Appayya Dīkṣita says in the invocatory verse of the *Siddhāntaleśa*, the *Sūtrabhāṣya*, having for its sole purport the non-dual *Brahman*, issued from the blessed lotus face of the Bhagavatpāda (i.e. Śaṅkara) and got diversified a thousandfold on reaching the preceptors who expounded it after him, in the same way as the Ganges, which originating from the foot of Viṣṇu, gets variegated on reaching different lands. Manifold are the ways disclosed by the post-Śaṅkara Advaitins. But all of them are intent on establishing the unity of the Self. They never lose sight of the central doctrine taught by Śaṅkara, that *Brahman* is real, the world is illusory, and the so-called *jīva* is non-different from the Absolute.

brahma satyam jagan mithyā
jīvo brahmaiva nā 'paraḥ ।

Glossary

abhāva: non-existence.

adhidaivata: cosmic.

adhyāropā-'pavāda: superimposition and subsequent withdrawal.

adhyātma: personal; individual.

adhyayana: learning (from the lips of a teacher).

adṛṣṭa: unseen potency generated by rites for helping to bring about their fruit in a hereafter; also called *apūrva*.

Advaitavidyācārya: Probably Raṅgarāja, Appayya Dīkṣita's father.

Agnihotra: the name of an obligatory rite enjoined on all twice-born persons, so long as they are alive.

Agnīṣomīya: relating or sacred to Agni and Soma.

anaikāntikatva: inconclusiveness.

anavasthā: infinite regress.

antaryāmin: internal ruler; cosmic form of the Self as associated with *māyā*.

anvaya-vyatireka: co-presence and co-absence.

apaccheda-nyāya: the principle of the later sublating the earlier; so called because it is formulated in the Pūrva-Mīmāṁsā in connection with the expiatory rites which are to be performed when different priests let go their hold of the tucked-up waistcloth of the priest in front, while going round the sacrificial fire.

atiprasaṅga: undue extension.

Atirātra: an optional part of the Jyotiṣṭoma sacrifice.

Avacchedavāda: the view that the *jīva* is the appearance of *Brahman* as defined by *avidyā*.

avidyā: nescience; the same as *ajñāna* which is translated as ignorance; it has a twofold potency of obscuring the real (*āvaraṇa*) and projecting the non-real (*vikṣepa*).

barhis: a variety of sacrificial grass.

Bhagavatpāda: a term of respect applied to Śaṅkara.

Bhaṭṭa: Kumārila Bhaṭṭa (700 CE), author of the *Ślokavārttika*: from him originated one of the two main schools of Pūrva-Mīmāṁsā; Advaitins generally follow the Bhāṭṭa view in matters empirical.

bhedābheda: difference-cum-non-difference.

Bhṛgu: one of the Upaniṣadic seers; the Bhṛguvallī of the *Taittirīya Upaniṣad* narrates how he learned the nature of *Brahman* through the instruction of his father, Varuṇa, and through inquiry.

Brahmā: God as creator; one of the Hindu Trinity, the other two being Viṣṇu, the protector, and Śiva, the destroyer.

brahmaloka: the world of Brahmā; in special contexts like *Chāndogya Upaniṣad* VIII.iii.2, *Brahman* itself is referred to as *brahmaloka*.

Bṛhaspati-sava: the name of a sacrifice by which, according to the *Taittirīya Brāhmaṇa*, the priest who desired to become a *purohita* obtained that office; the *Āśvalāyana-Śrautasūtra* regards it as the sacrifice to be performed by a priest after the Vājapeya, while the *Śatapatha Brāhmaṇa* identifies it with the Vājapeya.

Buddha: the enlightened: the name by which Prince Siddhārtha (b. *c*.567 BCE) is known; there are other names like Sugata, Śākyamuni, Gautama, Tathāgata, etc.

Cārvāka: Indian Materialism; means probably "sweet-tongued" (*cāru-vāka*) from the pleasure-philosophy it teaches; the classic authority to whom the system is traced is Bṛhaspati; hence also called the Bārhaspatya doctrine; another name is Lokāyata.

dhyāna: concentration or meditation.

guṇa: excellence; the three constituents of *prakṛti*, viz. *sattva, rajas* and *tamas;* quality.

guru: literally preceptor; according to tradition this title was given to Prabhākara (650 CE) by his teacher, Kumārila, in recognition of his extraordinary powers; it is urged now that he preceded Kumārila who differs from him in interpreting the Jaiminīya system.

hetv-asiddhi: non-establishment of the *probans*, a logical fallacy.

Hiraṇyagarbha: the cosmic form of the Self creating the subtle universe; also called Sūtrātman.

Indra: the ruler of the gods; the *Chāndogya Upaniṣad* narrates a dialogue between Indra and his preceptor, Prajāpati.

*indriya*s: the organs of sense and action.

iṣīkā: a reed.

Janaka: the lord of Mithilā and father of Sītā; reputed as a *rajarṣi*, philosopher-king.

jina: from *ji* "to conquer"; means "victor", i.e. one who has gained, mastery over himself; a title applied to Vardhamāna or Mahāvīra (born about 540 BCE), the last prophet of the Jainas; Ārhatas and Kṣapaṇakas are the other names by which the Jainas are known.

jīvan-mukti: release while being embodied.

jñāna-lakṣnaṇa-sannikarṣa: super-normal sense-contact or the contact through the cognition of an object revived in memory; one of three such super-normal (*alaukika*) contacts recognized by Nyāya, the other two being *sāmānya-lakṣaṇa* and *yogaja*, it is that contact by which we can associate the perceptions of other senses when perceiving by any one sense, e.g. the perception of fragrant sandal without any direct contact of the object with the organ of smell.

Jyotiṣṭoma: name of a sacrifice, a variety of the Agniṣṭoma.

kalhāra: the white lotus.

karma: rite; deed; certain actions are prescribed (*vidhita*) and certain others are prohibited (*pratiṣiddha*) by the Vedas; *kāmya-karma* is an optional rite, *nitya-karma* is an obligatory rite and *naimittika-karma* is an occasioned rite; the accumulated effect of deeds in lives past and present.

kuśa: one of the varieties of grass held sacred and used in religious rites.

mahā-vākyas: major texts of the Upaniṣads like "That thou art" declarative of non-difference as between *Brahman* and self.

māyā: the indeterminable principle that brings about the illusory manifestation of the world; some Advaitins distinguish between *māyā* and *avidyā*; the *Vivaraṇa* view identifies the two.

Mīmāṁsā: literally inquiry; short for Pūrva-Mīmāṁsā, one of the six systems; the aphorisms as commented on by Śabarasvāmin gave rise to two main schools of interpretation, that of Prabhākara and that of Kumārila Bhaṭṭa.

mumukṣu: one who longs for release.

Nārada: an Upaniṣadic seer; the *Chāndogya Upaniṣad* records a conversation between him and Sanatkumāra.

Nighaṇṭu: a vocabulary.

nirguṇopāsanā: meditation on the attributeless *Brahman*.

Nyāya: one of the six systems; the word which literally means "going back" indicates the emphasis laid in the system on argumentation and logic; metaphysically it is realistic and is coordinate with the Vaiśeṣika; other designations are *hetu-vidyā, tarka-vidyā, vāda-vidyā,* etc.; the followers of this school are also referred to as the Logicians.

Pāñcarātra: a monotheistic faith with an Āgamic basis; same as the Ekānta, Bhāgavata, Sātvata or Ekāyana system; according to the *Padmatantra*, it is so called because "the five other great Śāstras are like darkness in the presence of this".

parasparāśraya: reciprocal dependence, a logical fallacy.

Parīṇāmavāda: the theory of transformation; according to Brahma-Parīṇāmavāda, the world is a transformation of *Brahman*; and according to Prakṛti-Pariṇāmavāda, it is a transformation of Primal Nature.

prājña: the individual form of the Self as the witness of the bare nescience in the state of sleep; also called *ānandamaya*.

prakaraṇa: chapter, section, topic.

prakṛti: primal nature; in the view of the Sāṁkhya, the *prius* of creation; also called *pradhāna*.

pramāṇa: evidence; means of valid knowledge; sometimes signified valid knowledge.

prārabdha-karma: that part of the accumulated effect of past deeds which has begun to take effect with the creation of the present body and which is responsible for the continuance of the body even after release is attained through knowledge; it is destroyed only when its force is spent by suffering.

prasaṁkhyāna: continued meditation; the instrument of the intuitive experience of *Brahman*, according to the view of Maṇḍana and the Bhāmatī school.

Pratibimbavāda: the view that the *jīva* is the appearance of *Brahman* as reflected in nescience.

Rājasūya: a sacrifice for the sake of universal empery; only kṣatriyas are eligible to perform this.

Rāma: the hero of the epic *Rāmāyaṇa*; one of the incarnations of Viṣṇu, the son of Daśaratha and consort of Sītā.

Śākāyanya: the *Maitrāyaṇī Upaniṣad* relates a conversation, between Śākāyanya and Bṛhadratha.

samādhi: the superconscious state where there is complete absorption of thought into the one object of meditation.

sāman: a metrical hymn or song of praise; a text of the *Sāmaveda.*

saṁsāra: empirical existence, transmigration.

Sāṁkhya: one of the six systems; ascribed to Kapila; exhaustive enumeration and philosophical reflection are the meanings suggested for the name.

śara: a sort of reed.

śiṁśapa: a kind of tree (*aśoka*).

sopādhika-bhrama: delusion due to external adjunct, e.g. crystal appearing red in the proximity of the hibiscus flower or the conch seeming yellow due to jaundice.

śravaṇa: hearing, i.e. study (of the Vedānta).

śrīmukha: an epistle.

śrīpāda: of adorable feet.

Śruti: literally what is heard; scripture.

Śuka: son of Vyāsa; said to have been a *jñānin* even from birth.

Śūnyavāda: one of the four main schools of later Buddhism; the doctrine that nullity is the ultimate nature (*śūnyam tattvam*); it is also known as Asadvāda and Mādhyamika from the fact that the Buddha called his ethical teaching the middle (*madhyama*) path.

Sūtrabhāṣya: Śaṅkara's commentary on the *Vedāntasūtras*.

Śvetaketu: Son of Uddālaka; in the *Chāndogya Upaniṣad* he is taught the major text "That thou art" by his father.

taddhita: some noun-endings of that name.

taijasa: the self having a conceit in an individual subtle body in dream-experience.

tatkratu: the principle that one who meditates becomes one with the object of his meditation.

tripuṭī: the triple forms involved in all cognitive experience, viz. the cognizer, the object cognized and the means of cognition.

upakrama-nyāya: the principle that the earlier is stronger than the later.

Vaiśyaṣṭoma: a sacrifice intended to be performed by the vaiśyas.

Vāmadeva: name of a sage, a *jīvan-mukta* from birth.

varṇaka: chapter.

vārttikakāra. the author of the *Bṛhadāraṇyaka-Upaniṣad-Bhāṣya-Vārttika*, i.e. Sureśvara; also referred to as Viśvarūpācārya.

vāsanā: residual impression; also called *saṁskara*.

vivaraṇakāra: Prakāśātman (twelfth century CE), the author of the *Pañcapādikā-Vivaraṇa*, a commentary on Padmapāda's *Pañcapādikā*.

Vedānta: end of Veda; a term applied to the Upaniṣads which form the final portions of the Vedas; popularly it is used to signify the Advaita philosophy.

Vidyāraṇya: "forest of learning"; probably an epithet common to Mādhava and Bhāratītīrtha; tradition regards it as the *saṁnyāsa* name of Mādhavācārya, the minister of the Vijayanagara kingdom.

Vijñānavāda: one of the Buddhist schools; it is the idealist view, otherwise known as Yogācāra.

Virāṭ: the cosmic form of the Self as the cause of the gross world.

viśeṣaṇatā: the mode of contact (*sannikarṣa*) which, according to the Naiyāyikas, leads to the perception of non-existence.

viśva: the individual form of the self having a conceit in a gross body while awake.

Vivartavāda: the Advaita theory that the world is an illusory appearance superimposed by *māyā* on *Brahman*.

Yājñavalkya: an Upaniṣadic seer; in the *Bṛhadāraṇyaka Upaniṣaḍ*, he teaches his wife Maitreyī, that the Self is the seat of supreme love.

Yoga: path; discipline; one of the six systems, which while taking over Sāṁkhya psychology and metaphysics admitted the existence of God and prescribed a course of discipline of the mind; Bhāratītīrtha regards *yoga* as meditation of the formless, in contrast with Sāṁkhya as inquiry.

Bibliography

Bhāmatī (*Catussūtri*) of Vācaspati, ed. with an English tr. S.S. Suryanarayana Sastri and C. Kunhan Raja, Madras: Theosophical Publishing House, 1933.

Bhāratītīrtha-Vidyāraṇya, *Dṛg-Dṛśya-Viveka*.

Bhāratītīrtha-Vidyāranya, *Pañcadaśī* with the commentary of Rāmakṛṣṇna Paṇḍita, Bombay: Nirnayasagar Press.

Bhaṭṭārakācārya Ānandabodha, *Nyāya-Makaranda*, Benares: Chowkhamba Sanskrit Book Depot, 1907.

Bheda-dhikkāra (or A Critique of Difference), Narasiṁhasrama, Benares Sanskrit Series vol. 22, Benares: Braj B. Das, 1904.

Bradley, F.H., 1908, *Appearance and Reality*, London: Swan Sonnenschein and Co.

Carlyle, Thomas, 1837, *The French Revolution: A History*, London: Chapman & Hall.

Cidghanānandagiri, *Tattvānusandhāna*.

Das Gupta, Surendranath, 1922, *A History of Indian Philosophy*, vol. I, Cambridge: Cambridge University Press.

Datta, D.M., 1932, *The Six Ways of Knowing*, London: George Allen and Unwin (retypesetted edn, D.K. Printworld, New Delhi, 2018).

Descartes, René, 1901, *Discourse on Method and Metaphysical Meditations*, tr. G.B. Rawlings, London: Walter Scott.

Hiriyanna, Mysore, 1932, *Outlines of Indian Philosophy*, London: George Allen and Unwin. (retypesetted edn, D.K. Printworld, New Delhi, 2022).

Indian Historical Quarterly, vols VI (1930), VII (1931) and XII (1936).

Joachim, Harold H., 1906, *Nature of Truth*, Oxford: Clarendon Press.

McTaggart, J.M.E., 1921, *The Nature of Existence*, vol. I, Cambridge: Cambridge University Press.

Mādhava-Vidyāraṇya, *Parāśara-Mādhavīya*.

Mānameyodaya, ed. with tr. C. Kunhan Raja and S.S. Suryanarayana Sastri, Madras: Theosophical Publishing House.

Mīmāṁsā-Śloka-Vārttika with Sucarita Misra's *Kāśikā* commentary, Benares: Chowkhamba Sanskrit Series Office.

Müller, Max 1899, *Six Systems of Indian Philosophy*, p. xii, London: Longmans, Green & Co. (reprint edn, D.K. Printworld, New Delhi, 2016).

Naiṣkarmyasiddhi, by Sureśvara, ed. with an Introduction M. Hiriyanna, Bombay Sanskrit and Prakrit Series, XXXVIII, 1925.

Nilakaṇṭha, *Dipika* on *Tarkasaṁgraha*.

Niścaladāsa, *Vṛttiprabhākara*, 1901.

Nyāyasāra of Bhāsarvajña; ed. Mahāmahopādhyāya Paṇḍit Vāsudeva Sastri Abhyankar and C.R. Devadhar.

Nyāyakusumāñjali of Udayana, ed. Pandit Laxman Sastri Dravid.

Padmapāda, *Pañcapādikā*, (Vizianagaram Sanskrit Series, 3), Benares: E.J. Lazarus and Co., 1891.

Prakāśātman, 1892, *Pañcapādikā-vivaraṇa*; ed. Ramasastri Bhagavatacharya (Vizianagaram Sanskrit Series, 3), Benares: E.J. Lazarus and Co.

Pringle-Pattison, 1917, *Idea of God*, London: Oxford University Press.

Radhakrishnan, S., 1923, *Indian Philosophy*, vol. I, London: George Allen & Unwin.

———, 1929, *Indian Philosophy*, vol. 2, London: George Allen & Unwin.

———, 1932, *An Idealist View of Life*, London: George Allen & Unwin.

Rama Rao, R., 1930, "Vidyāraṇya and Mādhavācārya", *Indian Historical Quarterly*, VI(4): 701.

———, 1931, "The Origin of Mādhava-Vidyāraṇya Theory", *Indian Historical Quarterly*, VII(1): 78-92.

Robinson, E.S. and F.R. Robinson, 1923, "Alfred Binet on Perception", and "Lightner Witmer on Perception" *Readings in General Psychology*, Chicago: University of Chicago Press.

Śaṅkara, *Commentary on the Bṛhadāranyaka Upaniṣad*, tr. Svami Madhavananda, Mayavati: Advaita Asrama, 1934.

———, *Adhyāsa-Bhāsya*.

———, *Commentary on the Chāndogya Upaniṣad*, tr. Ganganath Jha, Madras: V.C. Seshacharri, 1923.

———, *Memorial Edition of His Works*, Srirangam: Sri Vani Vilas Press, 1910.

Sarasvatī Madhusūdana, *Bhaktirasayana*.

———, *Gūḍhārtha-dīpikā*.

———, *Siddhāntabindu*, tr. P.M. Modi, Allahabad: Vohra Publishers, 1929.

Sarvadarśanasaṁgraha of Sāyaṇa-Mādhava, ed. Mm. Vasudeva Sastri Abhyankar, Government Oriental (Hindu) Series 1, 1924.

Sastri, S. Kuppuswami, 1932, *A Primer of Indian Logic according to Annambhaṭṭa's Tarkasaṁgraha*, Madras: P. Varadachary and Co.

Sastri, S.S. Suryanarayana and T.M.P. Mahadevan, 1936, *A Critique of Difference: A Free English Rendering of the Bhedadhikkāra of Nṛsiṁhāśramin*, Madras: University of Madras.

Siddhāntaleśa-saṁgraha of Appayya Dīkṣita:, 2 vols, ed. and tr. S.S. Suryanarayana Sastri, Madras: University of Madras.

Sinha, Jadunath, 1934, *Indian Psychology: Perception*, London: Kegan Paul, Trench, Trübner and Co.

Sureśvara, *Bṛhadāraṇyakopaniṣad-Bhāṣya-Vārttika*, Poona: Anandasrama Sanskrit Series.

Suryanarayana Sastri, S.S. and T.M.P. Mahadevan, 1936, *Critique of Difference*, Madras: University of Madras.

Tattva-Cintāmaṇi of Gaṅgeśa Upādhyāya, ed. Paṇḍit Kāmākhyā Nātha Tarka-Vāgīśa (Bibliotheca Indica Series), Calcutta: Asiatic Society of Bengal, 1910-22.

Tattva-Pradīpikā of Citsukha, ed. Pt. Raghunath Kasinatha Sastri (second ed.), Bombay: Nirnayasagar Press, 1931.

Tattvaśuddhi of Jñānaghanapāda, ed. S.S. Suryanarayana Sastri and E.P. Radhakrishnan.

Taylor, A.E., 1920, *Elements of Metaphysics*, London: Methuen & Co.

Upaniṣads (108), ed. Vasudev Laxman Shastri Pansikar, Bombay: Nirnayasagar Press.

Vedānta-Paribhāṣā of Dharmarāja, ed. Mm. Anantakrishna Sastri, Calcutta: University of Calcutta, 1927.

Venkata Ramanayya, N., 1933, *Vijayanagara: Origin of the City and the Empire*, Madras: University of Madras.

Vimuktātman, *Iṣṭa-siddhi;* Gaekwad's Oriental Series, No. LXV, Baroda: Oriental Institute.

Vivaraṇa-Prameya-Saṁgraha of Bhāratītīrtha-Vidyāraṇya, ed. Ramasastri Tailanga, Vizianagaram Sanskrit Series, 7, Benares: E.J. Lazarus and Co., 1893.

Whitehead, A.N., 1933, *Adventures of Ideas,* Cambridge: Cambridge University Press.

William, James, 1892, *Psychology: A Briefer Course,* New York: Henry Holt.

———, 1922, *Pragmatism,* London: Longmans, Green & Co.

Index